# BEYOND THE BAYONET: INDIAN SPECIAL OPERATIONS FORCES IN THE 21st CENTURY

# BEYOND THE BAYONET
## INDIAN SPECIAL OPERATIONS FORCES IN THE 21st CENTURY

**Brigadier Deepak Sinha**

United Service Institution of India
Field Marshal K.M Cariappa Chair

GYAN PUBLISHING HOUSE
NEW DELHI-110002

Beyond the Bayonet:
Indian Special Operations Forces in the 21st Century

Rs. 690

ISBN: 81-212-0861-0



Photographs Courtesy: The Parachute Regiment Training Centre.

Published in 2006 in India by
Gyan Publishing House
5, Ansari Road, Darya Ganj, New Delhi-110002
Phones : 23282060, 23261060, Fax : 011-23285914
E-mail : gyanbook@vsnl.com
Website : http://www.gyanbooks.com

*Laser Typesetting at* : Shiva Infosystem, Delhi
*Printed at* : Salasar Imaging System, Delhi

*Dedicated to my late father, Major General Samir Chandra Sinha, PVSM, and his fellow "band of brothers" whose spirit of adventure, courage, sacrifice and determination made the Parachute Regiment the best there was, an ethos that continues to this very day...*

# Contents

# Preface

The increasingly complex nature of a dynamic threat covering the entire spectrum of warfare from nuclear to low intensity to the unconventional requires an interface of all operating components of the conservative civil and military establishments as also necessitates the requirement of and dependence on an elite band of troops: highly trained and motivated, possessing sophisticated weapons and equipment and capable of operating in varied conditions and diverse terrain to ensure a measured response to sensitive politico-military situations.

Most armies of the world have Special Operations Forces on their order of battle. These forces can meet unorthodox security needs that conventional military organisations find difficult to accomplish, if at all. In fact, the significance of such forces has progressively increased, especially in the West, where they are perceived to be able to produce favourable results with limited inputs or fallout in terms of financial outlay, casualties or repercussions.

India has had extensive experience with the employment of such forces. Chhatrapati Shivaji's guerrilla campaigns against the Mughals is the stuff of legends and would surely qualify as classical use of irregular troops to achieve outstanding success. The Indian Parachute Regiment along with a Parachute Brigade was first formed in 1942. This force had expanded up to a division by the end of the war. Some of these have now evolved into Commando units, which have a more specialised task. In addition different Services and ministries have raised a vast array of such forces. The Marine Naval Commandos (MARCOS), National Security Guards (NSG) and Special Frontier Force (SFF) to name a few, are other such forces having overlapping responsibilities. In our context there does not appear to be a national perspective for the raising, command and control or employment of these forces. This assumes all the more importance to ensure the utilisation of such forces in an optimal manner for getting the maximum bang for minimum bucks.

Thus the urgent need to examine and suggest a framework within which the type of forces needed, the tasks they would be required to perform, and the command and control aspects that would require to be addressed to ensure that such forces are optimally utilised, keeping our geo-political concerns and economic capacity in mind, is inescapable. This study addresses these very aspects along with their relevance in our context and suggests the way forward in the next decade, more so, since published literature within the country, on the subject is extremely limited.

This book, in its first part, examines the definition of special operations and the necessity for forces that can undertake them. It also goes on to differentiate between special operations that can be undertaken by regular conventional forces and those that require use of specialist forces. The Special Operations Forces of the UK, the USA, Israel, the Russian Federation, China and Pakistan are examined in detail along with an emphasis on their organisational and command and control structures and operations carried out by their units to realistically gauge their capabilities and performance, including their employment in the ongoing US operations in Iraq and Afghanistan.

The second part of the book goes on to trace the history and development of such forces in India and abroad that included units manned by Indians, such as forces that served with the Germans and Italians in the Second World War. It then carries out a critical examination of Indian Special Operations Forces and their employment since Independence. The institutional drawbacks that exist in the manner these forces have been organised which has prevented them from being used with more optimal effect, especially with regard to their employment in low intensity conflict, terrorism and in operations other than war have also been enumerated.

The final part of the book examines future battlefield environment in the Indian context and the manner in which these forces can best be integrated with conventional forces as also their employment independently to achieve the nation's politico-military aims. Changes in the organisational and command and control structures are suggested which will ensure their optimal utilisation and greatly enhance their capabilities. Providing the Government with unique options for countering threats on the horizon in a pro-active manner, preferably without having to resort to the use of large-scale conventional forces. All the more important as India emerges on the world stage as a power to be reckoned with that will not only have to look beyond its immediate borders but also develop the capacity to influence matters to its own advantage in these regions.

**New Delhi** **Deepak Sinha**
**January 2005**

# 1

# Introduction

*"But who are ye in rags and rotten shoes,*
*You dirty bearded blocking the way?*
*We are the Pilgrims, Master, we shall go*
*Always a little further: it may be*
*Beyond the last blue mountain barr'd with snow*
*Across that angry or that glimmering sea."*

James Elroy Fleckers "Hassan"

From times immemorial, human society has required heroes it can look up to and believe in. The Ramayana, the Mahabharat, the Bible and any number of epics have introduced us to the world of warrior heroes who with their sacrifice and valour have turned "defeat into victory". The stories of the 'Knights of the Round Table', the 'Three Musketeers' *et al* are a familiar part of growing up. In more recent times, the romantic image of the "Dirty Dozen" or a "Rambo" and numerous comic book heroes fighting against heavy odds has stirred the imagination of generations and led to innumerable movies where "a few good men" have taken on the might of the evil empire. Such movies hold a fascination that is easy to understand as they enable us to experience the vicarious thrills and pleasures of being masters of our own fate, even if, for just a few hours. Not much has changed since then and our hunger for heroes in this "*age of anxiety where men lead lives of quiet desperation, torn from the soil; victims of blind forces and heedless cruelties; debased physically and mentally by repetitive and meaningless work, synthetic food; spectators of tawdry thrills; fearful of death in an age without gods,"*[1] as Roger Beaumont calls it, is even more pronounced than before. We truly need heroes who can make this world a better and safer place to live in and can give a meaning to our lives. Without doubt, members of the Special Forces, the world over, have today been thrust, perhaps willingly, as replacements of the mythic warrior kings and knights of yester- years.

A need therefore arises to define special operations and the forces that carry them out, as that will enable us to better understand these shadowy warriors in our midst, to separate fact from fiction and to comprehend fully their role in future conflicts. Moreover, Special Operations Forces (SOF), worldwide, by their very nature, tend to be secretive and close-mouthed. Thus, more often than not, information regarding their employment and conduct in operations remains vague, at times, bordering on the realms of fantasy. To some extent such secrecy and hype is deliberately promoted by such units and their leadership elements because it plays a vital role in ensuring that the modus operandi of such forces are protected from the opposition, as also, in building up of intense psychological pressures on such groups to deter and curtail their activities. Terrorist groups worldwide think twice before initiating any action if it is likely to be countered by the British Special Air Service (SAS). Such is the fearsome reputation that this unit has built for itself, not only because of its operational successes, which undoubtedly are many, but also because of deft media management that makes them appear larger than life. However, secrecy also detracts from accountability and allows units and the establishment to wriggle out of failures by judicious use of the truth and media spin. Finally, there is also the likelihood that in some cases, such ignorance enables the leadership elements of such forces, given their proximity to the top-most rungs of political and military hierarchy, an opportunity to take unfair and unwarranted benefits, even of a personal nature. Such a policy has its own pitfalls as this lack of knowledge, especially within the politico-military leadership, results in the incorrect appreciation of the capabilities and limitations of such forces resulting in their wrongful employment, sometimes with disastrous results, and the subsequent loss of faith in their abilities.

However, probably more important than the usual questions as to what are SOF and how are they different from other regular units, is the question of why do we need them. Interestingly, apart from the belief that there is a need for special troops for specialised tasks, there is a school of thought that believes that the requirement for such forces involves a more fundamental issue, that of the political survival of ruling elites. "*Emphasis in modern political systems on progress and immediate results and the endless competition of promises has led to an increasing gap between the being and the seeming*".[2] This has been the very genesis of conflict and invariably modern governments have increasingly failed to control the course of such conflicts leading to loss of life and property. However, as long as the loss is borne by personnel of elite units who have volunteered to be in 'harms way', or, by regular forces recruited from the politically disenfranchised, there has been no backlash or threat to the political elite. However, once casualties have mounted to an unacceptable level leading to involvement or casualties among other more politically powerful sections of society, the political leadership has not been able to survive for long. Results of this hypothesis are more visible in the West where smaller populations, higher standards of living and empowerment amongst the people, have bred an increasing aversion to casualties. President Lyndon Johnson's defeat to Richard Nixon over the course of the Vietnam conflict is a case in point. Larger populations and greater under-development, as in India, show that despite clear indications of failure at the political level, during the Punjab problem of 1984, the Sri Lanka imbroglio, in Jammu and Kashmir or in the Kargil conflict of 1999, these still did not lead to change in the political leadership despite the casualties suffered. However, development and the consequent increase in the value placed on human life will increasingly require volunteer forces capable of dealing with brushfires before they get out of hand, as on-going operations in Afghanistan and Iraq show. The increasing dependence of the West on air superiority and SOF on the ground, whatever be its effectiveness, along with the strategy of pre-emption clearly show a shift in focus towards war prevention.

Another aspect that needs consideration is that of change in the very nature of war. For much of the past, warfare was governed by the nature of weapons at our disposal, whether it was the crossbow or longbow, gunpowder or canon, the repeater rifle or the machine-gun, the tank or the aircraft, and, their impact on time and space. Firepower and movement were the two essential components of warfare and armies that were able to take full advantage of technology to formulate and adapt strategy and tactics were more likely to succeed. The equation changed somewhat with the development of nuclear weapons as existing parameters reduced in their importance, as deterrence became the key, especially among nuclear adversaries. Despite improvement in the lethality and effectiveness of weapon systems and the organisations and tactics to go with it, the one constant factor was the nature of the threat that nations faced. Thus, war was seen as an extension of a nation's ability to destroy or neutralise the opposing forces and enable a nation to impose its will on others. More lethal weapons and superior technology, training and tactics enabled nations to wage war in a most cost effective manner but still required the capture of territory to enable destruction of the enemy's forces and their economic ability to wage war to finally be able to impose its will. This, however, no longer holds good and since World War II though more than half the world's nations have seen wars and conflicts of different intensities and scales, global struggle has moved from being a definable line or 'front' to a more dispersed battlefield. Operational tactics now cover the global screen and contested terrain encompasses the world. Moreover, conventional wars have become less favourable options in pursuing national interests. Smaller nations are bridging force asymmetry by resorting to proxy wars and supporting cross border terrorism. Another characteristic of our age has been a continuous increase in the fissiparous tendencies around the world. Invariably, after a brief incubation period such dissent or ethnic pressure erupts into a militant and violent struggle. Non – State actors fired by religious and ethnic fundamentalism have emerged as significant players on the security horizon. There is an increasing sophistication in the use of weapons and tactics employed by such terrorist or separatist groups and there is all likelihood now of the use of weapons of mass destruction by terrorists. Ironically, the on–going information revolution that has literally transformed the world into a global village has also made knowledge, information, communication and the sinews of our inter-dependent economy easily available to rogue nations, the smallest of trans national religious or ethnic group, and, even to individuals. Such elements have the ability to initiate actions that can have national or even international ramifications or repercussions.

The Chambers dictionary defines 'Special' as something *"distinctive, peculiar, exceptional, beyond the ordinary."*[3] In the context of the military this would imply operations that are different from the conventional and could therefore be termed as unconventional operations. While the Chambers defines unconventional as *"something that does not follow convention or custom"* and is therefore out of the ordinary and reasonably similar to the definition of special, the US military views it in a much narrower context. The Dictionary of US Military Terms defines unconventional warfare as that which *"includes the inter related fields of guerrilla warfare, evasion and escape and subversion conducted within enemy or enemy controlled territory by predominantly indigenous personnel usually supported and directed by personnel from an outside country."*[4] However, way back in 1941, former United States Army Colonel, William J Donovan, the first Director of the Office of Strategic Services (OSS), the forerunner to the Central Intelligence Agency (CIA), had a far more all-encompassing view of the issue. He visualised that the first phase of operations against the enemy involved "intelligence penetration," with its results available for strategic planning and propaganda. This would be followed by special operations in the form of sabotage and subversion, commando raids, coup-de-main operations in the rear and guerrilla actions by behind the lines resistance movements. All this, in his view, represented the softening up process prior to invasion by friendly armed forces and was an attempt to unify the functions of intelligence gathering, sabotage, psychological warfare, guerrilla operations and commando actions in support of conventional operations to forge a new *"instrument of war"*.[5] In essence, such a definition covers almost all actions in the enemy's rear areas, both in war and peace, including small-scale tactical actions in immediate depth that can be carried out by the commando platoons of any well trained infantry battalion. To differentiate between operations that can be carried out by well-trained conventional forces and those that require the use of specially trained and organised forces, SOF, requires adding a caveat to Colonel Donovan's definition, in that, such operations must be aimed at achieving results at the operational, strategic or national sphere. To this there is also a need to add conduct of specialised Counter Terrorist Operations or Counter Revolutionary Warfare that have developed into their own in the past two decades. In fact, it can be suggested that in the present day context, while actions of conventional forces would be decisive in the event of war, the SOF should enable us to achieve our national aim without the necessity to resort to war or even by preventing war. Towards this end Alexander David's definition, "*a special operation is conducted by forces specially trained equipped and supported for a specific target whose destruction, elimination or rescue (in the case of hostages) is a political or military imperative*",[6] would be more appropriate. Such actions could range from covert actions by small detachments in third countries to clandestine reconnaissance and direct action behind enemy lines to deep operations by airborne forces, whether dropped by helicopter or aircraft.

This increasingly complex nature of a dynamic threat covering the entire spectrum of warfare from nuclear to low intensity to the unconventional requires an interface of all operating components of the conservative civil and military establishments as also necessitates the requirement of and dependence on an elite band of troops: highly trained and motivated, possessing sophisticated weapons and equipment and capable of operating in varied conditions and diverse terrain to ensure a measured response to sensitive politico-military situations. Most armies of the world have SOF on their order of battle (ORBAT). These forces can meet unorthodox security needs that conventional military organisations find difficult to accomplish, if at all. In fact, the significance of such forces has progressively increased, especially in the West, where they are perceived to be able to produce favourable results with limited inputs or fallout in terms of financial outlay, casualties or repercussions.

India has had extensive experience with the employment of such forces. Chhatrapati Shivaji's guerrilla campaigns against the Mughals and their clique is the stuff of legends and would surely qualify as classical use of irregular troops to achieve outstanding success. The later employment of irregular cavalry, such as Skinners Horse and Hodsons Horse, by the British, especially during the First War of Independence, tells us much about the use of such forces in a counter revolutionary role. Closer to the present, Indian *Frei Corps* personnel, formed from POWs captured in North Africa, were dropped by the Germans into Iran in 1941 to organise and conduct resistance movements within India which would assist the Germans in their march towards India after they had pushed the Allies out of Egypt. The inability of the Germans to follow through on this ambitious plan resulted in this Special Unit having to merge with the population to fade into anonymity. On the Allied side we formed the Indian Parachute Regiment along with a Parachute Brigade in 1942. This force had expanded up to a division by the end of the war. Some of these have now evolved into Commando units, which have a more specialised task. In addition different services and ministries have raised a vast array of such forces. The Marine Naval Commandos (MARCOS), National Security Guards (NSG) and Special Frontier Force (SFF) to name a few are other such forces having overlapping responsibilities. In our context there does not appear to be a national perspective for the raising, command and control or employment of these forces. This assumes all the more importance for an impoverished nation such as ours, to ensure the utilisation of such forces in an optimal manner for getting the maximum bang for minimum bucks.

Organisations that we raise to give us some specific capabilities tend to develop group dynamics of their own and continue to grow regardless of their need. A prime example of this is the NSG, which was not utilised to prevent the hijack of an Indian Airlines aircraft to Afghanistan. The ignominy of witnessing that incident live on television is still fresh. Despite clear evidence of delay on the part of our decision makers to take decisions rather than slow reaction on the part of the NSG, there has been talk of 'enhancing NSG force levels to hasten its reaction capabilities' wholly ignoring the more critical issues that emerged as such stereotyped and conservative reactions tend to suit all concerned. For example, the lack of a coordinated SOF command and control structure precluded the Government from considering the option of intervention by force at Kandahar as the NSG is only tailored to react with the permission and assistance of local authorities, in this case the Taliban, which was not forthcoming. An intervention of this nature was only feasible if in conjunction with the NSG assault, actions had been taken by other SOF to secure the airport to prevent reaction by the Taliban, a capability that is available at short notice if properly synchronised.

Thus, the urgent need to examine and suggest a framework within which the type of forces needed, the tasks they would be required to perform, and, command and control aspects that would require to be addressed to ensure that such forces are optimally utilised, keeping our geo-political concerns and economic capacity in mind, is inescapable. This study aims to address these very aspects along with their relevance in our context and suggest the way forward in the next decade, more so, since published literature within the country, on the subject is extremely limited.

**End Notes**

1. Roger A Beaumont, *Military Elites*, London, Robert Hale & Co., 1976, pp. 4-6.
2. *Ibid*, p. 12.
3. Kirkpatrick, EM, *Chambers 20th Century Dictionary*, UK, WR Cham bers Ltd, 1983 p. 1242.
4. Joint Chiefs of Staff, *Dictionary of US Military Terms for Joint Usage*, Washington, D.C., August 1968.
5. Kermit, Roosevelt, Ed, *War Report of the OSS*, 2 Vols., New York, Walker & Co., 1976, 1:16.
6. David, Alexander, *Special Operations*, New York, Berkley Publishing Group, Penguin Putnam Inc, 2001.

## 2

# Development and Organisational Models

*"People sleep peaceably in their beds at night only because rough men stand ready to do violence on their behalf."*

- George Orwell

### HISTORICAL PERSPECTIVE

Special Operations Forces are not a new phenomenon. Mention of special soldiers can be found even in the Old Testament, tales that would fit neatly into any account of modern SOF operations. King David while fighting the Philistines sent his forces on countless forays behind their lines to disrupt their plans and cause confusion in their ranks. For example, in Chapter 2 of the Book of Samuel Verse 12, David sent Joab with a small force to capture the water supply of the city of Rabah while he led the rest of the Army to lay siege to the town. The successful capture of the water supply led to the fall of the town to King David's forces.

Operations such as these are too numerous to recount and can be found in the histories of all nations from that of the Vikings to the Mongols. Every age has produced its special soldier, from the Greek Hoplite to the English Archer, from the American

Minutemen of 1776 to the Green Beret of Vietnam, from the paratrooper of Indian Parachute Regiment of 1942 to the Para Commandos of today. The fundamental reason for the existence of such troops has been aptly summed up by the Mongol Warlord, Yasotay, who led Chengis Khan's elite irregular cavalry and scouting forces well ahead of his main army –"*You do not need more Generals, but when the hour of crisis comes remember that forty selected men can shake the world;*"[1] reinforcing the enduring belief that numbers are not everything, and, much can be achieved by having the right soldier at the right place.

**The Early Years**

Special tasks do not in themselves make a special unit or create a need for a specially trained soldier. By the 18th century, armies gradually became more professional, more rigidly disciplined and more conventional and were standardised into three main arms – the Infantry, the Cavalry and the Artillery. Battles between regular armies became a set routine – the opening artillery barrage, followed by the infantry attack and subsequent breakthrough and pursuit by the cavalry. This, increasingly resulted in stalemates, as both sides were able to anticipate each other's actions resulting in prolonged conflict with massive casualties with little to show, what with wars being decided more by exhaustion than military genius. The First World War was an excellent example to illustrate this point. The Battles of the Somme between 1 July 1916 and 18 November 1916, for example, resulted in more than a million casualties on both sides in less than six months with capture of just 12 kilometres of ground by the French and British allies.[2] Thus, a need came to be felt to specially equip and train forces to carry out unconventional manoeuvres, actions that would change the set piece format and create opportunities for conventional forces to achieve victories without debilitating casualties among them. The raising of Storm Trooper Units by the Germans, Tank Units by the Allies and the employment of Australian infantry for amphibious landings at Gallipoli, were all attempts at breaking this stalemate with varying degrees of success. It was probably the Russians who were the first to understand the value of and exploit such forces in the modern context. During Napoleon's invasion of Russia in 1812, they developed guerrilla forces and stay behind parties that operated behind enemy lines that harassed communication and supply lines to great effect.

The Boer War, however, is of importance since it was then that the term "commando" came to be extensively used and the true worth of such forces operating against a conventional army was there for all to see. According to the Chambers Twentieth Century Dictionary, the word 'Commando', first used in South Africa, is described as " a unit of a special service raiding brigade"[3]. These were the part time irregular units of the Transvaal and the Orange Free States of South Africa, which took on the might of imperial Britain in the Second Anglo-Boer War of 1899 –1902, events, which Sir Arthur Conan Doyle, a volunteer doctor at that time, described as "*stirred the minds of our people more than anything since the Indian Mutiny, and humiliated our arms as they have not been humiliated in this century*". It needed some 450,000 British Empire troops to defeat a population half that size (of whom only a fraction; 50,000, were in arms as part-time soldiers).

The Dutch had been in South Africa since 1652, when they first settled at Cape of Good Hope to supply ships to and from the Dutch colonies in the East Indies. By 1814, when the Cape Colony was added to the British Empire as the result of the Napoleonic wars, some thirty thousand Dutch, French and German colonists were already in South Africa, the Dutch among them commonly referred to as Boers. By 1820, five thousand British emigrants landed there, settling on the eastern border of the Cape Colony. To escape what seemed to be English encroachments, as well as the freeing of their slaves in the 1830s, about a quarter of Dutch settlers, some five thousand or so, left the coastal areas with an equivalent number of slaves. They moved into what came to be known as the Transvaal and Orange Free States, leaving the coastal areas of Cape Colony to an ever-increasing number of British immigrants and the remaining Dutch, German and French settlers. Soon Natal too became a British colony and pushed out many of its Boers into the two Boer Republics in the north. Thus was set the pattern of two English-speaking provinces in the south and two Afrikaan-speaking provinces in the north. At the time of onset of hostilities, there were about 500,000 people of British extraction in the Cape Colony and Natal and fewer than 250,000 people of Dutch extraction in the Boer Republics. Gold was discovered in the Transvaal hills in 1886. A gold rush ensued, with engineers, miners and merchants from England, America and European countries flocking to the scene. An ill-fated uprising by these outsiders, masterminded by Cecil Rhodes, involving an invasion of the Transvaal, the Jameson's Raid as it came to be known, failed, and, led to war between the British and the breakaway Boer Republics, on 11 October 1899.

In the initial phases of this war, the Boer Commandos used tactics of manoeuvre to include ambushes and raids behind the lines to inflict a number of resounding defeats on the British forces. By September 1900, however, the British were in control of both Republics, except for the northern part of Transvaal. They, however, found that they only controlled the ground their columns physically occupied for as soon as the columns left a town or district, the control the British had there faded away. The huge territory of the Republics made it impossible for the 250 000 British troops to control it effectively. The vast distances between the columns allowed the Boer commandos considerable freedom to move about. The Boer commanders also decided to adopt a guerrilla style of warfare. The commandos were sent to their own districts with the order to act against the British there whenever possible. Their strategy was to do as much damage to the enemy as possible, and then to move off and vanish when enemy reinforcements arrived. In the months following the start of the guerrilla war, the Boers under Generals De Wit, Botha, De La Rey and Beyers made unsuccessful attempts to invade the Cape Colony. The invasion attempts were aimed at drawing the battle away from the Republics' territory to British territory and relieving the tension there. It was believed that the presence of Boer commandos south of the Orange River would also serve as an encouragement to many Afrikaners settled in the Cape region to join the Republican commandos. To counter this policy of guerilla warfare and hit and run attacks by the commandos, Lord Kitchener, who succeeded Lord Roberts in November 1900, realised that a new approach was necessary. His new strategy consisted of three measures. Firstly the two Republics were systematically destroyed - farmsteads and some towns were burned down, food supplies destroyed and livestock driven away or killed in what came to be known as the 'scorched earth policy'. Secondly, all the women and children, who provided logistic and other support to the commandos, were placed in concentration camps where they perished in thousands. Thirdly, large drives using cavalry were begun with the aim of hounding out and capturing the Boer commandos while infantry supported these drives by establishing lines of blockhouses or posts that restricted free movement.

The scorched earth policy was particularly effective and resulted in causing great hardship to each man, woman and child in the Transvaal and Free State. Deprived of food, weapons and ammunition the Boer commandos attacked British columns and confiscated their food supplies, weapons and ammunition and helped themselves to clothing and other necessities. Considering these circumstances, however, members of the Transvaal and Free State Governments came to the conclusion that the only way out was the cessation of hostilities and the commencement of negotiations for peace with the British. Though the coming years brought new life to the Boer war effort and a number of well known victories including the capture of Lord Kitcheners second in command, British superiority in numbers ensured that the outcome for the Boers was inevitably nothing but defeat, with hostilities ending in 1902. In addition to the beginnings of modern strategies used by both sides, the Anglo- Boer War also saw the use of machine guns and the repeater rifle for the first time along with such innovations as trench warfare, establishment of concentration camps and the use of railways to move troops. It was, in fact, the first modern war, using tactics and weapons fairly similar to the ones in use even today. Thus, the effectiveness with which the Boers with a small extremely mobile force using unconventional tactics were able to match a conventional force ten times their size for about four years, is worth serious study. The fact that neither the British nor the Axis powers learned their lessons from this war was amply made clear from the fact that neither side thought it necessary to reorganise their forces to fight battles of manoeuvre instead of the battles of attrition that came to characterise the Great War.

An examination of the circumstances that led to the formation of the Storm Battalions, the first true SOF of the modern era by the Germans, is instructive. As time went on and the cost of war in terms of the killed and wounded became unbearable and victory ever more elusive, there came about a gradual breakdown in discipline, unit cohesion and morale. Troops mutinied and refused to attack with increasing frequency. The Russian Army, for example, collapsed. The frustration of military deadlock became the source of social revolution and a revolution in tactics. This was the tactics of attacking by infiltration. The designers of infiltration tactics visualised trench warfare from a higher plane than the advocates of the slugging attacks. The goals of the infiltrators were the weak points in the line and then, the nerves and arteries of the enemy army, such as headquarters, crossroads, supply and communication centres. It required reliable, aggressive, intelligent troops to carry out individual assaults.

To meet this requirement, the Germans formed the Storm troopers (Strosstrupps), who, unlike the Storm trooper thugs (Sturmabteilung) of the twenties and thirties, were considered to be an elite fighting force. They started out in 1916 at Verdun as a detachment within the normal infantry regiment, hence the name Strosstrupps. They were at the vanguard of the assault and were launched before the main assault to infiltrate and capture positions in depth. To ensure surprise they were launched without any artillery support. They were extremely successful at Verdun and the German High Command increased their numbers by forming companies within their assaulting regiments. Further successes saw the developing of the 'Sturmcompanie' into a 'Sturmbattalione' at the scale of one per division. At the end of the war in 1918 the Sturmbattalione consisted of four assault companies, a gun battery, mortar detachment and machine gun company. The personnel of these elite units were required to be volunteers who had successfully qualified in the assault course and had then been accepted by the unit. In addition he needed to have above average skills in weapon handling and physical education. It was also planned to raise them as a secret branch of infantry to be designated as grenadiers with the personnel authorised to wear a badge on the lines of the pilot badge, which had been instituted, with the raising of the Air Corps. Some of these actions were not undertaken due to the abrupt end of the war. The Soviet Union too had gone on to form elite units known as "Chasti Osobogo Naznacheniya or ChoN"(English translation: Detachment of Special Troops) by the end of the civil war in 1919. However, these units were primarily for Internal Security and were extensively used to quell rebellions against the Communist government.

There are no records of the Allied powers raising specialised units similar to those raised by Germany for conduct of assaults. There is a passing reference to the parachuting of two-man demolition teams by the French Army in the spring of 1918 for raiding and destroying German communication sites. In addition, Brigadier General Billy Mitchell, the Aviation Officer of the American Expeditionary Force, was able to convince General John J Pershing, the Commander of the Force, to permit him to tentatively plan an airborne attack using a complete infantry division for the capture of Metz in the spring of 1919. This planning ceased with the signing of the Armistice in November 1918.[4] Interestingly, Mitchell subsequently went on to organise a demonstration drop at Texas but was not able to convince the top brass of its efficacy. Even Winston Churchill is reported to have suggested the use of parachute troops behind enemy lines for destruction of bridges but to no effect. Possibly, the emphasis on technology involving the invention of the tank and the armoured car was seen as a more favourable approach to ending the stalemate of trench warfare. Its use in the Battle of Cambrai for the first time proved its effectiveness beyond doubt but the Allies were neither able to produce them in sufficient numbers nor evolve a suitable doctrine for their employment, thus not being able to fully exploit its potential. However, tank units could probably have been considered as part of SOF but for the fact that they replaced the cavalry as the arm of decision and became an integral part of the set piece battle. Probably, in a similar context, personnel manning attack helicopters and remotely piloted vehicles (RPVs) should be seen as a part of SOF. The Allies did, however, form and employ SOF with great effect in the Arabian Peninsula under T E Lawrence, an unconventional soldier whose use of partisan troops against the Germans and Turks greatly influenced the course of the War in the Middle East.

**Post World War I Developments**

One of the main lessons that most participants of the Great War, especially the vanquished, took back with them was the utter futility of the stalemate that they fought themselves into for five long years and the bloody cost of trench warfare. Most armies began to look for means by which such a situation could be avoided in future. Emphasis on manoeuvre warfare by developing more lethal and reliable tanks and aircraft and a doctrine for their joint use, "the Blitzkrieg", was adopted along with innovative use of forces that would be able to provide the initial break in which the tanks could then exploit. The period prior to the Second World War, thus, saw much work on forming of airborne forces, mainly by Italy, the Soviet Union and Germany. In 1927, Italy became the first country to try practical military parachuting using an improved parachute, the "Salvatore," which for the first time utilised a static line to deploy the parachute instead of the individually pulled ripcord used by pilots. By 1930, the Italians had several battalions trained in parachuting, though they were not thus employed during World War II.

The Soviet Union, however, was the most developed with regard to raising of such forces and by end of 1933 had formed sizeable forces amounting to approximately ten thousand personnel in twenty nine battalions and up to five corps by 1941. There are reports of use of small airborne detachments against Muslim bandits or "Basmachi" in the Central Asian republics as early as 1925 as also their employment in 1929 to repulse an offensive by the Afghan Army into Tajikistan [5] In 1935, as part of the Kiev manoeuvres, the Soviets demonstrated to the world the air transportation of a Division from Moscow to Vladivostok. These troops along with their equipment were air-landed following the seizure of the airfield by a regiment of airborne troops. Similar exercises were conducted in 1937, but it still remains one of the more interesting and enduring mysteries of that period as to why these forces were never employed in large-scale airborne operations of this nature right through the War. In all likelihood, the political importance of such forces, which, incidentally, remains even to this day if reports of the Russian Chief of General Staff, General Anatoly Kvashnin, about attempts to curtail these forces are to be believed[6] may have felt the effects of Stalin's putsch to a very great extent. The other possibility could be that since the airborne units were seen as offensive troops for employment in the enemy's rear areas in his territory and since most Soviet operations were restricted within their own area where large-scale partisan units were already in action thus obviating the need to employ airborne units. Moreover, these units were also fully committed in countering the German offensive due to its massive scale and success in the initial stages. Incidentally, it was around the mid thirties that Special Purpose or Spetsnaz units were also formed as a part of the airborne forces and were employed extensively in support of the partisans to carry out reconnaissance, surveillance and demolition and mine laying tasks. The operations by the Soviets in Manchuria against the Japanese are worth recounting as extensive use of Spetsnaz was made. In the course of this campaign, Soviet troops operated over vast territories with more than a million and a half soldiers who took part in the operation supported by over five thousand tanks and nearly four thousand aircraft resulting in approximately 84,000 Japanese officers and men being killed and 593,000 taken prisoners. In this campaign Spetsnaz units were inserted by air, ground and submarine well ahead of the conventional forces to provide intelligence on terrain and Japanese deployment. The Spetsnaz followed an extremely high-risk technique in that "senior GRU officers, with the rank of Colonel or even Major-General, were put in charge of small groups. Such a group would suddenly land on an airfield close to an important Japanese headquarters. The appearance of a Soviet Colonel or General deep in the Japanese rear never failed to provoke astonished reactions from both the Japanese high command and the Japanese troops, as well as from the local population. The transport planes carrying these were escorted by Soviet fighter aircraft, but the fighters were soon obliged to return to their bases, leaving the Soviet transport undefended until it landed. Even after it landed it had at best only one high-ranking officer, the crew and no more than a platoon of soldiers to guard over the plane. The Soviet officer would demand and usually obtain a meeting with a Japanese General, at which he would demand the surrender of the Japanese garrison. He and his group really had nothing to back them up: Soviet troops were still hundreds of kilometres away and it was still weeks to the end of the war. But the local Japanese military leaders (and the Soviet officers too, for that matter) naturally did not realise this. Perhaps the Emperor had decided to fight on to the last man. "In several recorded instances, senior Japanese military leaders decided independently to surrender without having permission to do so from their superiors."[7]

During this period, while the United States, France and Britain remained complacent of developments in the field of vertical envelopment, Nazi Germany went on to energetically develop their airborne forces as an added element to the armoured thrusts of the blitzkrieg style of warfare that they had evolved, determined to strike the first blow and cognisant of the value of surprise in destroying the enemy's morale. By the beginning of the war they had two divisions worth of airborne troops. Additionally, by 1935, Lufthansa, the German commercial airline, had over 250 dual use aircraft available that provided these divisions the needed airlift. Operationally these forces were used for the first time against Czechoslovakia in 1938 when they were dropped behind the Czech fortifications near the town of Bruntal as a demonstration of German might that forced the Czechoslovak government to give in without a fight.

Subsequently, the April 1940 invasion of Denmark and Norway depended heavily on surprise achieved by the use of SOF. One parachute battalion captured four airfields and a key road bridge, providing the security needed for the build up of follow-on forces. Within two hours, the Luftwaffe was operating from these airfields while air landed troops built up a force large enough to compel the surrender of the two countries. Following the success of the Scandinavian campaign, a similar attempt was made against the "Low Countries". On 10 May 1940, the German SOF that tried to seize the airfields around The Hague, were met with heavy fire. The defenders were ready and the parachutists were quickly rounded up. As the air landed units came in to land they were decimated. However, south of The Hague, the 7 Flieger Division fared much better and seized a number of airfields, several key bridges (intact), and the "impregnable" Belgian fortress of Fort Eban-Emael. This assault provides an excellent example of their effectiveness.

Fort Eban-Emael was a large underground fort dominating three well-defended bridges over the Albert Canal manned by over 1,200 soldiers. A 400-man strong glider force silently attacked at dawn with nine gliders landing on top of the fort. Using hollow-charge explosives, they blasted their way through the roofs of the gun emplacements and quickly disabled the guns. With the guns out, the remainder of the force was able to quickly secure two of the three critical bridges over the canal allowing armoured forces to get across in a matter of hours leading to a Dutch surrender in four days.

The German employment of SOF reached its zenith with the successful airborne invasion of the island of Crete in May of 1941. This ushered in a new era in warfare as only SOF were utilised with no planned assault from the sea. It involved the capture of four airfields by parachute and glider assault that was to be followed up by air-landed forces. Though successful despite relatively heavy casualties (Germans lost 5,678 while the Allies lost 17,325), it sealed the fate of further large-scale use of SOF as Hitler deemed the day of the paratrooper to be over. By this time the German Airborne Forces consisted of nine divisions under the Luftwaffe along with one additional parachute unit, the Fallschirmjäger

Battalion 500/600, of the Wafen SS. All these units ended up fighting ground actions till the end of the war except for a number of coup-de-main missions that included the unsuccessful attempt to capture Marshal Tito and the subsequent successful kidnapping of the Hungarian leader Admiral Horthy to prevent him throwing in his lot with the Soviets.

However, the most high profile of these was the successful rescue of the Italian dictator Mussolini from Gran Sasso where he was imprisoned, in a joint operation involving the Fallschirmjäger Lehr battalion under the command of Major Mors with fifty men of the Jagdverband der SS led by Otto Skorzeny. The Duce was being held in the hotel Albert Rifugio on Gran Sasso that was only accessible by a railway that passed through the mountains. Frontal assault was out of question so an airborne landing was planned with troops designated to occupy the railway terminal to prevent reinforcements. Despite loss of half the glider force during the assault, the force was able to land next to the hotel and free Mussolini who was then flown out in a Fiesler Storch light aircraft back to Germany.

While large number of Fallschirmjäger or parachute units available met the requirement of SOF for providing support for conventional operations, the Germans had also realised the need for units capable of covert action and accordingly formed the Brandenburg Commando Division. In 1919-20, the German government created a special unit of men identified as "Industrieschutz Oberschlesien". This group was ordered to do all it could to prevent Polish insurgents from being able to influence the Silesian plebiscite in Poland's favour. In about 1938, the unit "Industrieschutz Oberschlesien" was redesignated as the "Deutsche Kompanie". During the Sudetentland crisis of 1938, the "Deutsche Kompanie" participated in numerous covert actions. A sister unit, the "Sudetendeutsche Freikorps" was then added to the units' roster. Subsequently, realising that such forces needed to be under a formal military structure, in 1939, the Abhwer or German Intelligence under Admiral Canaris formed two companies of what subsequently became the Brandenburg Division. Canaris recruited Germans who had lived abroad or in the countries around Germany's borders. These people known as 'Volksdeutsche' came from Silesia in Poland, Czechoslovakia, Hungary and the Sudetentland and could pass themselves off as locals for operations in that country. In fact, there wasn't a part of Europe that the Brandenburgers were not familiar with, the local customs and language, and contained men who spoke Russian, Ukrainian Latvian Estonian and Finnish. It also contained men who had lived in the German colonies in Africa and spoke local dialects as well as English, Portuguese and French. They were used for the first time at the very start of the Polish campaign being deployed even before the invasion to ensure the safe capture of factories in Silesia, which were vital for the German war effort. These troops were also employed during the opening phases of the invasion of Yugoslavia disguised as civilian Serbs, a routine tactic used by them, to capture the gates on the river Danube to keep German river traffic open.

In the opening stages of the Russian campaign, Ukrainian volunteers were recruited for a new detachment, the so-called 'Nightingale Group', and were instrumental in capturing a vital bridge across the San River. They were, however, disbanded when after the successful capture of a radio station in Lvov they proclaimed an independent Ukrainian State that was immediately denied by the Germans. The invasion of Russia also led to a new problem for the German Army — partisans who attacked supply lines and communication networks. The Brandenburgers became the obvious choice to counter such incursions. Russian volunteers who made up at least one company of each Brandenburg Battalion and who knew the local areas extremely well helped them. Apart from anti-partisan operations these units also raided the Murmansk rail route. In the spring of 1941 an African detachment with seventy personnel was formed to assist the Afrika Korps as a deep reconnaissance unit with little success. These units also participated in the failed attempt to capture the Yugoslav partisan leader, Marshal Tito. By the end of 1944, most of these units were converted into Panzer Grenadier units as a part of the "Groodeutschland" Panzer Corps with some personnel transferring to Otto Skorzeny's Panzer Brigade 150 or the "Jagdverband der SS", which went on to cause panic and confusion among the American forces during the Ardennes Offensive disguised in American uniforms. Interestingly, the Germans also formed the 'Indien Freikorps' from volunteers among Indian prisoners of war captured in North Africa. This included an SOF unit that will be discussed separately.

The superlative performance of the German SOF forced the Allies to rectify the situation on their side. On 22 June 1940, Prime Minister Winston Churchill directed the raising of SOF that included commando units in the army, parachute battalions (raised both in Britain and India) and commando units of the Royal Marines. Subsequently other forces such as the Long Range Desert Group (LRDG), Popski's Private Army (PPA) and the L Detachment Special Air Service (now the SAS) were also formed for operations in North Africa and the Chindits, Force 136 and Victor Force for operations in the Burma theatre. In addition, the Special Operations Executive (SOE), the forerunner to MI6, was set up for conduct of covert operations in occupied territories. The United States similarly established airborne forces and the Office of Strategic Services (OSS) that was to become the fore- runner to the Central Intelligence Agency (CIA) after the war along with other such forces like the Merrill's Marauders and Force space 101 that operated in South East Asia and Darby's Rangers and the Marine Corps Raider Battalions that operated in Europe, North Africa and the Pacific.

Eric Bagnold, had served in the trenches of France in the first World War and was stationed in Egypt during most of the inter-war years where he became an avid desert explorer, organising several long expeditions through the Sinai, the Trans-Jordan Desert and the Sahara and laying much of the ground work that would later benefit his patrols. When the war broke out, Bagnold was posted to Kenya, but a fortunate accident of his ship near Port Said delayed his passage and led to a meeting with General Wavell, who had an open ear for Bagnold's ideas of piracy in the desert. Subsequently, Bagnold called together his old explorer partners and proceeded to form the Long Range Patrol (which was soon renamed LRDG) that soon became one of the most successful Special Forces units of the war.

Vladimir Peniakoff was born in Belgium the son of Russian immigrants, but moved to Egypt in the 1920s where he became a successful businessman and spent his free time exploring the Western Desert. When war broke out, he tried to join the British Army as a volunteer but was initially rejected since he was a Belgian citizen and his country was still neutral. After the German invasion of Belgium, he was finally accepted and offered a post as a staff officer - but he had set his mind to working in the desert. After struggling with the Army authorities for a while, he was finally allowed to join LRDG late in 1941 and form a more or less independent subunit called "No.1

Demolition Squadron", which was intended to assist LRDG on sabotage missions. Since this concept did not work out too well as the LRDG's success was mainly attributed to stealth, and it was felt that raids may compromise the locations of patrols, Popski was authorised to form an independent strike force in March 1942, using jeeps armed with Browning machine guns. The unit's name, "Popski's Private Army (PPA)", started out as a joke ("Popski", by the way, was the nickname given to Peniakoff by LRDG's radio operators who obviously had some trouble spelling and pronouncing his name), but since nobody could come up with a better name, it stuck. The unit subsequently operated in Tunisia and served as an intelligence-gathering and surveillance unit behind German lines in Italy. One memorable anecdote, from his book, tells how Popski and his Jeep patrol got stuck somewhere in southern Italy on a mission to find out the troop strengths of several German camps. Not wanting to return to base without the required information, Popski discovered that the phone lines in the area were still working, and being able to speak German called up all the German camps and simply asked them for their troop strengths.

Captain David Stirling developed the concept of small team direct action units on lines of the PPA while recuperating from a parachute accident. The L Detachment No 2 SAS Brigade, as it was first called, was so named to deceive the Germans into believing that large scale airborne forces were available in the Middle East. It was initially created as a desert raiding force to weaken Rommel's North African logistics network as well as hinder aircraft operations. Their first successful raid was carried out in December of 1941, when two groups destroyed 61 aircraft at two airfields. When the force ran out of explosives, SAS soldiers began to use their personal weapons to shoot out the controls. One man, Paddy

Mayne, is reported to have ripped out the controls with his hands. By the end of the North African campaign the SAS had destroyed more aircraft on the ground than the Royal Air Force was able to. The SAS operated in Europe as well. All told, the SAS inflicted 7,733 German casualties in Europe. 4,784 prisoners were captured and 700 vehicles were destroyed or captured. 164 railways were cut, seven trains were destroyed and 33 were derailed. They were also successful to some extent in recovering downed Allied pilots in occupied France and arranging their return to Britain as also for the location, reporting and in some cases destruction of V1 and V2 rocket sites, all this in close cooperation and the assistance of the French Résistance. Towards the closing stages of the war and in its aftermath they were used to "mop up" German war criminals and hunted down important SS and Gestapo agents and brought them before the War Crimes Tribunal.

There were numerous other such forces operating in the South East Asian theatre, the largest being the two operations conducted by Wingate's Chindit Force against the Japanese. The success of these forces can be gauged by the fact that they were extensively used right through the war with some outstanding successes. Among the successful strategic missions were the destruction of the heavy water plant in Norway, the destruction of the German Rocket Development Works at Peenmude and the capture of a number of rocket scientists including Wernher Von Braun who subsequently went on to establish the US space programme, the parachute landings of D Day in Normandy and to some extent, Operation Market Garden, the attempted breakout through Arnhem. The Chindits, Merrill's Marauders and other such units in the Burma Theatre of operations also successfully undertook similar reconnaissance, surveillance and interdiction tasks. Teams of the SOE and OSS were successful in liaising, training and operating with the partisan and resistance movements in Yugoslavia, the Nordic countries and in France. These units provided valuable intelligence on troop movements and locations, interdiction and raids on lines of communication and sabotage and degradation of the Axis war effort through sabotage of factories.

## Post World War II Developments

The post war development of such forces which was restricted to a great extent by the war however saw a rapid demobilisation and winding up of most of these units, especially on the part of the Allies. However, basic capabilities were retained with covert capabilities being retained only by the intelligence services, with the UK, for example, reducing its airborne forces from two divisions to just one air assault brigade and reducing the SAS from three battalions to one with the other two being converted to Territorial Army units. The US similarly did away with its Ranger battalions only going on to reactivate them with the onset of the Vietnam conflict.

While the range of SOF operations have standardised over the years with minor variations brought in by various countries to suit their own environment, units required to conduct these can broadly be classified along the following lines:

- Units for offensive actions behind enemy lines that would assist conventional forces accomplish their missions at the operational, strategic and national levels. This would include coup-de-main missions, capture and holding of positions in depth, reconnaissance, surveillance and target designation (RSTAD) and direct action missions.
- Units for covert and clandestine operations behind enemy lines and in third countries in

support of national aims that include intelligence gathering, snatch operations, sabotage and assassinations.

- Units for counter terrorism (CT) operations against terrorists within and outside the country.

The conceptual development of these forces has been along three distinct approaches. The British have gone on to raise units that have capabilities spread over a broad spectrum of missions. The USA on the other hand has gone in for narrow "super specialisation" with a different type of unit for each type of mission, Delta Force being the only exception. The former Soviet Union, now the Russian Federation, has followed a unique pattern, in that they have raised units capable of broad-spectrum employment like the UK, but various departments have done this for their own purposes. Thus, while the GRU or Main Intelligence Directorate of the General Staff has such units so does the KGB, the Committee for State Security and the MVD, the Ministry of Internal Affairs. This was probably due to the large and disorganised bureaucracy that existed during the Soviet period and was inherited by Russia where each of these departments was a separate power centre with sometimes-conflicting interests. The Soviet Union, thus, had a large number of different forces with similar capabilities and little coordination. However, the unique aspect of the Russian model is that, unlike in the West, it has incorporated its SOF into its intelligence community "in the Soviet military concept razvedka: a seamless web of intelligence, reconnaissance, surveillance and other activities associated with the collection and processing of information about actual or potential enemies."[8] This includes elements of espionage, terrorism and large-scale partisan operations and covers a very diverse range of people: secret agents recruited from among foreigners for carrying out espionage and terrorist operations; professional units composed of the country's best sportsmen and units made up of ordinary but carefully selected and well trained regular soldiers. Furthermore, headquarters at all levels were required to generate their own intelligence, and though information was provided by higher and flanking headquarters, subordinate formations were not completely dependent on these inputs as is the case in most countries where SOF depends on central intelligence agencies to provide the necessary intelligence and attempts to work in close coordination with them. Moreover, while in the West SOF units are controlled at the highest level in the erstwhile Soviet Union, and now in Russia, the Spetsnaz units were placed under their Intelligence Services and allotted to various headquarters till the Army (Corps) level. Most other SOF's of the world have adopted one of these models with varying degrees of success. Interestingly, the Israelis did not have any SOF apart from their Parachute Brigade till quite recently. They believed in raising task-oriented units that were disbanded once the mission was accomplished. Thus, even the unit that carried out the successful hostage rescue mission at Entebbe was of a temporary nature. However, they did go on to raise the Sayaret Matkal for CT operations realising that hostage rescue techniques required expertise that needed to be honed over a period of time. They have also now gone on to raise other SOF units for reconnaissance and other direct action missions on the lines of the SAS.

There is also a prevailing belief among some that while the Western SOF have gone in for limited numbers, the Soviets on the other hand believed in mass. This is far from the truth, as we shall see when we compare the size of such forces in relation to the overall size of that nation's military. For example, the

UK has around ten thousand such troops in an army that is the equivalent of just three divisons. Similarly, the USA has approximately fifty thousand, excluding another ten thousand or so who are a part of their airborne forces, from a regular force that consists of around one million personnel. The Soviet Union and later Russia also had comparable numbers. Some countries such as Germany and France have trained police personnel for their incident response units, such as the GSG9 and the GIGN. These forces, however, have not found favour for dealing with incidents outside their respective countries and there are reports that these tasks are likely to be taken over by military manned SOF in the near future.

The post-Cold War era has seen an increasingly important role played by the non-state actors in the realm of special operations. The use of Private Military Companies (PMC) to carry out a variety of tasks in conflict zones, including some of those that are normally performed by the SOF. Such use was first observed in the 1950s in Aden and Dhofar where David Sterling, the founder of the SAS, led a PMC that assisted the SAS in its tasks. In fact most such PMCs are manned by ex SOF personnel. PMCs are increasingly employed to execute government military contracts and perform a variety of functions including providing military advisors (e.g. the training of the Croatian Army in the 1990s), providing military training to local police forces (e.g. in Iraq), providing security for oil installations (in Saudi Arabia), providing security for multinational companies, providing VIP security (e.g. to the present Afghan President, Hamid Karzai, and to the Coalition Authority Leader in Iraq, Ambassador Paul Bremer), conducting anti-narcotic operations (Colombia), convoy protection and supplementing conventional forces.

The literature on PMCs groups them in three categories: mercenary firms, private military firms and private security firms based on whether they provide combat services, military training and strategic advice, or logistics and technical support[9]. Some of the well-known firms operating in this field are[10] :

- Executive Outcomes (EO) was founded in 1989, initially as part of a larger corporation, Strategic Resources Corporation (SRC), which was later dismantled. It remained in existence until the end of 1998 when it was closed down after the passing of a more stringent law against such companies by South Africa.

- Sandline International previously known under the name "Plaza 107 Ltd.", but received its current name in 1996. Even though the company operates out of offices in London it is registered in the Bahamas. Sandline places (at least officially) great emphasis on having merely legitimate governments and international organisations among its customers. Its main activities to date have been in Papua New Guinea, but it has also been involved in Sierra Leone.

- Military Professional Resources Inc. (MPRI) is headquartered in the United States and closely linked to the US administration. Retired military officers founded it in 1987 and its staff includes, most prominently, former Chief of Staff of the US Army, General. Carl E. Vuono. MPRI has more than 350 employees and has stand-by arrangements with more than 2,000 former officers. Its main activities have been in the former Yugoslavia where it has, among other thinks, been involved in the training of the Croat and Bosnian (i.e. Croat-Muslim) armies. Under the auspices of African Crisis Response Initiative (ACRI), MPRI is also involved in the training of African armies.

The modus operandi of PMCs can be seen by the situation in Sierra Leone and the strategic role played by Executive Outcomes. In Sierra Leone, the Strasser government in March 1995 hired EO to fight the rebel movement Revolutionary United Front (RUF), which is almost universally regarded as common thugs with a reputation for a particularly nasty form of warfare, featuring amputation of civilians, etc. The initial assignment of the EO troops was the re-conquest of titanium and bauxite mines, which had fallen into the hands of the RUF, and the revenues from which amounted to more than half the export earnings of Sierra Leone. EO was initially merely supposed to provide training and technical support for the government forces, but after the RUF's seizure of important diamond mines its troops also became directly involved in combat. According to the EO, the total contingent of EO troops never exceeded 250 personnel. The results are generally assessed as a modest success, as the situation after ten months was sufficiently peaceful to allow holding of presidential elections in March 1996. The activities of the EO are also generally seen in a positive light, as EO personnel collaborated satisfactorily with both the government and international emergency relief organisations. A contributory cause to the acceptance among the local population may have been that most of the deployed troops were black. The peace did not last, and in 1996 attempts were uncovered to deploy other (in this case white) mercenaries, apparently on the payroll of the RUF, to seize control of a diamond mine being guarded by EO, presumably against payment in the form of diamond concessions, which were subsequently sold to BE.

PMCs have carved a space for themselves as market forces determine their interests and they are a repository for trained manpower—especially former SOF soldiers. There is a mutual convergence of interest between the PMCs and governments. The case of Iraq is important, as it is indicative of how far SOF tasks are subcontracted out to private actors. There are more than 15,000 contractors in Iraq making them the third largest combat deployed contingent in the Iraqi occupation. In fact operators of Blackwater Inc were working alongside US Marine and Special Forces in Najaf when the buildings they occupied came under attack. Subsequently, a company helicopter was used for fire-support, re-supply the soldiers and evacuate wounded SOF[11].

*"Who Dares, Wins."*

— British Special Air Service

## SOF OF THE UNITED KINGDOM

In the post war western world there can be no doubt that the United Kingdom has been the leading nation in evolving of SOF organisations, specialised equipment, training and employment doctrines. Their influence has been all encompassing and most countries of the developed world and not a few of the developing world as well, including ours, have tailored their SOF organisations based on the British model. The end of the Second World War left Britain's economy in devastated condition and the accompanying rapid loss of empire required massive reductions in the defense forces of the country. This led to only the very basic capabilities for special operations being retained that have since 1950, when the SAS was re-raised, evolved into a balanced well trained force under the Director Special Forces Group, who reports directly to Whitehall and the Chief of Defense Staff. He is also a part of the Cabinet Office Committee, normally attended by the Chief of Defense Staff, on matters pertaining to CT. Under him he has one active, the 22nd, and two Territorial Army Special Air Service (SAS) Regiments, the 21st, and 23rd along with the Special Boat Section (SBS) and the 14th Intelligence Group. Though how weekend soldiers can truly match up to their regular brethren is questionable. Neither the 16 Air Assault Brigade, which has two of the four parachute battalions (that includes one Territorial Army unit), nor, 3 Commando Brigade, Royal Marines, consisting of four Commando Groups, are a part of the Special Forces Group, probably because they also have officers of similar status in command. The command and control of the

Comacchio Group, Royal Marines, reportedly rests with the Headquarters of the Royal Marines.

The SAS have, over the years, developed into a highly professional force with clearly defined missions and well equipped, highly trained and motivated personnel to execute them. The first missions that the newly formed SAS where required to undertake was in, what was then Malaya, against communist insurgents supported by the local ethnic Chinese population. These were operations in what they referred to as 'Counter Revolutionary Warfare' or defensive CT operations in a low intensity conflict scenario. The primary tasks that they carried out in this campaign were area domination by establishing ambushes and winning the hearts and minds of the local population, especially in the tropical jungles of the heartland, along with covert surveillance and some snatch operations to either assassinate or capture insurgent sympathisers and their leaders. Interestingly, prolonged and continuous operations by small teams in the jungle for two to three months at a time with complete dependence on air maintenance enabled these detachments to dominate the area and force the insurgents into villages and towns where they could be easily targeted by conventional military and police forces. Similar tactics were again used in the campaign in Borneo against the Indonesians. Here the rugged terrain and dense jungle enabled the SAS to infiltrate behind the Indonesian front line positions and ambush elements deployed in depth. In Aden and Dhofar, however, the SAS operated in larger strengths carrying out cordon and search and area domination operations in conjunction with local pro government militia that they had trained. It was also in Aden that the British government used mercenaries led by the SAS founder, David Sterling, to carry out trans-border operations against Yemen. The likelihood of SAS personnel also being used covertly cannot be ruled out. Incidentally, tactics evolved in Aden to counter urban guerrilla operations referred colloquially to as 'Keeni Meeni' operations, Swahili for the unseen movement of a snake in the grass, came to be extensively used in northern Ireland where the SAS built up an excellent intelligence base and carried out covert surveillance, area domination, raids, snatch and assassination operations. There were some attempts at targeting IRA safe houses and elements located in the Irish Republic but a couple of unsuccessful attempts where SAS soldiers were picked up across the border led to a ban on cross border operations.

Its primary mission, however, remained unconventional military operations in general war. In this they were required to primarily take on the rear elements of the Soviet Armies in Europe providing stay behind parties that would provide intelligence of follow up forces and target Soviet administrative and communication elements. Fortunately such a situation did not arise and the first real opportunity that arose for such tasks were during the Falklands War with Argentina. The SAS inserted detachments from one of its squadrons into East Falkland, the more densely populated of the two main islands, for prolonged surveillance of up to six weeks prior to the main assault in rugged terrain in extreme weather conditions; no mean feat. Thus the assault force had reasonably accurate intelligence available for planning purposes. The Argentinean defensive strategy was based on a strong mobile reserve supported by helicopters that would move the force to suitable locations once the main assault had been identified. However, some of the SAS detachments were able to pinpoint the location of the Argentinean Chinook helicopter force and direct an air strike on to it thereby substantially reducing this capability. In these operations, the SAS had two of their positions compromised by foot patrols leading to two dead and one trooper captured. Another squadron was able to raid an airfield on Pebble Island that led to the destruction of eleven Pucara ground attack aircraft, out of the total of 33 available on the Island. However, their most politically and strategically sensitive mission was the attempt to raid the airbase at Rio Grande in the Argentine half of the island of Tierra del Fuego, approximately six hundred kilometres to the West of the Falklands. This was where intelligence had reported that the Exocet carrying Super Etendard aircraft of the Argentinean Air Force were based and these aircraft were considered to be the biggest threat to the safety of the fleet and the entire invasion plan. The fact that the mission failed due to a simple navigation error on the part of the mission commander after having been successfully inserted on to the Island, led to the loss of a number of ships in the attacks on the fleet once it was within range. The loss of one of the aircraft carriers instead of the Atlantic Conveyer could have very well changed the very course of the conflict.[12] The other conflict where the SAS were used to some effect was the Gulf War of 1990. In that conflict, however, the SAS were not as successful in conducting surveillance missions due to the open terrain and the large number of graziers who moved around with their herds in the vast open scrub. The exploits of Andy McNab and his patrol, Bravo Two Zero,[13] makes interesting reading. Despite difficulties the SAS were still able to pull off a couple of worthwhile raids against Scud missile sites and also locate and bring down air strikes against a number of armour units. By and large, most of their operations were at the tactical rather than the strategic level.

The third type of task that the SAS excelled in was incident response operations involving dealing with intervention in hijack or hostage situations. The spate of hijackings, bombings, kidnappings in the seventies by various terrorist groups, mainly Palestinian or their affiliates, led to the formation of the Counter Revolutionary Wing that evolved tactics and equipment to neutralise terrorist hijackings and kidnappings. In these operations close cooperation is maintained with the Special Patrol Group of the London Metropolitan Police. The first clear insight into their capabilities was provided by their intervention in the siege of the Iranian embassy at London. This siege began around noon on 30 April 1980 when six terrorists, belonging to the minority Arab community of Khuzestan Province of Iran, occupied the Embassy taking 26 people hostage. They demanded autonomy for the province and the release of 92 of the Arab minority in jail. Police negotiators attempted to get the terrorists to release their hostages while the SAS assault teams were kept on stand by in close proximity of the Embassy. In this period of five days the SAS was able to carry out reconnaissance of entry routes and place surveillance devices within the grounds to gain as much information as possible with regard to locations of hostages and the terrorists. On 5 May, negotiations broke down and the terrorists commenced murdering their hostages. After the first body was dumped outside and there appeared to have been another killing, the SAS assault team was given the go ahead and launched its assault. This was successfully carried out with only one other hostage being killed by the terrorists during the assault. It resulted in five of the terrorists being killed with the sixth being taken prisoner, while the SAS suffered only one wounded, a trooper who suffered burn injuries because of his proximity to the explosive charges used to break into the building. This troopers' abseiling mechanism jammed leaving him dangling outside the window he was to enter.

This successful assault close on the heels of the disastrous American Operation Eagle Claw made the SAS the premier incident response team in the World. Another low profile covert unconventional operation that never made headlines exemplifies what the SAS do best. The very next year, in July 1981, a Libyan-Cuban backed coup was attempted on the West African State of Gambia while the President, Sir Dawda Jawara, was away in Britain attending the wedding of Prince Charles. Rebel forces were soon able to take control of the capital, Banjul, and seize the country's radio station; airport and the palace as also take hostage one of the President's wives with her children and some members of the cabinet. While neighbouring Senegalese paratroopers intervened on behalf of the President and took control of the airport, the 22 SAS dispatched a three-member team, under their second in command, by commercial aircraft with communications and weapons to provide an update on the situation. This team was able to make its way to the Banjul airport by an Air France flight and link up with the Senegalese troops there. It subsequently crossed through the rebel lines made its way to the British High Commission where it was able to meet up with the High Commissioner who was able to give them information that the President's wife was admitted at the hospital as one of her children was unwell. They then made their way to the hospital, disarmed the guards and rescued the President's wife along with her children and transported them to the High Commission for safe keeping. They then went back to the airport, convinced the Senegalese to detach a sub unit with which they assaulted and broke the hold of the rebels leading to the collapse of the coup.

The high standing that the SAS came to be held in over the years added a lucrative money-spinner to their repertoire, that of providing training and advisory teams to a large number of Middle Eastern and African Nations. Apart from the huge amounts of money earned in this way, both by the personnel and the establishment, the British Government also had the added advantage of being able to establish close and intimate relationships with the leaders of these countries and thereby influence the course of events in the region to their advantage, far beyond what they could have otherwise ever hoped to have achieved in their prevailing economic circumstances. For example, President Jomo Kenyatta of Kenya, who was totally anti British in his initial years in power, because of the excesses he had faced at their hands during the independence struggle, completely changed his stance because of the active assistance of the SAS training team that was conducting training of his personal bodyguards and his secret police thereby ensuring he remained in power for decades. It was this ability to influence foreign affairs that gave the SAS tremendous clout within the British Government with direct access to the Prime Minister.

The parachute battalions along with the 16 Air Assault Brigade, though not a part of the Special Forces Group, do enjoy an extremely close and symbiotic relationship with the SAS. This is because they are the largest contributors of manpower to the SAS as also because of the fact that they work very closely with the SAS on most operational deployments. They provide the muscle while the SAS concentrates on acquisition of information and covert operations. This has been the case in Malaya, the Falklands, Ireland, Sierra Leone and Iraq. In operational terms these units are similar to the Ranger Battalions of the 75th Ranger Regiment of the US and our own Parachute Brigade.

The Royal Marines that form a part of the Royal Navy provide the other elements of the SOF in the UK.

They have the four Commando Groups under 3 Commando Brigade, which like the Air Assault Brigade, is not a part of the Special Forces Group but provides one important element of the rapid response force maintained by the UK. The Special Boat Squadron (SBS), formed from volunteers within the Commandos is an infantry company sized unit supplemented by specialist communication and logistic support units and is responsible for protection of maritime assets such as the oil rigs in the North Sea and for carrying out offensive maritime special operations including deep penetration, reconnaissance and sabotage tasks. They also have an Arctic Warfare Team that was deployed in the Falklands with limited success. In fact not much is known about the operational capabilities of the SBS except that commercial diving operations appear to have poached and drawn away experienced manpower thereby seriously affecting their effectiveness. Interestingly, technological advancements in early warning and surveillance equipment used for protection of maritime assets has increasingly forced the SBS to enhance its ability to operate on land and approach its targets from the landward direction, a capability in which it is still to reach the proficiency that army units such as the SAS and parachute units normally display. Finally, the Royal Marines also have the Comacchio Group that is quite similar to the SBS. This five hundred-man unit formed in 1980 has the task of protecting Britain's nuclear assets, especially the ballistic missile submarines at the Royal Navy Base at Faslane. The Comacchio Group is reportedly made up of two companies, all of whom would be at the disposal of the local police commander in the event of an emergency. The group is subrogated in this manner by law and could only take action with the permission of the police and necessary government ministers.

Operationally, the unit falls under the direct command of the Royal Marines Headquarters. Interestingly, Comacchio has deployed against possible threats posed by anti-nuclear demonstrators. Though the incident in question did not require use of force, it did highlight the possibility that an attack on a nuclear base or device need not come from foreign terrorists.

The 14th Intelligence Group was raised in the early seventies to coordinate and organise all intelligence activity on behalf of the army in Northern Ireland. Over a period of time it developed very close links with the SAS and became the main souice of intelligence for its operations in Northern Ireland. It has now reportedly been converted into the "I" Battalion of the Special Forces Group and is tasked with coordination with other intelligence agencies, acquisition, provision and assessement of all technical intelligence of the target area for the SOF. The SOF units then only carry out close and confirmatory receonnaissance of the target area prior to launching their operation. This grouping ensures a better integrated approach to CT operations and has important lessons in our context.

The Royal Air Force (RAF) has a dedicated squadron that includes fixed and rotary wing assets with state of the art navigational systems for operations in support of the SAS. It however does not have any dedicated squadrons in support of the 16th Air Assault Brigade. It also has a small independent parachute squadron for Combat Search and Rescue (CSAR) as a part of the RAF Regiment, the force responsible for providing air defence and ground protection to RAF airfields.

The British SOF has not always distinguished itself, as is the conventional wisdom on the subject. They were unable to prevent the hasty withdrawal of the British Army from Aden, similar in many ways to the hasty and disorganised retreat that the US beat from Vietnam. The refusal to obey orders, a mutiny no less, on the part of 'D' Squadron 22nd SAS tasked to react against the Rhodesian Unilateral Declaration of Independence in 1965 brought out the inherent racial bias of the British and did untold damage to the Commonwealth and to British prestige in the region and around the world.[14] Their performance in the Falklands also left much to be desired as a number of instances at self-glorification came to light. The decision to use the SAS to capture the Rio Grande airfield after the failure of the initial raid is an example. The SAS is neither trained, organised or equipped for such a task, which falls in the province of the parachute battalions, and were selected only because of the influence that the Commander SF Group had with Mrs. Thatcher, the Prime Minister. The fact that the operation had to be called off due to the Squadron Commander and most of the NCOs of the sub-unit nominated unwilling to participate, as was the reaction of the RAF, does not enhance the reputation of all those involved in the planning and execution of the mission.

In terms of operational results, the Gulf War in 1990 was marred by non-availability of equipment and lack of coherent planning, tasking and organisation. For example, the squadron that was initially deployed as a part of the coalition forces was replaced just weeks before the operation commenced by a squadron that had just come off a rotation in anti drug operations in the jungles of Colombia, not because of any operational consideration but on the grounds that the squadron commander had sufficient clout to convince his superiors that his squadron should not miss out on the action, as it had during the Falklands crisis. Not something that would do wonders for unit cohesion or espirit-de-corps.[15] Thus, over a period of time, the SAS has become a stepping-stone for ambitious officers willing to take on missions of doubtful value that give them personal contact at the highest levels, regardless of the cost to the rank and file, who are permanently posted, while officers continue to serve only on a tenure basis.

There can be no doubt that British SOF and rapid reaction forces are balanced, highly motivated and well-trained units that provide the British Government with an extremely potent capability to look after its interests. It is however ironic that Great Britain no longer has either the muscle or the money to really play an active part in world affairs despite what its political leaders believe. It has, therefore, over the years become subservient to the US and played second fiddle to ensure it continues to bask in the limelight. Unfortunately, most of its citizens, including those in the defence forces, fully comprehend this reality and must, therefore, lead to a lack of motivation and unwillingness to go in harms way on the part of the defence forces, including the SOF, who fully understand that their sacrifices are not for Queen and country, but for the President and citizens of a former colony who are unwilling to risk their own after their bitter experiences in Vietnam.

*"De oppresso liber"*

*(To free the oppressed)*

Motto US Army Special Forces

## SOF OF THE UNITED STATES

The United States has the most elaborate and well-organised SOF establishment in the world. It is also one of the largest with an overall strength of 45,690 personnel and a budget of over $ 3.7 billion as per figures available for the financial year 2001.[16] Operations in Afghanistan and Iraq could have only added to the budget and manpower in view of the extensive use that the US has made of these forces. While the performance of US troops in combat may be debatable, as experience in Afghanistan and Iraq show, there can be no gainsaying the fact that the systems approach that the US adopts to respond to problems and the speed with which they are implemented show up the bureaucracy in very good light along with the clarity of thought and determination of the leadership. A recent example of this is the establishment of the Department of Homeland Security for coordinating and controlling intra-departmental action to deal with the terrorist threat that emerged with the September 2001 attacks. As we shall see, legislative action has forcefully put in place systems not only for establishment, training, employment, command and control of SOF, but also for ensuring joint services cooperation in the conduct of all combat operations.

In 1941, former United States Army Colonel, William J Donovan, the first Director of the OSS, the fore- runner to the CIA, visualised that the first phase of operations against the enemy involved "intelligence penetration," with its results available for strategic planning and propaganda. This would be followed by special operations in the form of sabotage and subversion, commando raids, and guerrilla actions by behind the lines resistance movements. All this, in his view, represented the softening up process prior to invasion by friendly armed forces and was an attempt to unify the functions of intelligence gathering, sabotage, psychological warfare, guerrilla operations and commando actions in support of conventional operations to forge a new "instrument of war".[17] The agency was divided into intelligence, special operations and training divisions. While research and analysis, secret intelligence and counter espionage were a part of the Intelligence Branch, sabotage, psychological and guerrilla warfare formed a part of the Special Operations branch. Special operations in their context covered aspects pertaining to "*espionage, counter intelligence in foreign nations, sabotage, commando raids, guerrilla and partisan group activity ... various other forms of psychological warfare and underground operations.*"[18] Thus, while strategic tasks became the realm of the OSS, the US simultaneously went on to raise Ranger Battalions, Raider Units and underwater demolition teams for carrying out tactical commando tasks. They also, like the British, went on to raise a number of airborne divisions and all these units were at the forefront of operations till the end of the war.

The end of the war saw a drastic reduction in all such types of units with all covert operations continuing to be the responsibility of the newly formed CIA. It was only the growing involvement in Vietnam and President Kennedy's firm belief that there was a requirement for unconventional forces that saw the resuscitation of the Rangers and the formation of the Special Forces. It was only in 1977 with the raising of the 1st Special Forces Operational Detachment-Delta (Delta Force) that a CT operations capability was put in place. This capability was subsequently expanded with the raising of the Naval Special Warfare Development Group. It was however in 1987 with the passage of the Cohen-Nunn Amendment to the Goldwater-Nichols Act that the SOF came into their own. This amendment encouraged the revitalisation of the special operations capabilities of the Department of Defense, which had reached its nadir in the way Operation Eagle Claw was planned and executed, as a result of which the U.S. Special Operations Command, a unified command dedicated to the preparation of special operations forces for assigned missions around the world, was established. Also as its components the Army, Navy and Air Force, each established commands for their SOF units along with all the unified theatre commands establishing elements to control SOF allotted to them. More importantly the Cohen-Nunn Amendment also established the Office of the Assistant Secretary of Defense for Special Operations and Low-Intensity Conflict at the Pentagon as the policy and resource focal point for all special operations and low-intensity conflict activities of the Defense Department. Additionally and most importantly, it mandated a separate defense budget for all SOF.

Special Operations Forces in the context of US military philosophy today have a dual role. They are seen as the nation's penetration and strike force, able to respond to specialised contingencies across the conflict spectrum with stealth, speed, and precision. They are also seen as warrior-diplomats capable of influencing, advising, training, and conducting operations with foreign forces, officials, and populations. Broadly, the missions that the SOF undertake, as stated in the Posture Statement, are as follows: -

- **Counter Proliferation (CP).** Combat proliferation of nuclear, biological, and chemical weapons across the full range of U.S. efforts, including the application of military power to protect U.S. forces and interests; intelligence collection and analysis; and support of diplomacy, arms control, and export controls. Accomplishment of these activities may require coordination with other U.S. Government Agencies.

- **Combating Terrorism (CBT).** Preclude, preempt, and resolve terrorist actions throughout the entire threat spectrum, including anti-terrorism (defensive measures taken to reduce vulnerability to terrorist acts) and counter terrorism (offensive measures taken to prevent, deter, and respond to terrorism), and resolve terrorist incidents when directed by the National Command Authority (NCA) or the appropriate unified commander or requested by the Services or other government agencies.

- **Foreign Internal Defense (FID).** Organise, train, advise, and assist host-nation's military and paramilitary forces to enable these forces to free and protect their society from subversion, lawlessness, and insurgency.

- **Special Reconnaissance (SR).** Conduct reconnaissance and surveillance actions to obtain or verify information concerning the capabilities, intentions, and activities of an actual or potential enemy or to secure data concerning characteristics of a particular area.

- **Direct Action (DA).** Conduct short-duration strikes and other small-scale offensive actions to seize, destroy, capture, recover, or inflict damage on designated personnel or materiel.

- **Psychological Operations (PSYOP).** Induce or reinforce foreign attitudes and behaviours favourable to the originator's objectives by conducting planned operations to convey selected information to foreign audiences to influence their emotions, motives, objective reasoning, and, ultimately, the behaviour of foreign governments, organisations, groups, and individuals.

- **Civil Affairs (CA).** Facilitate military operations and consolidate operational activities by assisting commanders in establishing, maintaining, influencing, or exploiting relations between military forces and civil authorities, both governmental and non-governmental, and the civilian population in a friendly, neutral, or hostile area of operation.

- **Unconventional Warfare (UW).** Organise, train, equip, advise, and assist indigenous and surrogate forces in military and paramilitary operations normally of long duration.

- **Information Operations (IO).** Actions taken to achieve information superiority by affecting adversary information and information systems while defending one's own information and information systems.[19]

The SOF have also been given additional collateral tasks that include coalition support and security assistance that includes advice on tactics, communication support, training, provision of equipment and liaison with coalition forces. Combat search and rescue, primarily for SOF personnel and humanitarian activities include de-mining and counter drug activities. The last and probably most important task, which any Government publication will underplay for obvious reasons, is that of special activities that include "planning and conduct of actions abroad in support of national foreign policy objectives so that the role of the U.S. Government is not apparent or acknowledged publicly."[20]

The major variation in tasking between the US SOF and those of the British and other West European nations is the inclusion of psychological warfare, civil affairs and information warfare as a part of special operations. There can be no debate that these facets of warfare can play an important role in any conflict and can greatly enhance the performance of the SOF as well in certain situations, but their integration into the SOF may not be either necessary or justifiable. Civil affairs, for example, especially in the context of LIC become an important tool that all units need to utilise to enhance their performance and ensure an effective campaign to win the hearts and minds of the population. In a similar manner, psychological and information operations require greater interaction with intelligence and electronic warfare operations and would in all likelihood pay better dividends if integrated into the same organisation.

## Organisational Overview

To fulfill these missions, the SOF have an elaborate joint services organisational structure headed by a four star General that reports to the Joint Chiefs of Staff as also to the National Command Authority (NCA). Details of the organisation tree are given at Appendix A. Its important components are as follows: -

- US Special Operations Command (USSOCOM) located at MacDill Air Force Base, Florida, has all SOF of the Army, Navy, and Air Force, based in the United States placed under its command. USSOCOM has three service component commands: Army Special Operations Command (USASOC) Ft. Bragg, North Carolina; Naval Special Warfare Command (NAVSPECWARCOM) Coronado, California; Air Force Special Operations Command (AFSOC) Hurlburt Field, Florida; and one sub-unified command, Joint Special Operations Command (JSOC) Ft. Bragg, North Carolina. USSOCOM is responsible for providing SOF to the NCA, regional combatant commanders, and American Ambassadors and their Country Teams for successful conduct of special operations during both peace and war. USSOCOM prepares SOF to successfully conduct special operations, including civil affairs and psychological operations. Lately, it has also been given responsibility to undertake operations independently if authorised by the President or Secretary of Defence having been nominated as a "Supported Command" from its earlier status of a "Supporting Command".

• Each of the unified theatre commands has a separate Special Operations Command (SOC) to meet their special operations requirements. These provide the planning, preparation, and command and control of SOF from the Army, Navy, and Air Force. They ensure that SOF strategic capabilities are fully employed and that SOF is fully synchronised with conventional military operations, where necessary. They provide a clear chain of command and advisory support to the theatre commander. While USSOCOM provides funding and personnel for the SOCs, each SOC reports directly to the geographic Commander in Chief (CINC). There are six SOCs in support of the geographic commands worldwide; Atlantic, Central, Europe, Pacific, Korea and the Southern Command.

• The sub unified command, Joint Special Operations Command (JSOC), was established in 1980 and is located at Fort Bragg. JSOC is a joint headquarters that deals with organisational and training aspects and is designed to study special operations requirements and techniques; ensure interoperability and equipment standardisation; plan and conduct joint special operations exercises and training; and develop joint special operations tactics. There are however some reports that JSOC is also responsible for all "black" direct-action operations through three covert operations units—Delta Force, SEAL Team 6 and the Intelligence Support Activity Team (ISA), now known as Gray Fox. The latter is probably responsible for tasks such as assassinations and snatch operations.[21]

The army component of the SOF is under command of the US Army Special Operations Command (USASOC) at Fort Bragg, N.C., which is a major Army command and provides active and reserve Special Forces, Ranger, Special Operations Aviation, Psychological Operations and Civil Affairs forces to USSOCOM for deployment to combatant unified commands around the world. These are: -

- The 75th Ranger Regiment, headquartered at Fort Benning, Georgia, is composed of three Ranger Battalions, and is the premier light-infantry unit of the United States Army. Each battalion consists of three rifle companies with a Headquarters Company. Each battalion is authorised 580 Rangers. However, the battalions may be up to fifteen per cent over-manned to make allowances for personnel away on temporary duties and courses. The cornerstone of Ranger missions is that of direct action, in that they are the premier airfield seizure and raid unit in the Army. However, they are also required to be proficient in conventional infantry tactics of advance to contact, ambush, reconnaissance, airborne and air assaults, and hasty defense. A typical Ranger Battalion or Regiment mission would involve seizing an airfield for use by follow-on forces and conducting raids on key targets of operational or strategic importance. Once relieved, the Ranger unit is pulled back so that it may conduct planning for future SOF operations. On any given day, one Ranger Battalion is on alert with the requirement to be "wheels up" within 18 hours of notification. Additionally, one rifle company with battalion command and control can deploy in nine hours. Ranger units have a limited anti-tank capability (16 Carl Gustav Rocket Launchers and nine Javelin ATGMs) and some indirect fire support in the form of six 60mm mortars and a few shoulder based Stinger air defense artillery systems. They are, however, well supplied with a variety of machine guns at the battalion, company and squad levels — twelve, twenty seven and fifty four respectively. Ranger units have no organic combat support or logistic support and deploy with only five days of supplies and require logistical and mission support from other services and/or agencies.

• The US Army Special Forces Command (Airborne) is required to train, validate, and prepare Special Forces units to deploy and execute operational requirements. It exercises command and control over five active and two reserve Special Forces Groups. Each Special Forces Group is regionally oriented and comprises of a Headquarters Company, one Support Company and three Special Forces Battalion. The support company provides intelligence, electronic warfare, communications and logistic support to the Group. Each Special Forces Battalion (Airborne) comprises of a Battalion Headquarters detachment, one support Company and three Special Forces companies. Each battalion also has a detachment each of

Combat Diving and Combat Free Fall. The Special Forces Company is comprised of a Company Headquarters and six Operational "A" Detachments, the working twelve member squad. It consists of one Captain (Commander), one Warrant Officer (Detachment Technician), one Master Sergeant (Operations Sergeant), one Sergeant First Class (Assistant Operations Sergeant), two Weapons Sergeants, two Engineer Sergeants, two Medical Sergeants, and two Communications Sergeants.

• The 160$^{th}$ Special Operations Aviation Regiment (Airborne) provides aviation support to Army SOF. This Regiment holds modified OH-6 light observation helicopters, MH-60 utility helicopters, and MH-47 medium-lift helicopters and is based at Fort Campbell, KY. It is composed of four active duty battalions and one forward deployed company. It conducts specialised aviation operations in conjunction with other SOF that includes clandestine penetration for the insertion, extraction, and re-supply of SOF by air as also attack helicopter support as required.

• The US Army Civil Affairs and Psychological Operations Command (Airborne) is the headquarters for Army Civil Affairs and Psychological Operations units and is located at Fort Bragg. Of its approximately 9,000 soldiers, about 83 per cent are in the Reserve component and provide support to all theatre commanders in meeting their global commitments. The command has one active duty Psychological Operations unit, the 4$^{th}$ Psychological Operations Group (Airborne), with six battalions, and, one active duty Civil Affairs unit, the 96$^{th}$ Civil Affairs Battalion (Airborne), with six companies. Both units are also located at Fort Bragg.

In addition to the units mentioned above, the Army has Delta Force that reports directly to the Joint Chiefs of Staff and is the premier incident response unit available to the US Government. This unit is organised on the lines of the SAS and though primarily tasked for hostage rescue has participated in a number of operations not involving such tasks. The unit is located in a remote section of the U.S. Army's Fort Bragg, North Carolina. It is organised into three operating squadrons that are subdivided into three troops each. Troops, as the case with the SAS, specialise in a variety of skills such as Combat Free Fall, Combat Diving and other skills. Delta also maintains support units that handle selection and training, logistics, finance, and the unit's medical requirements. It also has a little known, but vital, technical unit that is responsible for covert eavesdropping equipment for use in hostage rescues and similar situations.

All US Air Force special operations are under the command of Air Force Special Operations Command, which is an Air Force major command and constitutes the Air Force component of the unified USSOCOM. The command provides Air Force SOF for worldwide deployment and assignment to regional unified commands for conducting the full spectrum of special operations missions and collateral activities. It is organised into one active component Special Operations Wing, two active Special Operations Groups, one active Special Tactics Group, and two reserve Special Operations Wings. Its missions include insertion, extraction, re-supply, aerial fire support, refueling, combat search and rescue, and psychological operations.

The special operations wings and groups are quite similar in organisation except for the fact that the wing has a larger number of squadrons on its organisation for battle. While the Wing is located in the continental US (CONUS), the two active groups are located in the UK, for operations in support of Central and European Commands, and in Japan in support of the Pacific and Korea Commands. The Special Operations Wing and the Special Operations Groups primarily have squadrons equipped with MC130E and H fixed wing aircraft for day, night and adverse weather infiltration, exfiltration, and re-supply of SOF in hostile or denied territory; squadrons equipped with MC130P tankers for clandestine aerial refueling of special operations helicopters; squadrons equipped with AC130U and H Spectre gunships that are equipped with 105mm Howitzers among other weapon systems and squadrons equipped with the MH-53J Pave Low III and MH-60G Pave Hawk helicopters for day or night, all-weather, low-level penetration of denied territory to provide infiltration, exfiltration, re-supply, fire support and combat rescue capability for SOF. The Special Operations Wing in addition has a squadron for foreign internal defence whose personnel provide US military expertise to other governments in support of their internal defence and development efforts. While the wing has approximately 90 aircraft the groups deploy approximately sixty aircraft each. The Special Tactics Group, with headquarters at Hurlburt Field, Florida, has special operations combat controllers; para-rescue personnel and combat weathermen who work jointly in Special Tactics Teams. The Group has six Special Tactics Squadrons and one Combat Weather Squadron on its establishment. Of these; two are co-located with the Special Operations Groups in the UK and Japan. In a similar manner, the Combat Weather Squadron has detachments with these Groups. Interestingly, since 1990, a number of EC130 Commando Solo aircraft have been allotted to one of the reserve groups for psychological operations. This aircraft is equipped to conduct psychological operations and civil affairs broadcast missions in the standard AM, FM, HF, TV and military communications bands. It supports civic actions by broadcasting via radio or TV programmes on educational issues, messages and speeches by government officials of friendly countries and entertainment and cultural programmes. These operations have been carried out with some success in the Gulf War, Afghanistan and, recently, in Iraq.

The Naval Special Warfare Command is located at the Naval Amphibious Base in Coronado, California, and is the Naval component to the USSOCOM. The mission of Commander, Naval Special Warfare Command is to prepare Naval SOF to carry out assigned missions and to develop maritime special operations strategy, doctrine, and tactics. It exercises operational control of all United States-based Naval SOF and responsibility for the training, equipping, supporting, and providing trained and ready forces to the theatre commands. The Commander, Naval Special Warfare Command is a Navy Flag Officer, a Rear Admiral. Under his command are the Special Warfare Groups, the Special Boat Squadrons, the Special Warfare Centre, Naval Special Warfare Development Group and logistics support elements. The Special Warfare Centre is the primary training establishment and conducts basic diving and advanced maritime special operations training for control elements located outside the continental United States, support other NSW forces assigned to theatre SOCs or components of naval task forces naval and other service SOF. The Naval Special Warfare Development Group provides centralised management for the test, evaluation, and development of current and emerging technology applicable to Naval Special Warfare Forces. It also develops maritime ground and airborne tactics for Naval Special Warfare application. In addition, SEAL Team 6, which specialises in maritime incident response and intervention operations, is in all likelihood under its command. The Special Warfare Groups, of which there are two, are the operational establishments and have under them SEAL Teams, Seal Delivery Teams (SDV) and Naval Special Warfare Units. Each SEAL Team has a number of SEAL Platoons, normally eight with a strength of sixteen personnel per platoon tasked for reconnaissance, direct actions and other operations in maritime or riverine environments. The SDV Teams operate and maintain submersible systems that deliver and recover SEALs in hostile areas as also conduct limited direct action and reconnaissance tasks. The Naval Special Warfare Units are small command and control elements located outside the CONUS, that support other Naval SOF assigned to theatre Special Operations Commands or components of naval task forces. The Special Boat Squadrons comprise of one or more active or reserve component Special Boat Units and CYCLONE Class Patrol Coastal ships that provide trained and ready special operations ships and craft to the theatre commands.

Interestingly, as is well known, neither the Airborne Forces nor elements of the Marine Corps Force Reconnaissance Units form part of the SOF Command. While both these types of units have a specialised role, it is more than likely that they have been kept out of USSOCOM purely because of internal politics within the Services and the Pentagon. Such a move gives the Service Chiefs options for utilisation for which they need not take clearances from the Pentagon, as is the present case with regard to employment of SOF. From all that has been stated above, one important fact that emerges regarding US doctrine and philosophy and its organisation and tasking of SOF is the manner in which clear cut and specific roles have been assigned to each of their forces with the probable exception of Delta Force. This reliance on 'super specialisation' appears to have played its part in some of their more spectacular failures. Successful operations require robust and reliable command and control structures, unified forces preferably from a single agency, unit or group and a simple plan as an essential ingredient. However, the US has, time and again, conducted operations involving multiple agencies with diffused command and control and complex plans with varying results. While employment of SOF has been a constant factor in all US deployments through the years, from the Vietnam period onwards, it has only been in the past few years that they have played an increasingly dominant and key role in US strategic doctrine as recent operations in Afghanistan and Iraq clearly show.

## Operational Employment

Though US SOF may have technological capabilities that are beyond our financial and developmental capacity as also responsibilities and tasks that have no bearing in our context, some of their experiences in special operations have lessons that are worth considering. Of particular relevance are some of their joint service operations of which Operation Eagle Claw, the Iran rescue debacle and Operation Urgent Fury, the intervention in Grenada, are of particular interest. The former operation led to a complete restructuring of their SOF, while the latter operation was launched after the revitalisation programme for the SOF had commenced. Both these operations give us an insight into their capabilities and functioning.

On 4 November 1979, militant students barged into the American Embassy in Tehran and took its 63 staff hostage demanding the return of the Shah to face trial in Iran. While negotiations were undertaken on the diplomatic front for the release of the hostages, an adhoc planning cell under a retired General, James Vaught, was established to plan and coordinate an appropriate military response if negotiations failed. Delta Force was alerted and commenced planning the rescue. From the outset operational security was given the very highest priority. The planners were confronted with a number of problems that included the lack of detailed intelligence on the layout of the Embassy and the location of the hostages, the vast distances involved from a suitable American Base in the region and the fact that Delta Force was organised and trained to operate with the permission of the host country.

The plan that evolved and was felt to have the most likely hope of success in essence involved the flying in of 70 Delta Force personnel by helicopter to a site outside Tehran where the helicopters would be refueled using rubber bladders dropped earlier. They would then fly on to a staging post prior to assaulting the Embassy the next night. After rescuing the hostages the complete lot would be picked up from another nearby airport by another aircraft and flown to safety. It was subsequently decided to insert a three-member team of Delta Force into Tehran, under the cover of an Irish business delegation, prior to the commencement of operations to arrange transportation for the assault force into the city and to provide real time intelligence of the target area. Also as the rubber bladders were found to be unreliable it was decided that tankers would be flown in which meant that a landing strip was required for the refueling stop. This in addition would require protection for which additional elements of Rangers were added to the assault force since the only suitable landing strip was next to a road used commonly by trucks and buses. In addition since intelligence revealed that some hostages were held separately at the Foreign Ministry, a separate force was nominated for their rescue, as Delta Force did not have the strength to undertake both actions. This force was nominated from the Special Forces Group located in Europe. It was then decided that aircraft would also fly in the Delta Force to the refueling stop where they would transfer to the helicopters and continue on to Tehran. Also, since the Army did not have helicopters with the required range it was decided to use Marine Corps helicopters with pilots who neither had the experience of desert flying nor of participating in special operations and all that it involved. The complete operation was to be controlled by General Vaught from Egypt with no clear nomination of the Force commander on the ground.

Thus, the force had separate commanders with the tankers answering to one, the helicopters answering to another, the Rangers to a third, the C130 transports to their own with Beckwith of Delta Force nominally coordinating the mishmash through General Vaught in Egypt since he was not in communication with any of the other elements due to incompatible radio communication equipment. Also the obsession with security ensured that the complete force never trained together. Instead each element rehearsed its part on its own only coming together for the actual operation. Even the additional element from the Special Forces Group in Germany did not train in concert with Delta Force but only linked up with them just three days prior to the operation. The lack of coordination was so complete that the helicopter pilots were not even aware that their route to their desert rendezvous would be through the middle of a sand storm even though this information was available to the planners from the meteorological department.

By mid April 1980, approximately after five months of preparation, the go ahead for the operation was given and the lead element successfully inserted into Tehran as planned. On 24 April, the operation was launched and the two C130s were able to land at the Desert One rendezvous by 2200 hours without any interference. The helicopters were not so fortunate as they were delayed by the sand storm and two turned back due to technical reasons leaving six helicopters available for the mission, the minimum required. They finally arrived at the rendezvous ninety minutes late and commenced refueling. At this stage it was found that another helicopter was having technical problems and would not be available for the mission but would instead go back to its launch base, a greater distance away than the objective. The reduction of the helicopter force to five meant that sufficient helicopters would not be available for extracting the hostages and the Delta Force and Colonel Beckwith in discussion with General Vaught recommended to President Carter that the mission be aborted, a recommendation he approved. This brought out clearly the fundamental flaw in all the operational planning carried out – the unwillingness of the commanders, mainly Colonel Beckwith, to give priority to the hostages as compared to the extraction of Delta Force. The five helicopters would have been sufficient to get Delta Force into its assault location and for extraction of the hostages and most of the Delta Force. The remainder portion of Delta Force could then have attempted to extract itself by land. Such a scenario was, however, not considered in the planning stages and, thus, not given any consideration when events did not go as planned. However, at the desert rendezvous things went from bad to worse as one of the helicopters crashed into a C130 while refueling leading to both aircraft going up in flames with most of the crew of these aircraft killed. The subsequent panic led to all personnel including the crew of the other serviceable helicopters abandoning their aircraft and getting into the remaining C130 and making a hasty departure out of the country. Subsequent inquiries pointed to the adhoc command and control set up, lack of coordination, poor intelligence and the claustrophobic emphasis on security to be the chief reasons for the disaster and recommended a complete overhaul of the SOF establishment including raising of its own air element and command and control structures as also an oversight committee of experts that would vet all operations prior to their being executed.

The genesis for the intervention in Grenada, a former British colony with a British appointed Governor General in the Caribbean, was laid in 1979 when Maurice Bishop led a peaceful coup against the unpopular Prime Minister, who had been strongly pro West. While promising to establish a modern democracy, Bishop went on to consolidate his own position and establish close ties with the Soviet Union and the communist bloc that went on to supply him with limited quantities of small arms and ammunition, much to the alarm of the USA— an incomprehensible reaction in view of the fact that Grenada with a population of one lakh, with its economy wholly dependent on tourism, was hardly in a position to threaten the USA. However, on 13 October 1981, events in the country took a turn for the worse with Bishop being overthrown by a more hard line group that led to the US to believe that the thousand odd American citizens, which included about four hundred medical students in the country faced danger that led to preparations for an armed intervention being ordered. At this stage intelligence estimates placed the opposition at approximately 1200 Grenadan Army and 3000 to 5000 militia supported by another 700 Cuban construction workers with military training. Detailed dispositions were not available despite the large American expatriate community and the fact that this issue had been worrying the US Government for over three years. It subsequently turned out at the end of the campaign that the opposition force consisted of approximately 2000 Grenadans and just fifty Cubans with military training. Against this rag-tag force the US deployed forces totaling 6500 that included Delta Force, both Ranger Battalions available at the time, two brigades of 82$^{nd}$ Airborne Divison, SEAL Units and a Naval Task Force that included a carrier group and a Marine Assault Unit. Interestingly, the Army alone awarded a total of 8612 medals at the end of the operations.

The highlights of the complex plan devised by the adhoc command set up established for the operation (the theatre commander responsible for the area was kept out of the loop to prevent the plan being compromised), to rescue all American citizens on the Island, neutralise the Grenadan Armed Forces and to establish conditions that would allow the people of Grenada to regain control over their governance, involved: -

- A pre dawn airborne assault by elements of Delta Force to secure the International Airport under construction at Point Salinas and clear the runway for subsequent elements of Rangers and 82$^{nd}$ Airborne Divison to be air landed. Another element of Delta Force, to simultaneously capture the local Richmond Hill Jail by heliborne assault and free civil servants and political prisoners held there. Tasks that should have been given to the Rangers or the Airborne. Interestingly, since both Ranger battalions wanted to be the one to lead the assault, a compromise was reached and a composite force comprising from both units was formed to lead the assault, completely nullifying existing command and control structures and espirit-de-corps of each of the units.

- At approximately the same time SEAL units were to assault the residence of the Governor General, Sir Paul Scoon, and take him off the island. Other SEAL units were to attack and capture the local radio station and recconoitre the landing strip at Pearl's Airport and the beach where the Marines were to subsequently land.

- The Rangers after being relieved by a Brigade of 82[nd] Airborne Divison were to advance and rescue American students at the True Blue Campus close to the International Airport.

- The Marine Battalion was to secure Pearl's Airport and Grenville Port and then commence advancing southwards to link up with the Rangers and secure the island.

Operations commenced on 25 October with the pre dawn assault by the Delta Force to capture the International Airport at Salinas that went wrong from the start as the small force dedicated for the task was seen landing by an alert sentry and was soon pinned down with heavy casualties just outside the airport. This led to an alert being declared by the Grenadan Forces that resulted in the ambush of the SEAL Team attempting to capture the Radio Station. The other SEAL Teams that were to recconoitre the landing strip at Pearl's Airport and the beach, suffered technical problems and were unable to complete their tasks forcing the Marine Battalion to assault blind. The failure of Delta Force to capture the International Airport delayed the landing of the Rangers, as mid flight they had to convert to dropping rather than air landing their personnel.

The aircraft stream, thus, reached the Airport that became the Drop Zone, in daylight and the leading two aircraft aborted their drop after dispatching twelve troopers because of small arms fire. The third aircraft carrying the command element of the force, being unaware of the situation, dropped its load leaving them isolated for another hour before the remainder aircraft dropped their loads. The Rangers on the ground consolidated themselves in the vicinity of the airfield and awaited reinforcements without any attempt at securing the airport or linking up with the elements of Delta Force landed earlier. The panic on the ground, mostly because of lack of any combat experience, led to a change of plans and the whole of 82nd Airborne Division was air landed with the airport still under fire that resulted in complete chaos on the ground. Finally, it was only by last light of the first day that the combined Ranger and Airborne forces were able to secure the airport and commence their advance towards the Capital, St Georges.

The second element of Delta Force that was to have captured the jail complex during the night commenced their operations only in daylight, five hours late, reportedly due to confusion over the timing of operations not having been specified in GMT or local time their orders, the most elementary of errors in staff work. This daylight assault resulted in one of the transport helicopters being shot down with a second remaining behind to assist, against orders. Thus, the force landed was too small to assault the jail and remained pinned down in the vicinity till relieved.

The only part of the plan that seemed to have gone reasonably well was the landing of the Marine Battalion and the SEAL Team to rescue the Governor. While both these elements completed their task without any mishap, the SEAL Team panicked and called for urgent assistance, stating that they had a large number of casualties and were surrounded and under fire. Three helicopters sent to their help were shot down by small arms fire and a reserve company of the Marine Battalion was finally able to link up with them the next day. It only emerged at that time that the SEALs had neither suffered casualties nor been under any fire as they had reported earlier. By last light of the second day, the Marines were able to advance and link up with the Airborne and Rangers close to the capital and secure the country.

Apart from the numerous mistakes committed during operations that clearly reflected the lack of combat experience, the biggest flaws that emerged were to do with aspects pertaining to command and control and logistics. The adhoc nature of the command and control structure, along with the emphasis on security that led to intense inter and intra services rivalry with each agency trying to get a piece of the action and to plans being made, with little attention to details and with every effort to satisfy all concerned showed clearly that lessons from the Iran Operation had yet to sink in. More damagingly, units planned operations in isolation with numerous instances of different units planning attacks on the same objective without any coordination, primarily because the issue of secrecy was stretched to ridiculous extents by the SOF units, especially Delta and SEALs, with disastrous results on a few occasions. There were also serious problems with regard to communications because of incompatibility of radio sets available with the different forces to the extent that one Ranger officer reportedly brought down covering fire by patching through to the fleet via the Pentagon on the civil telephone network by making an international call. Logistics also suffered greatly because all concerned staff elements were kept out of the loop for security reasons and were unable to provide the required logistics support at the last minute when required to do so. Subsequent efforts to show the operation in a favourable light, despite the systemic flaws that emerged, were probably to prevent embarrassment to the military and political hierarchy.

In our context, though, the Vietnam campaign has some relevance as it has many similarities to the situation that we face in Kashmir and the North East today, in terms of the type of war that the US was forced to fight, primarily against the Vietcong, as also the support that these cadres were given by the North Vietnamese—not only from their territory but also through the use of Laotian and Cambodian territory. Some of the cross border actions undertaken, not by the SF Group deployed in the area, but by the adhoc organisations raised for the purpose is instructive. Interestingly, the SF Groups were utilised to fight the insurgency inside South Vietnam very much in a similar manner as we use our SF today. Despite availability of limited data, the participation of the U.S. Military Assistance Command Vietnam's (MACV) Studies and Observation Group (SOG), and its ground reconnaissance component, Operations 35 (OPS-35), in strategic intelligence gathering is a historical fact. Although little has been written about the SOG and its troops, a picture of the unit's activities can be reconstructed and studied from several of the verbal and written sources that have been made public.[22] In keeping with security practices that required compartmentalisation for classified activities, SOG's ground reconnaissance element OPS-35 was, but one of its many secret component forces. Other components such as OPS-31, 32, 33 and 34 were responsible for conducting other unconventional and conventional warfare activities such as psychological operations (PSYOPS), maritime operations, and the training and direction of agent-operatives destined for infiltration into North Vietnam. The conduct of cross-border ground reconnaissance and its incumbent intelligence requirements were the purview of OPS-35. In addition to this mission, OPS-35's task also included locating and freeing friendly personnel captured or missing in action, assisting in the conduct of PSYOPS, and performing other tasks such as prisoner apprehension and equipment retrieval.

For the conduct of these activities it raised three command and control headquarters: Command Control North (CCN), Command Control Central (CCC), and Command Control South (CCS) located at Danang, Kontom, and Ban Me Thuot, respectively. To provide anonymity for the organisation and its personnel, OPS-35 had an administrative affiliation with the U.S. Army's 5th Special Forces Group (Airborne). Under this arrangement all of the OPS-35's U.S. Army personnel were listed on the strength of this group. Between 1964 and 1972, the SOG's OPS-35 was said to have had a strength of 2,000-2,500 U.S. personnel and 7,000 to 8,000 indigenous troops, most of whom came from South Vietnam's Montagnard, Cambodian (Khmer Krom), and Nung ethnic minorities. Although OPS-35's primarily concerns were with strategic reconnaissance, on special occasions its teams would conduct raids, prisoner apprehension missions, or seek-locate-annihilate-and-monitor (SLAM) missions. Frequently, the teams were sent into Laos to the home villages of ethnic minority team members to induce the villagers to aid in establishing "in country" bases for future operations. On other occasions, their task was to tap North Vietnamese Army (NVA) telephone lines or to plant acoustic and seismic sensors along the Ho Chi Minh Trail. The presence of the U.S. personnel on the teams insured accurate and reliable intelligence and to provide the SOG and the United States some form of plausible denial (albeit weak) for personnel who might be captured, the SOG units frequently had maps printed with distorted international boundary lines. In a further effort to conceal the nature of its operations, it was SOG's policy to report its casualties as having occurred in South Vietnam. Normally OPS-35 forces conducted reconnaissance missions with units known as "Spike Teams" comprising six to twelve men (two to four U.S. personnel and four to eight indigenous personnel). The North Vietnamese were well aware of the patrols sent into Laos to monitor their activities and their attacks on Khe Sanh and Kham Duc in 1968 were attempts to stop infiltration from these and other camps along the border. It was from these camps that American-led teams of Indo-Chinese mercenaries regularly infiltrated into Laos. These units had assigned missions in zones that extended 20 kilometres into the Laotian interior. The terrain in these areas was extremely, difficult, and they measured their movement in metres not kilometres. Using the least accessible regions as points of infiltration enabled the OPS-35 teams to enter the target areas with less chance of discovery by enemy patrols. After a team had infiltrated the area, it then moved to its specific reconnaissance site. Occasionally, the team monitored its target for as long as ten days in order to gather maximum intelligence. However, despite the good work done by the SOF units in Vietnam, the US was unable to change the course of events and suffered an ignominious defeat that led to the restructuring of its Army including the SOF.

The Gulf War of 1991, Operation Enduring Freedom, did not see extensive use of SOF except for "scud hunting" very much in the manner that the SAS adopted. There were also plans to use Delta Force to rescue American citizens. During the opening weeks of the Iraqi invasion, the Iraqi Army rounded up hundreds of foreign nationals and herded them off to various locations in Iraq. Many were relocated to strategically important facilities to be used as "human shields" against allied air attacks. Others were simply placed in detention facilities. In addition, the US Embassy in Kuwait was also expected to be overrun and its personnel taken hostage. Using existing blueprints and the latest intelligence from all available sources contingency plans were developed to use elements of Delta Force to assault and rescue the hostages. Operation Pacific Wind, as it was called, required three Delta operators to covertly infiltrate Kuwait City and coordinate the rescue. They were to be equipped with advanced electronic tracking devices so that their movements could be monitored. Dressed as American businessmen affiliated with an international oil company, it was hoped that they would be rounded up by Iraqi security patrols and taken to locations housing other hostages. From there, the concealed transponders would identify the location of the group to senior commanders to enable rescue operations to be mounted.

This operation, however, never progressed beyond the advanced planning stages for fear of reprisals if the operations were not successful. In any event, these hostages were released in December 1990, and no operation was necessary. The primary reason for the limited utilisation of SOF was the Allied Forces Commander, General Schwartzkopf's view of the SOF not as a viable tool in the wider scope of coalition military operations against Iraq, but, rather as support elements of his own conventional battle plan. Nonetheless, he did permit the use of U.S. Special Forces as liaison officers with several Arab nations. He also approved the use of Navy SEALs in mine clearing missions and Air Force SOF in the Combat Search and Rescue role. Schwartzkopf's distrust of SOF stemmed from his observations and experiences of their functioning during Operation Urgent Fury in Grenada, where he had been the commander of the Army element.

However, the events of 11 September 2001 changed perceptions within the military and the Government and the responsibility for the war against terrorism against the Al Queda and Taliban in Afghanistan was taken on by the SOF, primarily because of the distances involved and the fact that the SOF were chartered to support and train indigenous forces, in this case the Northern Alliance. From news reports of the Afghan campaign it is clear that US SOF supported by SOF from Australia, UK and the other nations participating from NATO have been extensively used for carrying out a complete range of SOF tasks with fairly encouraging results. Some experts, however, do blame the inability of the forces to capture the top Al Queda and Taliban leadership, on the over dependence on the SOF supported by the USAF instead of deploying larger numbers of conventional troops on the ground as was done in Iraq. This is probably true as the SOF being in limited numbers were wholly dependent on the Northern Alliance for the capture of Bin Laden and Mullah Omar. The Alliance was however unable to deliver because of a lack of internal cohesion with different warlords pulling in opposing directions. It however appears from the preliminary reports that have emerged in the media that the SOF has performed creditably despite the difficult terrain and weather conditions as also the uncertain political climate that prevails.

Similarly, Operation Iraqi Freedom has been very differently fought with extensive deployment of SOF when compared with the earlier Gulf War campaign. While the Coalition had the option of launching its offensive against Iraq using either just conventional troops or SOF, it chose a blend of both. This option appeared to focus not on the size of the Coalition Force, but rather upon the diversity of units attacking (armor, airmobile, special operations, marine), and very close coordination of air and ground attacks. Indigenous forces did not play a large role, though some effort was made through the CIA and the SOF units to gain their cooperation. Particular efforts were made to isolate and neutralize key Iraqi leadership, without much success. Targeting still emphasised command and control centres, suspected WMD capabilities, Saddam Hussein's palace complexes, and Republican Guards units. Extensive use of psychological operations was carried out to persuade regular Iraqi army units that resistance was futile. Heavy reliance was placed upon air power, particularly in the initial phase. While mechanised ground forces advanced from Kuwait in the South, some airmobile and airborne forces carried out airborne assaults in the North to seize high-value targets deep within Iraq. Interestingly, in addition to their normal tasking, SOF were mainly utilised to prevent damage to essential economic infrastructure, including securing oil installations, utilities and transport from sabotage and wilful destruction by Iraqi Forces; minimise and address adverse humanitarian consequences by demonstrating to the Iraqi people that they were not the enemy and that their security and well-being was of utmost concern; and most importantly, deny the Iraqi regime the use of weapons of mass destruction by identifying and securing the sites where weapons of mass destruction and their means of delivery were suspected to be located. Lastly, the SOF were utilised to act as liaison between various elements of the coalition forces and assist in the training of the new Iraqi Police and Army units. Examples of their utilisation that have been confirmed by the media include the employment of Navy SEALs and Polish "Grom" commandos to secure the Mukarayin Dam, 57Kms North-East of Baghdad, along with the adjacent power station and other facilities by helicopter assault to prevent the Fedayeen Saddam irregulars or Baathist loyalists from damaging or destroying the dam and possibly flooding Baghdad downstream. Other missions included "the capture of offshore oil terminals and the clearing of Iraq's only deep-water estuary in March. They also touched on other wartime missions - sniper-vs-sniper duels with Fedayeen Saddam loyalists in Baghdad, saving Army Pfc. Jessica Lynch, behind-the-lines reconnaissance and searching for weapons of mass destruction".[23] Subsequent to the invasion, the SOF have been utilised in a manner similar to our employment of such units in LIC and are reported to have been instrumental in the capture of Saddam Hussein. There has also been a groundswell of opinion, especially within the Armed Forces, that the size of conventional forces should be gradually reduced as more power is transferred to the Iraqi Governing Council, who should then be supported by an indigenous Army and Police force assisted by SOF units and personnel.

In the context of present SOF capabilities and functioning, especially in view of their performance in Afghanistan and Iraq, some of the important issues that have emerged, and which we need to consider in our context, have been aptly summed up by Colonel John Jogerst, USAF, holding the Special Operations Chair to Air University, on the faculty of Air War College, Maxwell AFB, Alabama : -

- "You don't know what you need until you need it. A wide range of capabilities in effective quantities is a good hedge against tomorrow's threat. Predicting the future is an enterprise with a very poor record unless predictions are so broad as to be useless for setting priorities." It may be worthwhile to ensure sufficient availability of SOF to meet unforeseen eventualities as these forces take extraordinary time and effort to raise.

- " Network-distributed may be more effective than network-centric warfare. The best way to speed up the observe, orient, decide, act (OODA) loop is to shorten it by getting it into the field. A battle against small, independent, and mobile formations may change too rapidly to allow centralized control in detail. The lesson from Afghanistan is that, with clear mission orders and appropriate technology, each tactical element can become a command, control, and execution node, greatly shortening the OODA loop.

- Interoperability comes by interoperating regularly, routinely, and often real interoperability requires constant testing and training not only to work out equipment problems, but also, and more importantly, to work out the human problems of command, control, and communications as well as unit tactics. SOF personnel conduct operations with elements from all services directly integrated in tactical formations— from SF or SEAL teams with integral Air Force air–control elements to tactical helicopter formations combining Army and Air Force aircraft. This makes SOF ideal for the kind of chaotic and diffuse warfare that probably awaits us in the future.

- Existing forces are nothing more than tools to provide the commander with combat capability. This capability and the ability to employ it are what matters— not the specific tool. The war in Afghanistan has seen Army, Navy, and Air Force helicopters, fighters, and long-range bombers providing interdiction and close air support to US, allied, and associated forces fighting from foot, horseback, high-mobility multipurpose wheeled vehicles, or light armored vehicles. The joint special operations team has been the key to linking these forces into an effective, interoperable tool to achieve the joint force commander's objectives. But interoperable does not mean identical. Each of these disparate forces brings particular capabilities as well as definite strengths and weaknesses to the fight. The Air Force's long-range bombers provide large weapons loads, precision, and endurance. Navy fighters provide forward forces in-theatre, precision, and reconnaissance. AC-130 gunships provide endurance; immediate, direct fire support; and real-time over watch of operations. Army and Marine conventional forces provide quick-reaction firepower and the ability to secure ground. The only important criterion for the joint force commander and troops on the ground is their ability to use these capabilities effectively.

• The "teeth to tail" ratio may no longer be a relevant measure of merit because it draws an artificial distinction between integral elements of US combat power. If the only "teeth" in Afghanistan were the few hundred SOF personnel and aviators who initially engaged the Taliban and Al Quaida, then the tooth-to-tail ratio was minuscule. Tens of thousands of US personnel flew reconnaissance, ran ships, moved logistics, processed intelligence, and moved information to support those few hundred troops at the sharp end. However, precisely because of that intricate and massive support structure, the few hundred troops on the ground were able to topple the Taliban regime in a few months with almost no US casualties. That same support structure allowed the US military to reach halfway around the world; commence combat operations in an unexpected, austere theatre within weeks; and succeed on an extremely chaotic battlefield. The only relevant measure of merit is the effectiveness of the entire US force structure. Is there enough "tail" to support full use of US teeth? Is the United States building enough of the "enablers" (tankers; air lifters; airborne warning and control system aircraft; joint surveillance, target attack radar system aircraft; unmanned aerial vehicles; communications bandwidth; information analysis capabilities; etc.) to allow effective employment of the latest generation of "shooters"? Does the force provide a complete capability worth the cost in people and material?

• Human beings are more important than hardware. The war in Afghanistan and the larger global war against terrorism are wars of people... The language skills, cultural orientation, maturity, and adaptability of SOF enabled the joint force commander to effectively co-opt Afghan anti-Taliban forces and incorporate them into his campaign. Their success is a result of human action and initiative in employing an extremely wide range of hardware— from horse cavalry to joint direct attack munitions — to conduct the campaign. Fundamentally, the global war against terrorism- indeed, any war, is about individuals. The war on terrorism features few traditional military targets, such as large military formations or key national infrastructure...The United States will need a range of tools— political, military, economic, legal, and informational— to exploit these individuals' vulnerabilities and achieve national objectives.

• The final lesson from the war in Afghanistan may be that the revolution in military affairs has already happened. Like most revolutions, this one went from the bottom up— not from the top down. While the generals debated how to mandate a revolution, the captains and majors quietly implemented one. Despite a decade of downsizing, parts of the US military have learned to exploit networked information and precision weapons to conduct real-time, coordinated, and precision joint/combined operations against an enemy dispersed over complex terrain in a chaotic theatre on the other side of the world. Troops have learned to use a networked, distributed force of coordinated but independent joint combat elements with a wide range of capabilities. They have demonstrated that command, control, communications, computers, intelligence, surveillance, and reconnaissance can be fused and focused directly on a small, effective formation at the tip of the spear, allowing US forces to apply the right tool at the right time in the right place. Ultimately, this capability will prove itself more important than raw firepower."[24]

*We're surrounded. That simplifies the problem.*

- Chesty Puller, USMC

## SOF OF ISRAEL

Special Operation Forces of the Israeli Defence Forces (IDF) (and the Israeli Intelligence, the Border Guard and the Israeli Police) play a crucial role in shaping the doctrinal development of Israeli domestic and external security. The SOF of the various security services have evolved tactics and strategies that are aimed at ensuring a multifaceted and targeted response to unpredictable incidents of terrorism and irregular warfare. The IDF have been continuously engaged in both high intensity and low intensity warfare ever since the creation of the state of Israel, and the SOF have been in the frontlines in all conflicts (1948, 1956,1967, 1973, Lebanon and Palestine). While the post-Cold War era has been marked by external peace, Israel has fought a continuous low intensity war against Hezbollah and various Palestinian groups such as Hamas, Islamic Jihad and the Al Aqsa Martyrs Brigade. While counter terrorism has evolved as a pillar of SOF doctrine, it remains to be seen whether Israeli SOF will be able to sustain the prolonged campaign against Palestinian nationalism without denting Israel's credibility in the international arena as well as counter new threats of suicide terrorism driven by religious fanaticism.

Israel has a long history of SOF activation and deployment, dating even before the official declaration of the Israeli State and the forming of the IDF in 1948. Between 1920-1945 the former Ottoman province of Palestine was under a British Mandate. The ethno-national and territorial disputes between the Arab and the Jewish people engulfed the region and culminated in the establishment of the state of Israel in 1948. Political developments in the period before the declaration of independence led to the overt and covert emergence of armed groups with the purpose of protecting Jewish communities. From 1920-1929, the Jews formed several underground resistance movements, with the main purpose of protecting fellow Jews from the Arab attacks and to eventually force the British out of Israel.

The largest and most powerful of those underground movements was the Hagana ("Defense" in Hebrew). In 1941, the Hagana formed the Smash Companies ("Plugot Hamachat'z – PALMACH", in Hebrew), which were the SOF Units of their time. Among the PALMACH were the Undercover Mistaravim teams (known then as the 'Arabic Platoon'). These special teams were dressed as Arabs and were used to covertly move weapons and equipment[25]. When the Israeli state was formed, and the IDF could freely and openly move its equipment, there was no longer a need for these teams and they were disbanded. But in 1987 when the Intifada broke out, the Israeli security services (the IDF, the Israeli Border Guard - MAGAV and the Israeli Police - IP) that were inspired by the success of PALMACH Mistaravim teams, formed new units of Mistaravim. While the PALMACH handled land-based assignments well, the Hagana also needed a dedicated maritime special unit. So, in 1943, the Hagana formed the Sea Companies ("Plugot Hayam" - PALYAM, in Hebrew). As their name suggests, the PALYAM were mainly underwater demolition and maritime activity units. In 1948, when the IDF was formed, the PALYAM evolved into Shayetet13 (Naval Commandos).

In 1948, on Israel becoming independent, all the resistance movements were joined together in order to form the IDF. One of the Hagana outfits - the Golany Unit became the Israeli Defense Forces' first infantry brigade in February 1948 and was called the Golany infantry brigade. On reassignment under the IDF command, the Golany infantry brigade formed the Special Reconnaissance Platoon. This platoon was a LRRP (Long Range Reconnaissance Patrol Unit) acting as pathfinder for the infantry brigade. But unlike the other reconnaissance platoons that existed in each of the Golany Brigade's Battalions, the Special Reconnaissance Platoon was also in charge of taking out key enemy strongholds, and executed more complex missions such as demolition and intelligence gathering. The Special Reconnaissance Platoon was in fact the first official Israeli SF unit. It later evolved into Sayaret Golany, which is considered as one of the finest SF units in the IDF. In June 1948, the IDF formed its Paratroopers airborne unit - the T'zanhanim Company. The T'zanhanim Company was designed as an elite infantry unit tasked with the most demanding missions.

In the early 1950's, Arab regular and irregular forces launched numerous assaults against Israel, aimed mainly at civilians. The IDF attacked in retaliation, but the conventional infantry units (including the T'zanhanim) were overstretched and not cognisant of the nature of unconventional tasks. In 1951, the IDF formed Unit 30 - a classified Unit that belonged to the IDF Southern Command. Unit 30 was designed to execute retaliation missions while operating in small and well-trained teams but was disbanded in 1952. In August 1953, the IDF tried again to form a dedicated new SF unit, and created Unit 101 as a SF unit designed to perform complex missions far behind Israeli borders. Unit 101 was composed of 20-25 men, most of them former T'zanhanim and Unit 30 personnel. The creation of Unit 101 was a major landmark in the Israeli SF history. Unit 101 established small unit manoeuvres, activation and insertion tactics that are utilised even today by Israeli Special Forces. Unit 101 only existed for five months and was disbanded after a raid in which the unit's members killed dozens of unarmed Arabs in an infamous brutal retaliation act. Once disbanded, Unit 101 was merged with the T'zanhanim Company. After the merger the joint outfit turned into a brigade size unit, composed of two battalions - 869 Battalion (made out of the original T'zanhanim company personnel) and 101 Battalion (made out of former Unit 101 personnel). With the increase in manpower, the T'zanhanim unit became an elite infantry demi-brigade rather than the elite infantry company as it was before. This merger was actually quite ironic since the T'zanhanim officers were originally the biggest opponents against the creation of Unit 101, as they simply didn't want another competitor for prestigious retaliation missions that they monopolised. With the increased strength in numbers of personnel, Ariel Sharon (former CO of Unit 101 and the new CO of the T'zanhanim Infantry Brigade) was able to launch full scale SF attacks against Arab irregulars, and the T'zanhanim Infantry Brigade pretty much ruled all the Israeli SOF operations in the rest of 1950's.

In the late 1950's, the IDF noticed that since the T'zanhanim Unit had turned into an infantry brigade rather then the SF unit it was before, it lacked a small dedicated SF unit. In 1958, Abraham Arnan formed Sayaret MATKAL, which answered directly to the IDF High Command. The formation of Sayaret MATKAL combined the operational experience gathered by Unit 101 and the unit structure of the UK SAS — the role model for SF units worldwide. Sayaret MATKAL was also formed one year after the IDF first helicopter squadron became operational in 1957. Close cooperation between the two outfits enabled the unit to deploy very deep into enemy territory.

After losing the prestigious SF title, the T'zanhanim Brigade formed it own SF unit - Sayaret T'zanhanim in October 1958, mainly as a response to the creation of Sayaret MATKAL. In the early 1970's, and especially throughout the 1960's, there was a new trend in the IDF – formation of the Regional Command Sayaret. Israel is operationally divided into three commands - South, North and Centre. After witnessing the successful formation of Sayaret MATKAL and Sayaret T'zanhanim in the late 1950's, each command also wanted an SF unit of its own as a result of which units like Sayaret Shaked (South Command), Sayaret Shoualey Shimshon (South Command), Sayaret Harouv (Center Command) and Sayaret Egoz (North Command) were formed. While those units were supposed to be skilled LRRP units, performing delicate intelligence gathering missions, most of them soon became raider units competing with Sayaret MATKAL, S'13 and Sayaret T'zanhanim on the raiding missions. The command-level raids; Sayaret were loose cannon units, acting as autonomous outfits, with no discipline whatsoever. These units were all disbanded in the 1960s once the IDF commands realised that they could get the same level of performance from the infantry brigades' Sayaret units (that already existed in each of the infantry brigades) without maintaining several, very expensive, independent SF units.

Until the 1970's, the Israeli SOF units (including Sayaret MATKAL) had a limited CT capability and no hostage rescue capability whatsoever. It was only after the setback suffered in the Mahalot massacre incident that this aspect was given the importance that it deserved. On 15 May 1974, three heavily armed terrorists took over the Mahalot High School north of Israel, taking several dozens of teachers and students as hostages in the process. Sayaret MATKAL that had the most advanced CT capability (together with Sayaret Golany), was selected to carry out the rescue attempt. At the beginning of the raid, a Sayaret MATKAL sniper was supposed to take out the terrorist who was guarding the room in which most of the hostages were being held. The sniper (who was equipped with a World War II era Mauser 98) was not used to short-range headshot sniping, failed to kill the target and only wounded him. The injured terrorist started throwing grenades and began firing at the hostages. More mistakes were made, both in planning and in execution and by the end of the raid though all three terrorists were killed, 21 children and four adults among the hostages had also died. Moreover, at least two civilians were killed by friendly fire from the Sayaret MATKAL entry team, which was under-trained in Closed Quarter Battle (CQB). The fiasco led to the formation of a civilian CT Unit created under MAGAV, on the lines of the German GSG 9 known as Unit YAMAM. In addition, the other SOF units also acquired advanced CT capabilities, with Sayaret MATKAL and S'13 as the cutting edge. These units were given the best personnel and weapons available and were extensively trained by instructors from the SAS, the US Navy SEALs and Delta Force.

The Israeli CT units are divided into three kinds of units[26]:

- **Takeover Units.** Takeover units are the units with assault being their primary specialty as is the case with our SAG units of the NSG. These include:
  - **Unit YAMAM.** In charge on domestic (within Israel) CT missions and is a part of the MAGAV or Border Guards.
  - **Sayeret MATKAL.** In charge of foreign (outside Israeli borders) CT missions.
  - **S'13.** In charge of foreign (outside Israel borders) maritime CT missions.
  - **LOTAR Eilat.** In charge of domestic (within Israel) CT missions in the Eilat city area.
- **Engagement Units.** Engagement units are the units that have CT capability as a secondary specialty. Their role is to close and secure the raid zone, gather intelligence and wait for the

designated Takeover unit to arrive. Engagement units are only allowed to perform a rescue attempt if the terrorists start to kill the hostages; other than that, they must wait for the designated Takeover unit to arrive. Each engagement unit belongs to an IDF Command, based on their geographic location with the following units under each of the commands:

- North Command: Sayeret Golany.
- Center Command: Sayeret T'zanhanim, Sayeret NAHAL and Sayeret Duvdevan .
- South Command: Sayeret Givaty.

- **Assisting Units**. Assisting units are the specialised units that help the engagement and takeover units in their CT missions and include an attack dog unit, intelligence and surveillance unit, a computer modeling unit, bomb disposal and an electronic surveillance unit. also an integral part of the CT team.

In a domestic CT scenario, the unit in the zone and command of the incident will respond. In a foreign CT scenario, the best-fitted units will be selected regardless of their home commands. For example, in the Thunderbolt Operation - the Entebbe airborne hostage rescue raid in 1976 - Sayeret MATKAL was the designated takeover unit with Sayeret Golany (belongs to the North Command) and Sayeret T'zanhanim (belongs to the Centre Command) designated engagement units. The two engagement units worked in the Outer Circle and were responsible for preventing Ugandan soldiers from getting close to the airport terminal while the rescue attempt (inner circle) was being conducted by Sayeret MATKAL. Aircraft hijacking is one of the most politically salient threats for any nation. The symbolism of an act of hijacking is extremely potent and lethal (e.g. 2001 attacks) especially in the era of the information revolution. The IC 814 hijack and the inadequate Indian response should be indicative of the fact that the lessons of Entebbe must not be forgotten. A prelude to the Entebbe operation was Operation Gift and proves to be an interesting case study for the need to innovate in Special Operations.

On 22 July 1968, terrorists hijacked an El Al airliner on its way from Israel to Rome, and forced the pilot to land in Algiers. Four months later, on 26 November 1968, two terrorists, who had arrived in Athens from the Beirut International Airport, fired at an El Al airliner about to take off from Athens Airport. As a result, an Israeli citizen was killed, a stewardess was wounded and the plane damaged. As Beirut was a major centre for Arab terrorist activity, the Israeli Defense Force (IDF) decided to attack Arab Airlines aircraft at the Beirut Airport in an airborne commando raid, in retaliation for attacks on Israeli civilian airliners. The raid, officially known as Operation Gift, is one of Israel's most famous (CT) operations.

The Beirut International Airport is located about 90 kilometres from the Israeli-Lebanese border. It is situated south of the city of Beirut, and about two kilometres eastward from sea. At the time of the raid there were 90 security personnel at the airport, armed primarily with handguns. A more potent Lebanese Army commando company was deployed three kilometres from the airport, standing by at five-minute alert status. Lebanese Gendarmes and Police in the Beirut area could also arrive at the airport in half an hour, and the Armoured Gendarmes Unit and Lebanese military forces could arrive within an hour after receiving an order.

The Planning for operation commenced following the El Al airplane hijacking on 22 July 1968. The initial intention was to hijack planes in Beirut. Since such a basic drawer plan existed, following the airplane attack on 26 November 1968, an order went out to the IDF to immediately revise the Operation Gift contingency plan for the possibility of destroying aircrafts instead of hijacking them. A similar order was issued to the Israel Air Force (IAF), whose aircraft were immediately placed on alert and their serviceability was increased. Two days later, on 28 December 1968, the task force assembled in Ramat-David Air Force Base (AFB), fully trained and ready.

The airport was divided into three primary operational sectors: the eastern sector, the western sector and the terminal area sector. Each sector was assigned a team of 20 operators plus a forward command group consisting of 12 soldiers. Accordingly, four teams were involved in the operation: three teams from Sayeret MATKAL and one team from Sayeret T'zanhanim. It was decided to sabotage the aircraft by two explosives charges: One charge placed in the landing gear under the aircraft's nose while another charge would be placed in the landing gear of one of the wings. The two charges would immobilise the aircraft and set it aflame. Each aircraft would be prepared for a separate explosion. The operational plan consisted of three Super-Frelon SA321K helicopters for landing the three main attack teams in three different locations, as well as extracting them at the end of the operation. Also assigned were two Bell 205 helicopters — one for landing the forward command party and another for airborne patrolling and transmission. Israeli Navy vessels and Shayetet 13 teams were also on stand-by in the event that a naval rescue would be required. So were Indian Air Force (IAF) attack fighter jets.

The helicopters took off from the Ramat David AFB at 20:37 hours. The helicopters grouped few kilometres before the target and approached the airport. At 2118 hours three Super Frelons landed inserting the three main attack teams. Few minutes later, the forward command party landed in a Bell 205. Another Bell 205 hovered above on a patrol and blocking mission. This helicopter dropped smoke grenades and flares, which created a heavy smoke screen on the eastern and northern perimeters of the airfield. The helicopter also dropped nails on the roads leading to the airport. This succeeded in halting six security cars traveling to the airport. Other vehicles who tried to escape from the airport northwards to the city of Beirut, and police and fire vehicles moving to the airport created a traffic gridlock which in itself constituted an effective block. In addition, the Bell also fired warning shots at vehicles trying to enter the airport. The entire operation lasted 30 minutes. A total of 14 planes belonging to Middle East Airlines (MEA), Libyan International Airways (LIA) and Trans Mediterranean Airlines (TMA) were destroyed in the operation with damage estimated at about hundred million dollars.[27]

*"Any mission, any time, any place"*

Motto of the Spetsnaz -

## SOF OF THE RUSSIAN FEDERATION

### Organisational Overview

Spetsnaz has had a long and colourful history with varying degrees of success. After the end of the Second World War the Spetsnaz, as was the case the world over, went into decline with all rear area diversionary missions being handled by the airborne forces. It was only in the mid-1950s with the deployment of tactical nuclear weapons by the West, particularly in Western Europe, that the SOF found for themselves a new and more dynamic role. Soviet strategic philosophy was always biased towards fighting wars of "liberation" on foreign territory, a practically impossible barrier with the advent of nuclear weapons. However, there was a growing belief that Soviet strategy could continue along the same lines if means were found to neutralise these tactical nuclear weapons without resorting to a nuclear strike. This required creation of forces that would be able to locate and destroy nuclear weapons discovered in the course of war or immediately before its outbreak, and it was felt that the Spetsnaz were trained and organised precisely for such tasks, interestingly, a task that has only recently been formally included in the charter for US SOF. Furthermore, since it was impractical to pinpoint and destroy every single nuclear weapon in the enemy's arsenal, the Spetsnaz were also tasked to neutralise the enemy's command, control and communication systems to substantially reduce that nation's capacity for action in the event of war. The Soviet High Command also came to believe that Spetsnaz could also be effectively used not only against tactical but also against strategic nuclear installations: submarine bases, weapon stockpiles, aircraft bases and missile launching sites as also against sources and distribution of energy - power stations, transformer stations and power lines, as well as oil and gas pipelines and storage points, pumping station and oil refineries. The neutralisation or loss of such assets would greatly reduce the ability of that enemy to react against Soviet offensive designs. The Soviet elite Airborne Forces, the VDV, which form a separate department within the Army and number around seven divisons along with Air Assault Forces (helicopter borne) are the other SOF strike elements available for deep penetration that work in close coordination with the Spetsnaz. In addition to these units that are under either the GRU or Main Intelligence Directorate of the General Staff, or the Army, or Navy, there are other Spetsnaz units subordinated either to the KGB, the Committee for State Security, or to the MVD, the Ministry of Internal Affairs. The KGB units are responsible for strategic social, political and economic targets while the units of the MVD are responsible for dealing with internal problems, though at the present time, units of the GRU and SPD, the successor of the KGB, are also committed for operations within the country in Chechnya.

It was, however, only in the 1970s, when the Cold War was at its height, that the West became truly aware of the existence of Soviet Spetsnaz troops, which were grouped into what were known as "diversionary brigades." The existence of Spetsnaz was a closely guarded secret even within the Warsaw Pact and individual troops were not allowed to admit membership, to the extent that army Spetsnaz wore standard airborne uniforms and insignia, while naval Spetsnaz wore naval infantry uniforms and insignia. It is only in the recent past that the Russian Federation openly acknowledged the existence of

Spetsnaz units and, permitted the wearing of special badges and berets identifying such troops. During this period, SOF units increasingly came to be raised by various ministries of the (then) Soviet Union. Further, such was the large and disorganised nature and wastefulness of the Soviet system that similar bodies with similar missions were set up by different parts of the same ministry, particularly within the Committee for State Security (KGB) and the Ministry of Internal Affairs (MVD). These special troops went under the generic title of "Spetsgruppe" and were paramilitary forces that had received special training and indoctrination for a variety of missions. Many of these units served in a variety of roles in the war in Afghanistan but for most of them a defining moment seems to have been reached during the 1991 coup, when they were forced to take sides, or at least to refuse to take action. After the coup had been defeated President Yeltsin transferred most of them to his personal control but they have since been transferred yet again back to various ministries. Many of these groups are now involved in the conflict in Chechnya. Though the Cold War is history, Spetsnaz units are still part of the Russian order-of-battle, although their missions may have undergone some change. Moreover some of the republics that broke away from the old Soviet Union took over the Spetsnaz units within their borders or have converted parachute units to the Spetsnaz role. Within the Russian Federation Spetsnaz units are reported less well trained and equipped, at a lower strength, and at a lesser degree of readiness than during the 1970s and 1980s and their numbers appear to be uncertain. Reports in the Eighties put the total number of Spetsnaz under the GRU at approximately 25 to 30,000. They were deployed at the scale of one Spetsnaz Company per Army; one Spetsnaz Regiment in each of the three "theatres of operations"; one Spetsnaz Brigade in each of the four Soviet Fleets, the Northern, Baltic, Black Sea, and Pacific fleets; and an independent Spetsnaz Brigade in most military districts of the USSR. There were also special Spetsnaz intelligence units, at the scale of one to each Front and Fleet: totaling approximately twenty. In addition there were a number of Spetsnaz Brigades directly under the GRU and the C in Cs of the Land and Naval Forces.

A Spetsnaz company reportedly consists of approximately 135 personnel, normally operating in 15 independent teams, although they could also combine for specific missions. A Spetsnaz battalion has approximately two to three companies with supporting elements and is numbered to be around three to four hundred. A Spetsnaz brigade is 1,000-1,300 strong and consists of a headquarters, three or four battalions, a communications company, and supporting troops. It also includes an anti-VIP company of 70 personnel whose mission is to seek out, identify and kill political and military enemy leaders. A naval Spetsnaz brigade similarly has a headquarters, two to three battalions of combat swimmers, a communication company, supporting units and an anti-VIP company. It also had a group of midget submarines designed to deliver combat swimmers to distant targets. It also has a battalion of naval infantry in support.

Spetsgruppe "Al'fa" (Special Group A) was set up by the KGB's Seventh Directorate in 1974, in response to the wave of terrorist acts that had swept across most of the world and had hit Western Europe especially hard. In forming "Alfa," a thorough study was made of other countries' experiences and it was formed on the lines of the British SAS and US Delta Force, as an incident response counter-terrorist and hostage-rescue group. The FSB or "Federal'naia Sluzhba Bezopasnosti" now controls Alfa; the Federal Security

Service that in general terms is equivalent to the USA's FBI. Current strength is estimated to be about 300, with the main group in Moscow and two smaller groups located at Krasnodar and Ekaterinburg. Its organisation includes specialists in explosives and underwater demolition, climbers, snipers, negotiations and psychologists. This unit has taken part in virtually all hostage rescue operations in Russia since its formation.

Another KGB Spetsnaz unit created in 1981 was "Vympel" or "Pennant", controlled by the First (Foreign Intelligence) Chief Directorate. It had and continues to have strength of approximately two hundred officers who are reportedly well versed in languages and have extensive experience of travel abroad. Its mission in the Soviet era was to fulfill the KGB's wartime role of assassination and sabotage in other countries. After the collapse of the Soviet Union it was initially transferred to the MVD but is now with the FSB and has reportedly been renamed as "Vega" and has been given the responsibility for dealing with nuclear terrorism.

The Ministry of Internal Affairs (MVD) in addition also has at least two groups of special troops known as the Omon or "Black Beret", which was originally raised to provide additional security and hostage rescue at the 1980 Moscow Olympics. Since then they have been used for counter-terrorist activities and defeating armed criminals, and are currently involved in campaigns against drug cultivation. In addition, these units have also reportedly been active in assisting the former Baltic republics as also the former Soviet republics of Uzbekistan, Azerbaijan, Georgia, and Armenia in anti-narcotic campaigns. The Ministry of Justice also has a special unit called Spetsnaz UIN that is responsible for tasks involving suppression of prison riots and revolts as also for rescue of hostages seized by prisoners.

Despite the numerous organisations that form a part of the contemporary Russian SOF apparatus, the Federal Government also has a quasi-private organisation working under exclusive contract to it known as GROM Security Company that is manned by former troops of various KGB SOF and provides security for selected government personnel and buildings, as well as for trains and aircraft. Despite the run down state of affairs of the Russian military, the SOF has continued to prosper, as it is looked upon as a crucial element available to the ruling political establishment to counter their opponents. Moreover, service in these units has always been considered prestigious and thus such units have never lacked suitable material. However, while in Soviet times this prestige was linked with a further career in the service, in recent years, it is defined by the fact that former Spetsnaz personnel are considered extremely valuable and offered well paying careers by a host of security firms and even criminal organisations on leaving service. This politicisation of the SOF however may result in its gradual degradation and loss of capability.

## Operational Employment

The Spetsnaz in conjunction with Airborne Divisions have been extensively used to promote state policy during the Soviet era. The examples of Czechoslovakia and Afghanistan, where Soviet Airborne Divisons were employed to capture strategic airfields to enable pacification of the country while Spetsnaz elements simultaneously went on to neutralise the political leadership, are well known. In 1968, the increasingly liberal-minded

Czechoslovak Communist Party government of Alexander Dubcek, for example, undertook major political reforms bringing to the fore fears within the Soviet leadership that such reforms could derail the Warsaw Pact and its other allies. After attempts by the KGB and hardliners within the country to prevent the reforms failed, the Soviet Union took the decision to intervene militarily.

On 16 August 1968, the Soviet Union informed the Czechoslovak government of impending Warsaw Pact manoeuvres along its borders. This warning enabled forces of the Soviet Union and other Warsaw Pact countries to concentrate in the vicinity without arousing suspicions, especially in the West. Some Spetsnaz elements were also inserted covertly for establishing surveillance over airfields and other places of importance. At 2300 hours on 20 August, a Soviet cargo plane made a distress call to Prague air control requesting for permission to land due to systems failures. Immediately on landing Spetsnaz elements disembarked from the aircraft and in conjunction with elements inserted earlier took over control of the airport. In this KGB agents serving in the Czech police and military establishments assisted them. Once control over the airport was established, other aircraft brought in elements of the VDV (Airborne Forces) that rapidly spread out through the town and took control of the radio and TV station as also Parliament. Similar actions were also undertaken in other towns across the country. In simultaneous actions elements of the Spetsnaz had also earlier, with the assistance of local agents, assaulted and taken Dubcek and his cabinet prisoners. By 26 August, Dubcek had accepted the futility of opposing the Soviet regime and signed an agreement allowing Soviet troops to be stationed within the country. "*The invasion provided an excellent example of Soviet covert operations. Working in apparently perfect harmony, the KGB with its agents in place and the GRU with Spetsnaz shock troops supported by overwhelming follow-on firepower, proved a devastating combination. Agents were already in place to take control of all communication centres. In addition, the isolation of the Czech leadership was correctly identified as being crucial to the whole enterprise...The tactics employed by the Soviets were to be put to good use again ten years later, during the invasion of Afghanistan."*[28]

One of the most notable operations involving Alfa took place in the opening phase of the Soviet invasion of Afghanistan during which it was tasked to carry out the assault on the Presidential Palace and capture President Hafiz Amin. This assault was carried out on 27 December 1979. This three-story building perched on a hilltop had only one road leading to it that was kept under constant surveillance by palace security personnel. The palace complex was well defended with some tanks dug in to cover the approach. In the vicinity of the Palace was the Afghanistan Army Headquarters with its own complement of soldiers and an air defense system. For the assault, Alfa's teams were supported by BMPs and ZSU 23-4 "Shilka" and an infantry battalion. Simultaneous assaults were also launched on the Army and Police Headquarters by other elements of Spetsnaz and Airborne Divisons that had earlier captured Bagram Airport. Within an hour of launching the assault the unit was able to force an entry into the Palace and kill President Amin and his family. The fact that Soviet involvement in Afghanistan went awry subsequently takes nothing away from the professional manner in which this intervention was carried out. The fact that the Soviet intervention in Afghanistan was primarily aimed at preventing the spread of Islamic fundamentalism and its impact on the Central Asian Republics is ironic, given the US reaction and subsequent history of the region.

This unit was also placed on alert for tackling the world's first incident involving unauthorised occupation of a nuclear submarine. On 12 September 1998, a 19-year-old sailor, Alexandr Kuzminykh, ran amok and killed eight of his fellow servicemen aboard a Akula Class nuclear submarine at the Skalisty naval base at Kola. He subsequently locked himself up in the torpedo bay and threatened to detonate some of the forty torpedoes on board. Such an explosion in all likelihood would have damaged the submarine's nuclear power plant as also damaged other nuclear submarines based there. His action resulted in the other submarines being evacuated while SOF, probably elements of Alpha Team, cordoned off the boat and attempted to negotiate with the sailor. In this they were assisted by the sailor's mother and brother, in addition to a psychologist and a priest who unsuccessfully tried to persuade him to give himself up. After a twenty-three hour stand off, the sailor killed himself even as assault elements were in the process of moving in to neutralise him.

Another important operation that stands out and deserves mention was the action on 23 October 2002 when approximately forty armed Chechen rebels led by Movsar Barayev occupied the Dubrovke theatre in Moscow at 2100 hours and took about seven hundred spectators hostage. They ringed the building with explosive charges while each of the eighteen women terrorists strapped themselves to chairs attached to explosives and demanded a stoppage to the Chechen conflict. They also threatened to blow up the theatre and kill all hostages if any attempts were made to assault the building. While Spetsnaz and police units cordoned off the theatre, SOF negotiators assisted by some Chechen members of parliament commenced negotiations to arrange for the release of the hostages. After two days of torturous negotiations that resulted in a few of the hostages, mainly women and children, being released, there was a deadlock and the talks broke down with the rebels threatening to commence killing hostages from 6 AM the next day. It was at this time that the go ahead was given for the Alfa Team to assault and neutralise the terrorists.

On early morning of 26 October surprise was compromised while the assault elements were still getting into position resulting in exchange of fire between the rebels and the Spetsnaz as also in a number of hostages being shot. The Spetsnaz were forced to change plans and immediately commenced a chemical attack that incapacitated all within the theatre. This was probably done through air conditioning vents and must have been planned for in advance. It resulted in the Spetsnaz being able to force an entry into the building without any opposition and kill all rebels except for three that were taken prisoner. It however resulted in a large number of the hostages falling sick due to the chemical used including over ninety fatalities. These fatalities may have been drastically reduced if the SOF had informed the local hospitals of the chemical used, which is still not known, or provided the necessary antidote. The lack of prior preparation to deal with the effects of the chemical attack leads to the conclusion that in all probability it was only a standby plan that was activated due to loss of surprise. Credit must be given to the unconventional plan of assault and the boldness with which it was executed resulting in over six hundred hostages being freed unharmed with forty-two rebels being killed and three others being taken prisoner. More importantly, it showed the firm resolve of the Russian Government to tackle terrorist attacks whatever the cost.

The extensive use of Spetsnaz elements of the GRU and the KGB in the training and advisory capacity to assist various "liberation movements" during the Cold War has been well documented. Their effectiveness in imparting training, especially in guerrilla and unconventional warfare, has been spectacularly successful as can be seen in the manner these groups have gone about their business in Africa and the Middle East. There are no reports at the present time as to whether the Russian Federation provides such training at present. There are, however, numerous web sites advertising adventure training by ex Spetsnaz personnel. In all likelihood, as is the case in the West, covert training to meet Russian political ends, if being provided, may have been "privatised" and is being imparted by any one of the private companies, with state concurrence.

*"He who knows others is wise"*

-Tao-te Chin

## SOF: REGIONAL STATES

### SOF of the Peoples Liberation Army (PLA)

Of particular interest to us are the SOF of the Peoples Republic of China and that of Pakistan, our neighbours and former adversaries. Their SOF, as is to be expected, are modeled on the lines of the Russian and the British pattern respectively. The Chinese have only given these forces attention in the past decade or so. While historically, the PLA was highly skilled in using special troops formed by specially trained and equipped soldiers to conduct various special and guerrilla warfare missions such as penetrations, tactical reconnaissance, raids on vital positions, rescuing prisoners, and capturing valuable enemy personnel it did not possess dedicated SOF, except for their airborne and marine units until the early 1990s, when the PLA commenced a doctrinal change from the "people's war" towards fighting "a local war under high-tech conditions".

In fact, the first "special mission, rapid reaction" unit of the PLA was established in Guangzhou Military Region based on the region's existing reconnaissance group and was used to demonstrate the capabilities of modern special operations warfare to the Chinese and PLA leaders. By the end of the 1990s, all seven military regions in China had a dedicated SOF unit under command deploying a "regimental" sized force of about a thousand personnel in three battalions. Also as a part of the PLA's strategic reserve and rapid reaction force, the PLA 15th Airborne Army was raised in 1961 consisting of three airborne divisions each of approximately ten thousand personnel and is reportedly equipped with the BMD3 Paratrooper Fighting Vehicle. It is directly under the command of the Central Military Commission and unlike in most other countries forms a part of the Air Force. The PLA is estimated to possess the capability to conduct airborne operations of at least regiment size against objectives within a 900 km radius and is expected to be employed for seizure of important areas, sabotage missions against WMD, their guidance equipment and support units, disruption of command and control, assistance to guerrilla warfare and special operations and internal security missions.

The People's Liberation Army Navy (PLAN) also has several elite units specialised in underwater special operations, officially called "Amphibious Reconnaissance Groups". They are similar to the SBS and the SEALs and each group is roughly equivalent to a battalion with about four hundred personnel grouped into three combat and one support company. In addition, the Marine Corps brigades also have such units organic to their establishment for conduct of reconnaissance and special operations.

For incident response situations, the Chinese established a dedicated anti-terrorism special police force in 1982 under the People's Armed Police (PAP) Forces that are also a part of the PLA. Originally known as the "Unit 722", the special police unit is presently known as "The People's Armed Police Special Police School" and is based in a Beijing suburb. It is a combat unit as well as an armed police college and recruits students from the regional police forces. Students receive three years of education and training in the college, and obtain a college diploma after graduation. The majority of the college graduates become officers in the PAP anti-terrorism units around the country, while those with best grades become members of the college's elite anti-terrorism unit.

**SOF of Pakistan**

Independence and partition saw Headquarters 14 Para Brigade along with 3rd Para Battalion 15th Punjab Regiment (MG), 3rd Para Battalion 1st Punjab Regiment and 3rd Para Battalion Baluch Regiment allotted to Pakistan. No further details on the fate of these units are available, but they were unlikely to have remained in the airborne role and in all probability contributed personnel to 312 Garrison Company, a hush-hush unit located at Cherat tasked for commando raids behind enemy lines that had been raised in the early 1950s. It was in 1954 that a decision was taken to expand these forces with the raising of 19th Para Battalion; the Baluch Regiment. In this assistance was sought from the US SOF and the CIA. It was initially raised at Cherat with twelve companies that also incorporated 312 Garrison Company and included a scuba company. In early 1965, the battalion was redesignated as the Special Services Group. In 1966, after a less than favorable showing against the Indian Army in the September war, SSG underwent major reorganisation and expansion. Two new battalions and a Group Headquarters were raised. In 1970, the SSG formed an independent combat diver unit by re-designating the old scuba company that was known as the Musa Company. This company was given the task of operating within Pakistani riverine areas while Pakistani Naval SSG undertook the responsibility of coastal operations to minimise overlap in their tasking. The Naval SSG reportedly has three 110 - ton mini submarines for conduct of covert operations in coastal areas.

In 1980, a decision was made to raise an additional company (Zarar) in the counter-terrorism role, which came up as a result of increases in terrorist incidents worldwide. For this new role, advisors from the British SAS helped train the Zarar Company operators. The current SSG strength has been enhanced to four battalions with approximately 700 men each. These battalions are further divided into four companies each that are split into platoons consisting of 10 man teams. The battalions continue to be commanded by officers of the rank of Lieutenant Colonel while a Brigadier (Commander SSG) oversees the SSG as a whole from the Group HQ in Cherat. Interestingly, the Headquarters apart from the usual staff officers for intelligence, operations, training, logistics and personnel also has an administrative officer handling finance, who in all likelihood, is responsible for budgeting all operational, procurement, training and administrative expenses. Apart from the Parachute Training School there are reports that this Group has dedicated air assets also available for its use. The organisation tree is at Appendix B.

The independent Zarar Company has evolved into a genuine and sole counter-terrorism capability within Pakistan. During any given year, the four SSG battalions are constantly rotated through bases at Cherat and Attock Fort. One battalion is generally kept in training while two are on operational duties along the Indian and/or Afghan border as well as on any UN peacekeeping deputation and the fourth battalion is used for security of strategic locations such as the nuclear power plants etc. As a result of exposure to a wide range of training, the SSG is capable of carrying out a variety of missions. These include unconventional warfare, long-range reconnaissance and intelligence gathering missions, riverine operations, counter-terrorism, and tactical assaults against enemy positions. Another possible role would be to act as target designators for the Air Force and artillery observers. SSG personnel are also tasked with protection of vital points (VP) such as nuclear installations and dams. SSG also provides a security detail for the protection of VIPs including the COAS. In the past, SSG members have also been deployed aboard airlines to act as Air Marshals, though this practice has reportedly been stopped.

There can be no doubting the fact that the SSG has performed extremely well in the commando role in the 1971 Indo-Pak War, where it was utilised for raids and coup-de main missions, such as in the Fazilka Sector, where a company was able to infiltrate Indian defences and occupy the Beriwala Bridge, which was a part of the depth defences, at the beginning of the campaign and hold it till the ceasefire despite numerous counter attacks. However, the battalion deployed in East Pakistan at that time, the 2nd Commando Battalion, was used primarily for conduct of counter insurgency operations against the local population prior to the war. It is reported to have also carried out a number of trans-border raids against the Indian Army and the Mukti Bahini without much success. During this period this unit came under severe criticism for its brutal and inhuman behaviour against the local Bengali population. In fact, its actions during this period have been selectively deleted from the Hamood-ur -Rehman Report thereby raising suspicions of a cover up. Interestingly, General Pervez Musharraf, the President of Pakistan, was also one of the company commanders in this battalion during this period. However, all operations undertaken were at the tactical level and had no effect on the overall campaign.

This, however, was not the case during the 1965 War when the SSG was utilised for organising Operation Gibraltar prior to commencement of the War and for raids against Indian airfields in the western sector. While both these operations failed because of amateurish planning and poor execution, there can be no gainsaying the fact that both operations represented strategic vision and foresight and were classic employment of SOF. In Operation Gibraltar "*the then Foreign Minister Mr. Zulfiqar Ali Bhutto, and the Foreign Secretary, Aziz Ahmed spurred on by Major General Akhtar Hussain Malik, who was commander of our troops in Azad Kashmir, pressed the Government to take advantage of the disturbed situation in the valley and direct the Army to send raiders into Indian held Kashmir for conducting guerrilla activities there and to help, on a long term basis, the locals in organising a movement with a view to eventually starting an uprising against the occupying power.*"[29] The SSG was given the task of coordinating the operation and providing the leadership elements for the "raiders". Apart from poor planning and execution by the SSG itself, the leadership had wrongly assessed the level of support for their cause as also miscalculated the Indian reaction, in this case massive retaliation. As the then Commander SSG, Colonel SG Mehdi, MC (Retd) , subsequently writes: "I decided to reduce my arguments in writing, as to the reasons why Gibraltar shall fail. These, in brief, were:

- No ground had been prepared before launching of the operation, in concert with people of the Valley.

- The raids were to be launched in a total logistical vacuum relying exclusively on what the troops would carry in their packs or living off the countryside. Without any covert support across the Ceasefire Line, this living off the land proved fatal to the security of the guerrillas. Most of them were betrayed.

• GHQ had mixed up classic guerrilla operations with Commando raids.

• All SSG and other officers, responsible for training and later leading groups across the ceasefire line was critical of the soundness of the plan, unsure of the means and uncertain of the end."[30]

As regards the abortive SSG airborne commando raids against the Indian Air Force forward bases of Adampur, Halwara and Pathankot, this operation conceived initially by PAF Chief was approved by President Ayub Khan in May/June 1965 and planned by the SSG. While Colonel Mehdi attempts to disassociate himself from the planning by having "emphatically pointed out that the concept of operation was faulty as no raids of this nature, after the breakout of war, could have even a remote chance of success against fully alerted targets,"[31] the fact is that instead of concentrating against one base in strength with a workable exfiltration plan, like for example, using an aircraft to land and pick up the raiding party, the attempt to hit the three bases, with small raiding parties that were to accomplish their mission and then exfiltrate on their own, was doomed to failure. In fact, the personnel were detected during the drop and eliminated by the army supported by the local police and the civilian population in the vicinity. The belief that small groups of personnel can operate covertly and avoid detection deep inside enemy territory in areas with a high population density, especially after hostilities have commenced, is questionable.

Subsequent operations in the past decade have been launched with much more finesse and sophistication. This can be seen from the manner in which the operations and training of terrorists in Punjab and Kashmir, as also of the Taliban, have been conducted. In addition, training teams also provide training in CT operations to a number of Middle Eastern countries and even for the Sri Lankan Commando Regiment. They have also fought well in Siachen though with no success and instead have taken very heavy casualties. Also, during the initial phases of the Kargil operations of 1999, the Special Service Group (SSG) performed well infiltrating relatively deep into Indian territory undetected. Subsequently, being used as stock infantry troops to hold defensive positions without reinforcements led to heavy casualties added to which they suffered the mortification of being 'denied' by their own country for political expediency. There are also reports that motivation and training standards have fallen with greater emphasis on the outward signs of toughness and ceremonial drills and demonstrations, if the first Commanding Officer of the Special Services Group (SSG) is to be believed, as has been stated by him in his incisive autobiography.[31]

## NOTES

1. Heral, Ethan. "Yasotay and the Mangoday of Genghis Khan." *Armed Forces Journal Intl* (January 1985): pp. 38-39, 42-43, 45, 47, 50, 54, 56, 60, 62, 64 & 68-69.
2. From the Net: Battles: The Battle of the Somme, 1916 First World War. Com.
3. Edit Kirkpatrick, EM, *Chambers 20th Century Dictionary,* W & R Chambers Ltd, Edinburgh, 1983, p. 252.
4. Gavin, John R, General, *Air Assault: The Development of Airmobile Warfare,* Hawthorne Books, New York, NY, 1969:
5. Burgess, William H, *Inside Spetsnaz: Soviet Special Operations–a Critical Analysis,* Presidio Press, USA, 1990, pp 2-4.
6. Whither Russia's Elite Airborne Forces? *Monitor,* Volume 7, Issue 156, August 28, 2001.

7. Suvorov, Viktor, *Spetsnaz: The Story Behind the Soviet SAS*, Hamish Hamilton Ltd, 1987.
8. Burgess, *Op Cit* p1.
9. Krahmann, Elke "Controlling Private Military Companies: The United Kingdom and Germany", *International Studies* Association Annual Convention, February 25- March 1, 2003,Portland, Oregon, p.3.
10. Møller, Bjørn, "Private Military Companies And Peace Operations In Africa", Paper for the seminar on Private Military Companies (PMCs) in Africa: To Ban or Regulate,Department of Political Sciences, University of Pretoria, 8 February 2002, pp. 6-7.
11. http://seattletimes.nwsource.com/html/nationworld/2001896454_security06.html
12. Connor, Ken, Ghost Force: The Secret History of the SAS, Cassel & Co, London 1998, pp. 357-414.
13. McNab, Andy, *Bravo Two Zero*, Bantam Press, London, 1993.
14. Connor, op. cit. pp.175.
15. Ibid, pp 463.
16. From the Net, US SOF Posture 2000, Spec Ops.Com.
17. Kermit, Roosevelt, ed, *War Report of the OSS*, 2 Vols. Walker & Co, New York 1976, 1:16.
18. Ransom, Harry Rowe, *Central Intelligence and National Security*, Harvard University Press, Cambridge, 1958, p. 64-65.
19. SOF Posture 2000, op. cit., pp. 43-44.
20. *Ibid*, pp. 44.
21. Kibbe, Jennifer D, *The Rise of the Shadow Warriors, Foreign Affairs* March-April 2004, pp.102-115.
22. Stanton, Shelby I., *Vietnam, Order of Battle*, U.S. News Books, Washington 1981, pp. 239-253.
23. Crawley, James W, SEALs Give Glimpse Of Missions In Iraq, San Diego Union-*Tribune* 27 June, 2003.
24. From the Net: Jogerst, Colonel John, USAF, What's So Special about Special Operations? Lessons from the War in Afghanistan, Global SpecOps.com.
25. From the Net, Home Page Israeli Special Operations Forces, Misaveret.Com.
26. *Ibid*.
27. *Ibid*.
28. Adams, James, *Secret Armies: The Full Story of SAS, Delta Force and Spetsnaz*, Century Hutchinson Ltd, UK, 1987, p. 68.
29. Musa, General Mohamed, *My Version*, Oxford University Press, Pakistan, 1993, pp 48-50.

30. From the Net: Mehdi, Col (Retd) SG, MC, Operation Gibraltar: Role of SSG Para Commandos, defencenotes.com.
31. *Ibid.*
32. Mitha, Major General (Retd) A O, *Unlikely Beginnings: A Soldier's Life*, Oxford University Press, UK, 2003, pp. 225-226.

# 3

# Overview of Indian SOF

*"It don't matter if the cat is black or white*
*As long as it catches mice..."*

Anonymous

## HISTORY AND DEVELOPMENT

In the rigid caste system of the Services, elite units are detested not for what they do, as all regulars understand and accept the necessity of forces operating behind enemy lines who will divert the attention of the enemy and improve their own chances of success, but for what they are. Special units are not only a drain on regular units in terms of taking away their best manpower, leadership and budgets, but also, more importantly, for their lack of acceptable 'social behaviour'. Personnel from these units tend to dress differently, are more outspoken, have divergent views on discipline and tend not to follow the accepted chain of command. In other words, they tend to create excessive and infructious work for commanders and staff. All this is, of course, well known and accepted as a necessary evil.

However, what is less well known is the fratricidal tendencies that exist among such elites for a variety of reasons—the reasons for conflict ranging from unit pride to ego and conflict over share of the budget pie. However, the major bone of contention, especially in our case, has been the differences in perception of what constitute Special Forces which has in many ways detracted from the otherwise exemplary performance of one of the Indian Army's most battle hardened and premier regiments — the Parachute Regiment. This, to a great extent, happened because of our excessive use of American terminology without taking into consideration the relevant language, cultural or historical context. Thus, we 'borrowed' the term Special Forces to describe our parachute commando units and have then attempted to make these units perform a mix of tasks for which the US employs a host of *Special Operations Forces* including Special Forces. Since the US does not follow the 'Regimental System', it has no unit, per se, called the Special Forces. What it does have are a number of Brigade (Regiment in their case) sized formations called *Special Forces Groups*. These along with the 75th *Ranger Regiment*, another brigade sized formation and some *Civil Affairs and Psychological Warfare Groups* form a part of the *Army Special Operations Command* and are referred to as *Special Operations Forces*. In their context, interestingly, the Parachute Infantry Regiments and the 82 Airborne Divison do not form a part of the Special Operations Forces as they are meant for conventional tasks of a strategic nature. Interestingly, in our context, some of the tasks our Parachute Brigade is required to take on, such as capture of an airfield or out of area contingencies, are quite similar to that of the 75th Ranger Regiment.

This misunderstanding of terminology on our part has resulted in our Parachute (Special Forces) units attempting to take on ranger tasks as well, without the requisite wherewithal, such as ground holding capability. In consonance with these views, an effort was made by some to separate special forces units from the other parachute units and equate them in a similar manner as has been done with the US Airborne Regiments/Division to keep them out of the special operations field. This resulted in a debilitating internecine battle effecting morale and regimental cohesion that set back the Parachute Regiment by years.

This is something that other armies have faced as well. The SAS for example raised their fourth sabre squadron, 'G' Squadron, when the need for the unit to be expanded was felt not by getting additional volunteers from their Parachute Regiment, which otherwise contributes in large numbers, but by converting the Guards Independent Parachute Squadron of the Brigade of the Guards to the SAS role without any selection procedures being implemented. This was done by senior officers of the SAS to ensure enhanced influence at the highest levels through the Guards, who tend to be intimately connected to the aristocracy, and partially to stop the Parachute Regiment from increasing their considerable influence over the Regiment. The fact that the 'G' Squadron is even to this day required to be led by officers and senior NCOs from the Brigade of the Guards is deeply resented by many. Thankfully, in our case, attempts at the present time to resolve this issue and place it in the correct perspective will pay dividends.

As stated earlier, Special Operations Forces or Special Forces are units that have specially selected manpower, with unique skills, trained and equipped for a specific purpose that utilises unconventional and unorthodox tactics to achieve its aims. Thus, if we accept this definition, armour in its infancy could be considered to have been a part of Special Forces till it became the conventional arm of decision and replaced horsed cavalry in its entirety. Similarly, in our context today, the Rashtriya Rifles should rightfully be considered as a Special Force since it is specifically trained and equipped to fight a Low Intensity Conflict. However, since these units follow standard doctrine and tactics that are now universally employed the world over, it may be more appropriate to consider them as conventional forces for Low Intensity Conflict.

In addition the Dogra and Kumaon Scout Wings and the Ladakh Scouts are manned by personnel from the region and organised to act as stay behind parties and engage enemy logistic and command and control elements in the region they belong to. These units also have a ground holding role in their area of deployment. Despite the unconventional nature of their tasking, these units have till now not been considered a part of the Special Forces because of the broad based nature of their tasking, akin to other infantry battalions, the fact that the primary requirement is that the personnel are from the region where they are required to operate and their operations are by and large restricted to within our own territory. If the role of such units is amended to employment for trans-border guerrilla operations in addition to their stay behind role, it may be worthwhile converting them into Territorial Army Special Forces units that are activated only as required. In addition, various Para Military Forces, Central Police Organisations, ministries and state governments have raised "commando" units that are better trained and equipped than their counterparts within the Force. However these units are in fact carrying out normal police functions, albeit more efficiently, and, therefore, cannot really be considered as a part of Special Operation Forces.

In these circumstances, therefore, only the Parachute and the Parachute Commando battalions along with the Marine Commandos (MARCOS), National Security Guard (NSG), Special Frontier Force (SFF) and the Aviation Research Centre (ARC) have been considered as Special Forces. However, since the Parachute Commando units are now designated as Parachute (Special Forces), it may be appropriate to refer to all generic Special Forces units as Special Operations Forces (SOF), as has been done here and is the case in the US. This will also enable us to distinguish between the PARA and the PARA (SF) battalions with regard to their organisations and roles though both have been taken to be part of the SOF in the context of this study.

In the historical context employment of SOF in India can probably be traced back to ancient military text. Closer to the recent period, Shivaji's use of partisan warfare and employment of small forces to infiltrate enemy strong points to turn their defences is well documented. He had thoroughly studied the strengths of the Mughals as well as their weaknesses, and tempered his diplomacy, military doctrine, organisation, and tactics to capitalise on the latter. The rugged terrain of the Western Ghats, where he operated, could be counted on to slow down large conventional columns. His cavalry, swift and decisive in battle, had great stamina, dedication and skill. It used the raid, hit and run tactics, hounding and harrying but never offering set piece battle. Shivaji's defensive pivots were his famous hilltop forts, eminently suited for defence against anything but a long investment siege. A commander of incomparable pluck and acumen, he exploited every facet of the military art including deception, to appear where he was least expected and in sufficient strength to carry the day. Subsequently, in the 1800s the irregular cavalry units raised by the East India Company, such as Gardner's Horse, and Hodson's Horse copied Shivaji's employment of cavalry and went on to harass, raid and destroy rebel forces, fortifications and communications during our First War of Independence.

In terms of establishment of modern SOF, Winston Churchill's directions for raising of parachute units in India was implemented in September 1941 with the raising of 50(Independent) Parachute Brigade with three parachute battalions that by the end of the war had become the 44 Airborne Division. In addition the LRDG went on to raise an Indian squadron for employment in North Africa while the Chindits, Force 136 and Victor Force were raised for employment in the South East Asian theatre of operations. The 50(Independent) Parachute Brigade was intimately involved in the battle of Shangshak that preceded the Japanese attacks on Kohima and Imphal and was subsequently used for the first time to launch a composite battalion level airborne operation in 1945 in support of the amphibious landings at Elephant Point that were carried out to hasten the capture of Rangoon. Incidentally, this Parachute Brigade is today the oldest airborne formation to have continuously remained in an airborne role in the world.

The employment of the Assam Rifles during this period is of interest. It was tasked to organise a resistance group on the Indo-Burmese border to counter the Japanese invasion and to disrupt their lines of communication. The whole concept was contained in Plan Number V, and the Resistance Force so formed and organised, came to be known as 'Victor Force'. The Assam Rifles, which formed the nucleus of this Force, covered itself with glory with the exemplary performance of its platoons. They fought gallant independent actions far into Burmese territory behind the enemy lines and later during the battles for Kohima and Imphal. As part of the V Force, a number of Assam Rifles platoons acted as covering forces both during the defensive and the offensive phases of the operations in Burma. One of the platoons of the 4th Battalion was also trained as paratroops and dropped near the Sittang River behind Japanese lines during the latter part of the Campaign.

Another such unit was Force 136, a British Intelligence organisation composed of military personnel working behind enemy lines. Its objectives were to gather important information on enemy movement and to organize local underground resistance groups to disrupt enemy communication and supply lines. It was an offshoot of the SOE and operated in Burma and Malaya. Another similar group known as "Operation Oblivion" was stationed in Australia and operated in Borneo and Sarawak. The personnel recruited for these organisations were required to blend in with the local inhabitants. Personnel of this Force received training in tactics, demolition, weapons, communications and parachute jumping. They normally operated in groups of eight with each agent a specialist in his party. Besides the commander and his second in command, there were two demolition experts, a wireless operator, a coder/ decoder and two scouts. Their mission was changed at the end of the war and groups were instructed to control the immediate disengagement of the Japanese army in their respective areas, prevent the guerrilla groups from taking revenge on the surrendering Japanese troops, and care for the released Allied prisoners of war until the arrival of Allied forces.

The Chindits were the largest of the allied Special Forces of the Second World War. They were formed and led by Major General Orde Wingate, DSO. The Chindits operated deep behind enemy lines in North

Burma in the War against Japan. For many months they lived in and fought the enemy in the jungles of Japanese occupied Burma, totally relying on airdrops for their supplies. There were two Chindits expeditions into Burma, the first in February 1943, Operation Longcloth, which consisted of a force of 3,000 men who marched over 1,000 miles during the campaign. The second expedition, Operation Thursday, in March 1944 was on a much larger scale. It was the second largest airborne invasion of the war and consisted of a force of 20,000 British and Commonwealth soldiers with air support provided by the 1st Air Commando USAAF. Tragically their leader, General Wingate, was killed a few weeks after the launch of Operation Thursday. The Force was divided into a number of columns each consisting of about four hundred men built around a infantry company with reconnaissance and a commando platoon and signalers and medical personnel.

The second operation had fewer mules than the first as it was planned to provide it with extensive aerial re-supply. Each of the columns was tasked to attack and cut supplies lines and generally harass the rear of the Japanese forces on the frontline facing British, American and Chinese forces. The column formations were designed for movement through the jungle that was to be their main source of strength. A column would emerge from the jungle to blow up a dump or ambush an enemy convoy and then slip away again into the jungle where the enemy would be unable or afraid to follow. When necessary, the columns would reform into battalions and brigades to attack and seize larger targets or to repel attacks from a large enemy force. Though these operations were launched from India, no Indian troops, except for Gurkhas, participated as Wingate reportedly had a poor opinion of Indians and Indian troops.

It is of utmost interest, however, that while Wingate refused to employ Indian troops for special operations, the first Indian SOF personnel to be launched into operations belonged not to the British Indian Army as should have been the case, but to the "Legion Freies Indien" of the German Army. German Military Intelligence, the Abhwer, had envisaged this new military force as accompanying an Axis campaign via the Caucasus through Iran into India to end British rule there. As early as the end of August 1941 they had formulated a scheme to fly the Indian Legion to India and using parachute landings start an anti-British revolt. To this end some Indians appear to have been recruited by Rittmeister Habicht of the Abhwer and incorporated as a part of "4.Regiment, 800.Bau Lehrdivision zur Besonderen Verwendung Brandenburg" (Special Purpose Construction Training Division Brandenburg), which despite its innocuous sounding title constituted the Special Forces of the Wehrmacht. In January 1942 Operation "Bajadere" was launched and one hundred Indians were parachuted into Eastern Persia in order to infiltrate into India through Baluchistan and commence sabotage operations against the British in preparation for the anticipated national revolt. Oberleutnant Witzel in Afghanistan reported to the Abhwer station in Kabul that the Indians had been effective and this information was passed on to Abhwer headquarters in Berlin. Axis reverses at Stalingrad and El Alamein at the end of 1942 made an attack into India by the European Axis powers appear an increasingly unlikely scenario and nothing more seemed to be heard about these detachments subsequently[1].

To go back a bit, around the time the British had commenced raising of the Parachute Brigade in India, the Italians also commenced raising a SOF unit from disaffected Indian Prisoners of War held by them, though their efforts were comparatively short-lived. On 10th May 1942, the Italian Army established a "Ragruppamento Centri Militari", a special unit composed of foreign military personnel, ex-prisoners-of-war, foreign nationals living in Italy and Italians who had been resident abroad, with the intention of using them for intelligence gathering and sabotage operations behind enemy lines. Under Tenente Colonello di Stato (Staff Lieutenant Colonel) Massimo Invrea, it had three companies, the 'Centro T' consisting of Italians from Tunisia, the 'Centro A' consisting of Italians from Egypt, Palestine, Syria and Arabia and also Arabs and Sudanese ex-prisoners-of-war and, lastly, the 'Centro I' consisting of Italians from India and Iran and Indian ex-prisoners-of-war. In all, the Ragruppamento Centri Militari collected together approximately 1,200 Italians, 400 Indians and 200 Arabs. In August 1942, the Ragruppamento was renamed as Ragruppamento Frecce Rosse (Red Arrows Group) and each of the companies enhanced to battalion strength with the Centro I being redesignated as 'Battaglione Azad Hindoustan' (Free Indian Battalion). The units of the Ragruppamento Frecce Rosse were intended to be delivered behind enemy lines by various means including infiltration on the ground, via submarine and by parachute; this last means of transport leading to the establishment of a Platone Paracadutisti (Parachute Platoon) within the Battaglione Azad Hindoustan, with its members receiving their parachute training at the Parachute School at Tarquinia. By August 1942, the battalion consisted of a motorised rifle company, a motorised machinegun company, a parachute platoon and a platoon of overseas Italians who had lived in India. However, despite their investment in the training of Indians, the Italians considered the Indian troops of Battaglione Azad Hindoustan to be of doubtful loyalty; this view was confirmed when the Indians mutinied on learning of the Axis defeat at El Alamein in November 1942. Following this the battalion was disbanded and the Indians returned to their prisoner-of-war camps. Thus ended the disappointing Italian efforts to recruit Indians for service in the Axis armed forces.[2]

Their German partners, who had begun to recruit Indians earlier, were not put off by the negative Italian experience, as they were greatly assisted in their endeavour by Netaji Subhas Chandra Bose, who had established himself as leader of the Indian "Government-in-exile", in Berlin. In April 1941, some of the members of the British 3rd (Indian) Motorised Brigade taken prisoner by the Afrika Korps in Libya were flown to Berlin together with the establishment of a special camp for about 10,000 Indian POWs at Annaburg. There, the Indian prisoners were visited by Bose and exposed to intensive propaganda with a view to their enlistment into the proposed unit, variously referred to as the Indian Legion, Azad Hind Legion or the more exotically sounding, Tiger Legion. Subsequently, six thousand of the Indian prisoners who were considered most receptive to Bose's ideas were transferred to the camp at Frankenburg where they underwent military training under German officers and NCO's. These men now constituted the Legion Freies Indien of the German Army and by mid-1943 consisted of approximately two thousand personnel and were also referred to as 'Indisches Infanterie Regiment 950'.[3] The personnel parachuted into Iran belonged to this force. Incidentally, the leaders and best personnel of the Indian Legion were subsequently transferred to Singapore to join the Azad Hind Fauj in two ships of which one was successfully able to run the blockade and link up with the Japanese at Singapore while the other was never heard of ever. Subsequently, the British captured the personnel of the Legion that remained behind in

Germany in the closing stages of the War while they attempted to unsuccessfully cross over to neutral Switzerland.[4]

The end of the War and subsequent partition led to 50(independent) Parachute Brigade with three battalions remaining as the only SOF on the order of battle of the Indian Army. These units were extensively employed in the 1948 war with Pakistan and subsequently in all wars and conflicts that this country has fought. These battalions also participated in United Nations peacekeeping operations in Korea and Gaza. The 1962 War with China led to an increase in the number of units to eight with an additional parachute brigade headquarter as well. However, a need was felt for units that would be organised for hit and run raids and surveillance and reconnaissance behind enemy lines that led to the raising of two commando units.

It was in the late seventies that a need was first felt for a sub unit organised and capable CT tasks, primarily for countering hijacking of aircrafts. An adhoc company was formed within 50 Parachute Brigade with selected personnel from within the brigade. This force, however, did not have suitable equipment nor specialised training for such tasks and based on other such forces world wide a new organisation was formed within the Special Frontier Force (SFF) from volunteers mainly from the Parachute Regiment. Subsequently, this force formed the core elements of the Special Action Groups of the National Security Guard (NSG) when that was formed in the mid 1980s.

It was also in the early 1980s that a need was felt for a unit capable of carrying out a range of Special Forces missions on the lines of the SAS. This led to the conversion of the 1st Battalion. The Parachute Regiment to convert to a new and more sophisticated organisation. Subsequently, the other commando battalions adopted the new organisation and this was followed by the conversion of 21st Battalion the Maratha Light Infantry and 2nd Battalion the Parachute Regiment. There are now reports of additional parachute battalions being reorganised for this role.[5]

*"Men Apart, Every Man an Emperor"*

—Field Marshal Montgomery of Alamein

## PARACHUTE BATTALIONS

### Organisation and Employment

The Army has three different types of SOF on its order of battle, which between them, provide specialist support covering the complete spectrum of conflict from operations other than war to total nuclear war. The oldest units available are the Parachute Battalions. The existing units were either converted from infantry battalions in 1945 with elements of the erstwhile Indian Parachute Regiment being amalgamated into them or were raised as parachute units after the Sino-Indian Conflict of 1962. There are presently five such battalions of which three form a part of the only strategic rapid reaction capability available to the country, in the form of 50 (Independent) Parachute Brigade. This brigade group has elements from all arms and services in terms of artillery, communication, combat engineering and logistic support integral to its establishment. Air Defence elements have been provided by attaching adhoc elements from other formations, an aspect that needs reconsideration.

The parachute battalions, though organised in a similar manner to standard infantry units, have some crucial differences that greatly enhance their combat potential. It has a mechanised platoon equipped with BMP2 and additional Anti Tank missile launchers that greatly enhances its anti tank potential along with additional manpower. Moreover, in terms of value addition where these units really score is in the fact that all their personnel are volunteers selected after having undergone a tough three-month selection capsule in respective units, which ensures that all personnel are physically tough and well motivated. The policy permitting volunteers to opt out and transfer to their original or parent unit after a mandatory period, as also the authority with the commanding officer to transfer out personnel who may suffer from physical, mental or motivational deterioration goes a long way in ensuring that these units remain at their optimal efficiency. Unfortunately, perceptions, which exist in the receiving units that personnel not selected or returned from these units are likely to cause problems with regard to either integration within the unit or affect promotion prospects of other personnel or cause disciplinary problems leads to opposition towards accepting these personnel. There is a requirement to explain the existing policies in detail to regular units so that personnel there are made aware of the reasons for keeping parachute units at optimum efficacy. They need to view personnel from these units in a more positive light and take advantage of their varied experience, abilities and technical proficiency. Moreover, a unit at any time will not have more than a sprinkling of such personnel and that will in no way upset unit integrity.

These units are organised, trained and tasked for offensive action behind enemy lines and for out of area contingency tasks which includes capture and holding of ground for limited periods. They are trained for insertion by parachutes or by helicopters. The old adage that such units are a 'threat in being' has been most seriously adhered to, and more often than not, in past conflicts, the Parachute Brigade has been kept as a reserve at the Army Headquarter level or employed in bits and pieces in a ground role. This in itself has been justified to some extent if one is to go by the account of Lieutenant General Gul Hassan, the then Director Military Operations of the Pakistan Army, who hints to the fact that in the 1965 Indo- Pak conflict the offensive operations of Pakistan's First Armoured Division were delayed at the commencement of the campaign based on rumors that Indian paratroopers had been dropped in the vicinity of Lahore.[6] This, however, needs to be balanced with the aspect of utilising one's complete combat potential, especially in short duration wars, where employment of such forces can enhance momentum and depth of operations.

The employment of the Para Brigade against the Portuguese in Goa in December 1961, the earlier employment of a company sized Task Force to establish a forward post at Bara Hoti along the Indo Tibetan border to neutralise Chinese offensive actions in the area in May 1961 and the use of the brigade in the Kutch Operations in April 1965 are all examples of how rapid reaction forces can and should be applied, though in all these cases, it was in the ground role. Their subsequent successful employment in the Indo Pak War of 1971 in the Eastern Sector for launching a battalion level airborne assault at Tangail is also an appropriate case in point, since in most respects it was a defining moment for the Regiment. Field Marshal (then General) Manekshaw was keen to finish the campaign in Bangladesh with utmost speed. His aim was to minimise damage to the Bangladesh economy and avoid unnecessary bloodshed. His efforts were, therefore, directed at the early capture of Dacca. Tangail, northwest of Dacca, was an important communication centre linking Mymensingh and Jamalpur to the capital. Its capture could check the flow of reinforcements to the North; also, when these troops fell back, they could be bagged with ease. India's 95th (Infantry) Brigade Group was advancing on Dacca from the North and a foothold on Tangail would have greatly assisted its progress. Also the presence of Indian troops in the heart of Bangladesh was bound to give a fillip to the activities of the Mukti Bahini (freedom fighters) in the area. Based on these considerations a prompt decision was taken to capture Tangail by airborne assault.[7] The battalion tasked was so enthusiastic that even those personnel who had just joined the unit and were yet to undergo their basic parachute training volunteered. From among these men one officer and one other rank were selected and jumped for the first time directly into action.

The operation was conducted at 1600 hours on 11 December 1971, about one hour prior to last light, in view of the overwhelming air superiority that the IAF had achieved and the objectives, the Poongli Bridge and the Ferry site, were captured by 2000 hours, despite a fairly dispersed drop due to strong winds. The Commander of the retreating Pakistani Brigade and his staff, who initially thought that the Chinese were sending reinforcements to assist them in dealing with the Indian offensive in the sector, witnessed this drop. Sound of gunfire soon persuaded them that this was not the case and they hastily withdrew cross-country towards Dacca without even informing the units under their command[8]. Within the hour the unit was able to ambush an artillery battery withdrawing southwards causing extensive losses in men and equipment. Subsequent unsuccessful counter attacks by the Pakistanis resulted in massive losses on their part amounting to over three hundred and fifty personnel being killed, wounded and taken prisoner against the battalion sustaining just four casualties. This airborne drop, which the BBC wrongly reported as involving the complete Parachute Brigade instead of just one battalion, played an extremely crucial part in forcing Lieutant General Niazi, the Pakistani theatre commander, suing for an unconditional surrender despite the majority of his forces being intact.[9]

Their employment in an earlier time frame and on a larger scale would have, in all likelihood, hastened the fall of Dacca. However subsequent procurement of new generation of aircraft by the Air Force, both for heavy and medium lift, led to the establishment of a viable strategic airlift capability, the effect of which, was visible in the Parachute Brigade action against the rebel coup attempt in the Maldives in 1986.The Brigade was first alerted for the intervention at 1000 hours on 3 November 1986. It was estimated from all available information that Tamil mercenaries numbering between 150 and 400 controlled Male, the capital. The NSS- Maldivian National Security Service, comprising the land forces, the two plane Air Force, Coast Guards and even customs, were besieged in their headquarters. The whereabouts of the President was not known though information was available that he was in hiding. The only silver lining was that Hulule International Airport was still functional and in loyal hands.[10]

The plan envisaged that 6 PARA reinforced by a company from 3 PARA would fly in to secure the airport and jetty and go on to rescue the President. In a subsequent phase the remainder of the Brigade would be landed for further operations as required. For this task the initial aircraft, which carried the company tasked to secure the airfield and the Brigade Commander with his tactical headquarters accompanied by the Indian Ambassador to the Maldives who fortuitously was in India at the time, was to attempt a landing in case the airfield was open and in loyal hands, and, in this not being the case, drop the company on the runway of the airfield—a 40 to 60 metre wide strip with the sea on both sides. Fortunately, the parachute drop was not required and the aircraft were able to land and reinforce loyalists holding the airfield by 2200 hours, just 12 hours from the time the initial warning was received by the

Brigade. By 0230 hours the next morning President Abdul Gayoom had been rescued. By 0730 hours most elements of the Brigade had arrived at the airfield and by mid-day the situation had been stabilised with the coup defeated and the Government in full control. No mean feat for a force launched over three thousand kilometres away with little information or time to prepare, especially when compared to the manner in which operations were conducted by the US SOF in Grenada.

Unfortunately, increasing perceptions within the Air Force especially, that conventional airborne operations are unviable in the existing air defence environment, has led to a steady degradation of our strategic and tactical lift capability. This coupled with unwillingness and inflexibility on our part to try out and adopt new tactical concepts for conduct of airborne operations can only harm our special operations capability in the future. As in most things, it may be wise to remember that it is easier to destroy than to build, and degradation of our airborne capability through lack of awareness will be shameful.

In Low Intensity Conflict scenario these units are presently used in a similar manner as other infantry battalions despite the fact that they have a higher quality of manpower, more focused training and better leadership that has ensured that these units have performed more effectively than other regular infantry units. This is but a logical and expected result of existing policies to enhance the capability of these units by providing them higher quality manpower. This in no way reflects on the performance of regular units nor is it a disparagement of their abilities as our infantry has time and again proved its mettle where it matters most, in battle. On the other hand, inability of parachute units to produce better results would instead have been a cause of concern and reflected poorly on our manpower policies in vogue. However, the utilisation of such units in a conventional manner by either giving them areas of responsibility or making them guard vulnerable points such as ammunition dumps or headquarters is a colossal waste of trained manpower and has a deleterious effect on the morale of personnel serving with such units. Since there is similarity in manning and training policies of these units with that of the commando units within the Regiment it may have been more appropriate to have utilised these units also in a similar manner. In fact, in the North East where this was done these units produced outstanding results as the performances of both the 3rd and 5th Battalions of the Regiment have shown in the period 1992–1998.Similaly the 2nd Battalion, prior to its conversion, was also partially employed in a like manner in Kashmir with equally impressive results.

**Employment in Operations Other Than War**

Interestingly, for operations other than war, such as disaster relief or internal security, the parachute brigade is the only suitably organised and trained rapid response force available within the country. It may be of interest to note that as early as 1950, a reconnaissance team from the Parachute Brigade was dropped near Walong, Arunachal Pradesh, then the North East Frontier Agency, to make contact with the population and look for suitable landing sites and dropping zones in the vicinity of Walong. This group spent over a month in the area before making its way back to the road head, a 12 day walk back. There has, however, been little attempt to employ the Parachute Brigade in such a manner subsequently, except in one instance, as was done during the 1984 unrest by Sikh troops when elements of the brigade either established blocks along the routes being followed by the mutineers or to consolidate our hold and provide protection to military establishments affected by their actions. This is entirely due to perceptions and mindsets at the highest levels that Army Headquarter reserves must only be utilised once regional reserves have been employed. As any numbers of situations worldwide have shown, *the raison-de-etre for such forces is that they are the most suitable response available for intervention at the outset.*

Employment of such forces in this manner has a number of advantages. Firstly, many different options, from parachute to air transportation, are available for insertion of the force giving it inherent flexibility as utilisation of aircraft enable quicker responses within the limitations of time and distance. Secondly, these forces can be deployed regardless of the logistic support available in the area as they have the ability to remain self-contained for some period of time. More importantly, employment in such a manner will ensure that that the army is able to respond quickly to an emerging situation with limited availability of information with regard to the situation prevailing on the ground. In a number of cases such a rapid response will ensuret that the situation is neutralised and controlled before it assumes dangerous proportions. Such a force will also give important real time intelligence inputs as to the situation on the ground as required by military planners to organise a suitable long-term response. It also gives much needed additional time to the units nominated to respond to organise themselves for the task in hand.

Thus, for example, in the case of the earthquake or even the communal crisis in Gujarat, a better option may have been to insert by parachute or by helicopter self contained task forces of the Parachute Brigade consisting of elements of infantry, communications, engineers, medical and other logistics services throughout the state in the initial stages. These task forces would have been able to assist the administration in quickly regaining control or quelling violence as also providing humanitarian aid and first hand accounts of the situation prevailing on the ground. Moreover, in areas where the local administration was in paralysis, for whatever reasons, independent inputs and options would have been available to the central government.

Finally, this would have given the Army Headquarters adequate inputs with regard to the situation on the ground to be able to plan the next response and nominate the units and formations that would need to be deployed subsequently. It would also give these units additional time for preparation as also adequate information as to what they were likely to face.

In essence, such a deployment allows the Army Headquarters to gain control over the situation and prepare the area for subsequent deployment. In truth, more than just the reputation of the army or the services is in balance in such circumstances, the constitution demands that forces respond speedily, unequivocally and in an unbiased manner. It, therefore, behooves the services to institutionalise such a response, which is in place, but goes unutilised at present instance.

*"It is better to live one day as a lion than a hundred years as a sheep."*

- Italian Proverb

## PARACHUTE SPECIAL FORCES BATTALIONS

The Parachute Special Forces units, the second type of Army SOF, are designed for small team operations involving intelligence collection, hit and run actions and covert operations. At present we have five such units, which are affiliated to the four operational Army Commands with the fifth as the Army Headquarters reserve. These units were designed to support corps plans, both in the offensive and defensive roles, in conventional operations scenario and to carry out offensive covert operations in the low intensity conflict scenario. Till the late 1980s these units were expected to operate at a team (company) level primarily for carrying out raids and *coup-de-main* missions which may have even involved assaults against ill or lightly prepared enemy positions located in depth. An example of this was their employment in conventional operations in the 1971 War in the Western Sector.

Unfortunately, unlike in the Eastern Sector, wherein airborne operations had been integrated into offensive operational plans right from the initial stage itself, employment of these units in the western sector was of an adhoc nature restricted to the tactical level. This was disappointing, more so, since the only specialist commando units were both located in this sector at that time. In view of the overall defensive strategy adopted in the Western Sector, these commando units ideally should have been used behind enemy lines to degrade and disrupt enemy offensive plans by carrying out raids on headquarters and forward air bases, eliminating commanders and destroying communication nodes and other logistic elements. They could also have been employed in selected areas for gaining information with regard to deployment of enemy offensive formations.

This unfortunately was not done and instead they were utilised in an adhoc manner to carry out tasks that had limited tactical impact on the overall campaign. All assault teams of 9 PARA, for example, were used to assist various holding brigades in their operations. Thus, while one assault team was tasked to raid and destroy an artillery battery gun position at Mandhol in Poonch in conjunction with a battalion attack to capture a forward Pakistani post, which it did with utmost dispatch, the second was utilised for defence of the Mandiala Bridge in Chhamb, probably a first for commando units anywhere, and the third for capture of a ferry site held by Pakistani Para Military Force (PMF) in the Chicken's Neck area. This team was subsequently used for reinforcing the defences held by a Jammu and Kashmir Militia battalion. In the Rajasthan sector, 10 PARA was similarly tasked to conduct raids on the border townships of Chachro and Virwah, both of which had been evacuated earlier.[11] While the performance of the units involved was praiseworthy, the missions conducted appeared to have had only some propaganda value but little or no impact on operations, except probably at the tactical level.

The good performance of the Regiment, with all three commando battalions and two parachute battalions committed, as a part of the Indian Peace Keeping Force (IPKF) in Srilanka, in the late 1980s, was to greatly influence the military hierarchy and lead to the extensive use of these units for counter insurgency operations subsequently. All the units committed performed exceedingly well with a number of very successful missions to their credit and were extensively used by commanders as shock troops to deal with the LTTE. The attempted raid against the LTTE headquarters at the commencement of the IPKF campaign by 10 PARA (SF) and a platoon of 13 SIKH LI holds a special place despite its lack of success.[12] It clearly brings out the need for specialist units for conduct of heliborne operations. The specialisation required pertains more to the psychological conditioning and standards of training in operations behind enemy lines than proficiency in embarking or disembarking from helicopters.

Some intelligence was available that the Jaffna University (JU) was the tactical headquarters of the LTTE. At the beginning of the campaign against the LTTE, the Indian military leadership decided to launch a commando raid to round up the leadership and thus cut short the Battle for Jaffna. Units were quickly allotted and tasked on an adhoc basis with limited time being given for planning, coordination or preparation. While 10 PARA (SF) had the requisite skill for undertaking such operations at short notice, elements of 13 SIKH LI, infantry with limited exposure to such operations were not so fortunate and the lack of time for preparation was to effect them greatly.

The Jaffna University area was extremely built up. There were just two open patches, a football field and a smaller playground. The plan was to land a team from 10 Para (SF) and a platoon of 13 SIKH LI in order to secure a landing zone at the football field. A second wave was to follow with a company of the 13th Sikh LI that would replace the SOF elements while they launched an assault on the LTTE headquarters. If all went to plan the heliborne troops would subsequently link up with troops coming by land. But unknown to the IPKF, the LTTE had intercepted IPKF radio communications that led to the plans of operation being compromised. It enabled the LTTE to establish an ambush at the landing zone and bring down heavy fire on the heliborne force as they disembarked.

What followed is the most painful story of the Battle of Jaffna. In the dark with heavy machine gun fire the second wave of helicopters brought in a platoon of Sikh LI and landed on the other smaller playground. This was a few yards from the Jaffna University but was separated by several lanes of booby-trapped buildings. The Sikhs soon realised something was wrong as they landed within the LTTE's defences. Headquarters decided to abort the mission but were unable to contact the platoon and inform them of the decision. The platoon was however in contact with the paratroopers who asked them to break contact and link up with them, but like a good infantryman the platoon refused to move deciding to wait for the rest of their company. The troops fought valiantly against the LTTE assaults until they ran out of ammunition at approximately 1130 hours on 12 October, with the last bullet fired, the troops led a bayonet charge to try and break out. They were cut down to the last man but one. That man, Sepoy Gora Singh, was taken POW and later released. Sepoy Singh helped to reconstruct one of the most poignant battles in the history of the Indian Army.[13]

Meanwhile the commandos were still holding out. Their commander, Lieutenant Colonel Dalbir Singh, led a rescue mission with three T-72 tanks. The roads were hopelessly booby-trapped. The commander of the tank group, Major Anil Kaul, improvised brilliantly. Knowing the rail tracks passed behind Jaffna University, he drove his tanks on the Palaly-Jaffna rail line. Passing through the narrow lanes, an RPG-7 fired on him, hitting the turret. The explosion severed his wedding ring finger. Splinters hit him in the eye and arm. His men put him on morphine and they fought their way to the Para Commandos. A little later the 4/5 Gorkhas and remainder of the 13 Sikh LI linked up. The Para Commandos superior training saved the day. They conserved ammunition and even picked up all their dead and weapons. For 18 hours they prayed and fought. The LTTE leadership came perilously close to getting wiped out. Its Chief, Prabhakaran, was injured in the foot. The 13 Sikh LI now holds a special Ardas and Akhand Panth on 12 October every year to honour their 30 lonely and brave comrades on the brutal killing fields of Jaffna University.

By the end of the Indian involvement, these units became adept at small team actions involving establishment of multiple ambushes, covert surveillance, snatch operations, area domination and search and destroy missions. In these operations these units achieved some remarkable successes, something the IPKF was short of, and were able to achieve psychological dominance over the LTTE, who preferred to avoid contact to the extent possible. This experience was put to use with great effect over the last decade in Jammu and Kashmir and the performance of these and the other PARA battalions of the Regiment can be gauged from the fact that most units have been awarded the Chief of Army Staff Unit Citation with three units having been awarded it twice.

Subsequently, the increasing influence of western doctrine regarding employment of Special Forces within the army hierarchy, especially after the Gulf War of 1992, heralded a shift towards small team employment, primarily for reconnaissance and surveillance, which in time became the accepted tasking for these units. With this came the increased employment in low intensity operations in Srilanka, Kashmir and the North East, where these units operated, by and large, at troop (platoon) levels, primarily conducting ambushes, raids based on specific information, snatch operations and psuedo militant actions. All this gradually led to degradation of expertise and psychological conditioning within units to conduct operations involving launching of assaults at team and battalion levels. Personnel did not see themselves as being required to carry out missions other than those involving combat only as a last resort, especially in conventional operations. They came to believe that assault operations behind enemy lines were not specialised enough for employment of such units and would only result in wastage of highly trained manpower. This belief was further reinforced in the past decade in which their conduct of small team covert actions required avoidance of direct confrontation or contact with the opposition at all costs if success was to be achieved. The adverse effects of this belief, whatever its merit, were to be seen during the Kargil operations of 1999.

In the Kargil operations, all the Special Forces battalions less 2 PARA, which was undergoing reorganisation at that time, were moved to the area of operations. The fact that most of these units had little or no experience of mountain warfare, especially in high altitude, was overlooked. The units were required to attempt short hooks to outflank forward enemy positions and occupy dominating features in depth. The restrictions laid down on their transiting or capturing features across the Line of Control (LOC) did much to restrict the scope of operations that could be undertaken by these units. However, while there has been criticism of the performance of these units in some quarters, most agree that it was not performance at unit and sub unit levels that were in question – the personnel performed magnificently as the actions of 9 PARA for the capture of 'Zulu One'[14] clearly showed – but the inability of the unit commanders to meet the high expectations that the hierarchy had placed in their capabilities.

This can perhaps be blamed on a number of factors; the superlative performance of the units in the past decade had raised expectations with regard to their performance to exaggerated and unrealistic levels and commanders confronted with this unexpected and critical situation in this sector expected these units to produce results beyond what was expected of mere mortals. Their inability to do so was, therefore, excessively and unfairly criticised in the heat of the moment. Added to this was the fact that they had neither trained for such tasks nor developed the necessary psychological conditioning required. It would also be unwise to jump to hasty conclusions as these very units and the officers and men serving in them have time and again proved themselves in combat and continue to do so and probably constitute the most combat experienced group within the Army. There appears to have been a mis-match between the doctrines that were propounded and trained for and the reality that faced the commanders on the ground. If they had been tasked, in the manner they had trained, such as for intelligence collection, surveillance, raids on command and control elements, communication nodes and supply elements, the results achieved may have been very different. Whether such actions would have constituted either disregard for the government directive not to cross the LOC, or, led to any escalation, in view of the small numbers involved, continues to remain a matter of conjecture and speculation, as we are not fully aware of the prevailing politico-military dynamics of that time.

The requirement to balance out the need for terrain specific units against the necessity to ensure that they have a repository of knowledge to operate in other types of terrain, the need to rethink the type of tasks that our commando units should be employed for and whether a separate manning policy is required for parachute units and formations emerge as some of the major issues from this campaign and will be examined at length in a later chapter. Before an impression is created that these units are not capable of carrying out special operations in the conventional context, there is a need to reflect on the performance of one of the teams of 2 PARA that was employed for rescue of detainees belonging to one of the Indian Battalions and some military observers of the United Nations Peacekeeping Force in Sierra Leone. In a heliborne assault utilising Chinook helicopters of the Royal Air Force this team penetrated deep into rebel held territory, cleared pockets of rebels from the route of exfiltration and assisted and guided the detained UN personnel to a safe zone with minimal casualties. What is even lesser well known is the fact that one officer of this team undertook preliminary reconnaissance of the target area disguised as the driver of the local rebel commander.

Both these actions reflect highly on the skills, dedication and motivation levels of the troops involved. This action can be compared to any such operation attempted elsewhere and maybe one of the most successful operations undertaken by troops under the aegis of the UN. Probably, the only reason it has not been given the credit it deserves is the bias of the western press, which would most certainly have played up the action if their forces had been involved. As regards the Indian media, without its own sources on the spot and completely lacking in expertise with regard to military affairs, it had no other choice but to ignore the action except for publishing a couple of official handouts. An example of this biased reporting is the *Associated Press* report of 18 July 2000 which states "*But 222 Indian peacekeepers and 11 military observers of various nationalities remained besieged in a U.N. base inside the eastern rebel stronghold of Kailahun in eastern Sierra Leone — and exhaustive diplomatic and political efforts to free them failed. The RUF's recent decision to impede the delivery of supplies to the besieged troops was the final straw. A U.N. rescue operation was launched early Saturday when a team of Ghanaian, Indian and Nigerian troops supported by British and Indian helicopter gunships helped 233 peacekeepers and observers break out of Kailahun amid RUF fire...."* The British daily *The Guardian* of 17 July 2000 is even more biased when it states *"more than 200 other UN observers and soldiers were rescued from a rebel siege in Sierra Leone by forces acting on directions from SAS teams and backed by Chinook helicopters..."* The local Sierra Leone press however takes a more balanced view, *The Awoko*, for example, on the other hand goes on to say *"during his tenure as UNAMSIL force commander in 2001 General Jetley led the famous Operation Khukri to rescue Indian peacekeepers held hostage by the RUF rebels in Kailahun Districts. The Special Forces from India were able to rescue their colleagues after an eight-hour battle in which only one Indian soldier was killed alongside a huge number of RUF fighters. Operation Khukri's success saw a large cache of arms and ammunition being captured in Pendembu and eventually brought down to Freetown for public display at the UNAMSIL headquarters at Mammy Yoko. Another important aspect of Operation Khukri was that it paved the way to bring back the RUF to peace talks as it showed them clearly that the UN force was able to defeat them militarily if required to do so."*[15]

As has been stated earlier in the past decade the commando units have, like the rest of the Army, been involved in and continue to be deployed in low intensity conflict, primarily in Kashmir with some elements also being employed in the North East.

However, unlike their utilisation in conventional operations, their employment in low intensity situations has been more focused and effective with satisfactory results. This can be seen from the fact that most of the battalions of the Parachute Regiment have been awarded the Chief of Army Staff Unit Citation for their performance in such operations with four of the units having been awarded the citation twice. There are no such comparable examples available within the rest of the Army.

## Employment in Low Intensity Conflict

In the low intensity conflict scenario the employment of commando units has by and large been as "super infantry". They have been generally utilised as a rapid reaction force held at the divisional level to respond to specific intelligence by carrying out raids on hideouts. Apart from this they have been utilised for area domination, primarily in difficult terrain, involving laying of multiple ambushes which may last over three to four days, VIP protection and training of selected regular infantry personnel in special operations. In the covert role they have also been employed for carrying out surveillance, snatch actions and psuedo militant operations. Their success in the latter role has been commendable though the increased concentration of forces, especially in the Kashmir Valley, precludes such operations due to the difficulty of coordination among different units, formations and agencies. This is an aspect where difficulties exist at the working level since units when planning operations outside their area of responsibility tend to inform the concerned units only at the last moment, if at all, for fear of compromise of their sources as also because of the inherent inter unit rivalry caused by the primacy placed on 'body counts' to evaluate unit performance. The performance of the commando units and of other parachute battalions, where utilised in a similar manner, has been all the more commendable since by and large they have had to work under extremely difficult conditions with little assistance from units on the ground and the pressure of expectations of the higher commanders for them to perform miracles.

These units are generally deployed in small detachments that are superimposed on the existing counter insurgency grid. Though commanders at brigade and higher level are happy to have such troops available to them as they provide them with additional options while launching operations without the attendant responsibility if those units do not perform up to expectations. However, the unit and sub unit commanders on the ground tend to take umbrage and view such troop deployment with suspicion. This can lead to problems for these detachments as they are kept out of the information loop and employed by formations and units only for operations where the information is of a doubtful nature. Thus success would then not have to be shared with these detachments.

Commando units have however overcome this problem to some extent by carrying out joint operations with units on the ground and sharing the successes achieved equitably as also by building up their own intelligence network. In this 9 PARA has been particularly successful in view of its terrain specific deployment while the same can also be said to a lesser extent for 2 PARA, which due to its extended tenure had the time available to build up a suitable intelligence network and produce outstanding results. Against this, the prevailing system of deploying subunits or units for a one-year tenure has not produced the desired results since this is too short a time for them to set up an effective intelligence network and produce commensurate results thereafter. It, therefore, maybe worth considering extending deployment to a three year tenure for these units, as complete units, to give them a chance to settle down and produce the expected results.

Despite their outstanding performances in low intensity operations it can be seen that full use of their capabilities has yet to be made since they have till now only been employed in a defensive role. It is difficult to comprehend the reasons for these units not having been employed for trans-border clandestine operations either against terrorist training camps or for retaliation against hostile acts of some of our neighbours whether this be carried out as a part of their national policy, as in the case of Pakistan, or as an unwitting participant as may be the case with Bangla Desh, Bhutan and Myanmar. Employment of these battalions in this manner would also require our higher commanders getting out of the body count mindset and be willing to evaluate performance of these units based on other less specific factors, aspects such as the psychological effect of their actions on the sponsors, the terrorist leadership and its foot soldiers.

Before discussing how these units may be used in covert operations there is a need to correct the misperception that these units in their present avatar are unsuitable for use as "Special Forces" and are only organised to conduct commando type missions. There is a requirement to understand the difference between clandestine operations and covert operations, both of which have not been defined in our context. While US law defines covert action as activity meant *"to influence political, economic, or military conditions abroad, where it is intended that the role of the United States Government will not be acknowledged publicly*" it differentiates from clandestine missions as the term "clandestine" is used only to refer to the secrecy of the operation itself. Thus in their understanding of the issue an operation conducted secretly but subsequently acknowledged by US officials after the fact, would not be considered a covert operation.[16] This implies that deniability with regard to covert operations is of utmost importance because of the adverse political and diplomatic repercussions that is likely if the operations were to be linked to the sponsors of the action. This requires that such operations are extremely restricted in scale and use minimum personnel and support to ensure absolute secrecy and deniability, ideally operations that should be conducted by intelligence agencies. Clandestine operations on the other hand, while conducted with utmost secrecy, would not have similar repercussions if deniability were to be compromised and thus can be planned at relatively larger levels and can also be undertaken by SOF units. Thus, assassinations and snatch operations against high value targets in third countries can be treated as covert operations; trans-border raids against terrorist camps or support to indigenous movements could be referred to as clandestine operations. There is a need for us to also adopt a similar definition with regard to covert and clandestine operations, as that will enable us to correctly understand employment of SOF in actions. It, therefore, stands to logic that the existing organisational, personnel, training and equipment policies with regard to our PARA (SF) battalions more than meets the requirement of being able to conduct clandestine operations. They, however, are unsuitable for conducting covert operations, which requires a very different type of specialised unit similar to the ISA of the USSOF.

It is in the public domain that the Naga, Bodo and Assam terrorist groups have camps located in the dense jungles of Myanmar, Bhutan and Bangla Desh. It is of interest that despite the unequal military balance between these nations and us, similar perhaps to the Israeli–Palestinian/Lebanese situation, we have never launched trans-border operations against these camps despite accurate information as regards their location. If such information is not available, given the large amounts of money spent to build up such a capability, then there is an urgent need for the Government to reassess the performance of the intelligence agencies and their personnel tasked for this and initiate suitably drastic corrective actions. However, be that as it may, the employment of SOF units to neutralise these camps by conducting covert small team operations would have paid dividends. Ideally, raids to destroy these camps and create a sense of insecurity and fear among the terrorists that they are not safe anywhere would be the most appropriate action. However, if such operations are to be launched covertly without the knowledge or permission of the concerned countries, size of the force would have to be restricted. Moreover, keeping in view the thick jungles in the region, insertion of small teams, by free fall parachutes, at last light, would enable them to approach the camps under the cover of darkness; booby trap routes used and launch a "spoiling attack" on the camp using firepower.

Such actions would, even if they cause limited casualties, force militants to abandon their camps, increase psychological pressure on their personnel and leadership and all in all make it easier for us to combat these terrorist groups within the country. It would also convey the determination and will of the nation's political and military establishment to pursue and neutralise terrorists, who carry out actions against the country, despite the assistance they may receive from neighbouring countries. Such a course has risks, but then as the maxim goes "no pain, no gain". All this appears to be obvious and the normal methodology for employing such forces. There are numerous examples of this, the prime example being that of the Israelis. So what has prevented us from carrying out similar actions? In the case of Kashmir it is understandable for the Government and the Defence establishment to be circumspect in view of Pakistan's near parity in military strength in Kashmir, its nuclear weapons capability and the worry that the situation may get out of control and lead to unwanted consequences. However, such a reaction is not within the capabilities of our other neighbours and one can only speculate on the reasons for our political and military hierarchy not having acted firmly in this region. This inability to take pro-active action where it is feasible needs to be deliberated at the appropriate level and corrective action initiated at the earliest.

Finally, a word with regard to the organisation and equipment profile of these units. These units are reportedly being reorganised with their combat capability being enhanced substantially. Authorisation and procurement of new equipment is also proceeding apace though there is a case for reviewing the scale of some of the more advanced and costly weapons and equipment that are planned to be authorised to units. More importantly, however, simultaneous emphasis also needs to be given to providing these troops with basic equipment and packed rations of a high quality such as better boots, sleeping bags, ponchos, clothing, web equipment and rucksacks.

*"Kill one, terrify a thousand."*

- Sun Tzu

## RASHTRIYA RIFLES (COMMANDO)

The third SOF element within the Army is the 31 RR (Commando) Battalion that is a part of the Rashtriya Rifles, a specialised counter insurgency force, deployed in Jammu and Kashmir. By May 1990 it was clear that Kashmir valley was in the grip of a serious insurgency problem of an intensity not seen before. Based on its experience with low intensity conflicts in Nagaland, Sri Lanka and Punjab, the Army had formulated a doctrine of establishing the "grid system" to combat the insurgents. In this system the whole terrain is divided into a grid with a number of nodes, based on population centres, which enabled forces to carry out physical domination of their areas. This required forces in addition to those deployed on the LOC, manpower intensive but without the need for heavy weapons and equipment. This led to the creation of the Rashtriya Rifles (RR) in 1994. While conventional RR units were deployed on the CI grid, 31RR(Commando) was superimposed on the grid to provide commanders with additional rapid reaction forces.

This unit is organised on the lines of the Parachute Commando battalions and is manned by personnel from the Parachute Regiment and personnel from other Infantry Regiments hailing from the region. This unit is not airborne qualified except for those from the Parachute Regiment. Its primary employment is in a low intensity war scenario where it is tasked in a similar manner as other commando units. It however does not envisage being employed for offensive trans-border actions. Being permanently located in its area of operations, it has over a period of time, been able to establish an adequate intelligence set up which has enabled it to build up a fair reputation and has a number of successful actions to its credit.

The concept of raising such a unit with a fairly large percentage of troops belonging to the region, led by experienced Special Forces personnel, is praiseworthy. It has a number of advantages in the way it can operate in terms of local knowledge with regard to terrain, language, culture and people. It also provides the military commander with an option for carrying offensive unconventional counter terrorism operations in a defensive framework.

This battalion has in the few years of its existence carried out a number of very successful operations that have gone on to give momentum to defensive CT operations in their sector of employment. The drawback that this unit suffers from is that personnel posted from other Regiments are not volunteers but nominated by their units based on laid down criteria. This leads to some of the personnel lacking the motivation and dedication that such an SOF unit demands and requires. This aspect needs immediate corrective action. There is also a need to authorise personnel posted in this unit with some form of additional allowances that is the norm for SOF.

*"Not by strength, but by guile"*

- British Special Boat Service

## MARINE COMMANDOS

Planning for a special unit capable of naval special warfare started in April 1986. At the time the National Security Guards were created a requirement was felt for a complementary unit capable of maritime Counter Terrorism on the lines of the Royal Marine Special Boat Squadron and the US Navy's SEAL units. As a result three officers underwent training with the US Navy SEALs. Following this, further training was conducted through exchanges with British SBS. Finally, the Indian Marine Special Force (IMSF) was established in February 1987. The name was changed to Marine Commandos (MARCOS) in 1991. The MARCOS is numbered at almost 2000 personnel, with plans for forming 10 groups of 200 personnel each. At present there are three main groups at Mumbai, Kochi and Vizag.

Training for the MARCOS lasts almost two years in which after a one month selection phase personnel are put through a basic Combat Divers course, the Army's Ghatak Course and static line parachute jumps. On completion of this phase personnel join operational groups on a probation for 'on the job' training which lasts for a year in which specialised training is imparted on CT operations including storming oil rigs and hostage rescue in all environments.

Counter Terrorist operations are handled by the platoon sized Quick Reaction Sections, or (QRS), in each MARCOS group. In addition the units are tasked for carrying out beach reconnaissance, underwater demolitions and other operations in support of amphibious landings. Presently selected groups are also deployed in Jammu and Kashmir, primarily for "live training". Here they have been deployed along the Jhelum River and in the Dal, Nageen and Wullar lakes for area domination. They have also carried out joint operations with the Army Special Forces. Overall these units have been very professional in their approach and have successfully dominated the lakes.

In earlier operations they saw action in Sri Lanka as a part of the Indian Peace Keeping Force (IPKF) during Operation Pawan in 1987. The unit was attached to the 340th Independent Brigade whose task was amphibious missions. The MARCOS provided beach reconnaissance for the amphibious landings. It also provided security patrols along the costal road west of Jaffna. On 21 October 1988, the MARCOS conducted a successful raid against a coastal LTTE base. It also assisted in the capture of Jaffna and Trincomalee harbours from the LTTE. They also took part in the November 1988 Operation Cactus Lily in which elements of 50 Parachute Brigade thwarted a coup attempt in the islands of Maldives. When the islands were liberated, a ship containing 46 mercenaries and 27 hostages (including the Maldivian Education Minister) escaped. Indian maritime reconnaissance aircraft spotted the ship the next day and MARCOS personnel slithered on to the ship from helicopters and took control without any resistance.

In the overall concept there is a need for an institutional framework to ensure active cooperation and coordination with the Army's SOF elements that is presently carried out in an adhoc manner at the Service Headquarter level. The need for a joint doctrine is underscored by the lack of standardisation of weapons and equipment among the SOF units of the army and navy making planning and conduct of joint operations needlessly complicated.

*"Sometimes it is entirely appropriate to kill a fly with a sledge hammer."*

- Major Holdridge, 1994

## NATIONAL SECURITY GUARD

The National Security Guard (NSG) is the elite antiterrorist establishment in the country. Formed in 1986 under the National Security Guard Act (Act 47 of 1986), the NSG (or Black Cats, as they are popularly known) is one of the finest CT units in Asia. It has gained a wealth of experience over the years wherein its performance has been quite commendable. It comes under the Ministry of Home Affairs and is tasked with handling counter terrorism, anti-kidnapping, anti-sabotage, anti-hijacking and hostage rescue. Maritime Counter Terrorism is not the responsibility of this Force and is handled by the Navy's MARCOS. Interestingly, one of the most important tasks presently handled by the NSG is protection of VIPs, a task it is not chartered to do by law. Moreover, successive governments have not amended the NSG Act to include VIP security, as they are probably unwilling to face the adverse publicity this would generate. Unfortunately, this tasking has detracted from the NSG's ability to carry out its primary mission to its optimum capability, as we shall see.

The NSG has approximately 7500 personnel in three main groups with more than half being on deputation from the Army. The first element is the elite assault groups and their supporting groups, which are wholly manned by personnel on deputation from the Army. They consist of the two Special Action Groups (SAG), the two Bomb Disposal Units, the Dog Unit, the Communication Group and the Transport Unit. The second element, the three Special Ranger Groups (SRG), manned by personnel from the Para-Military Forces and the Central Police Organisations has the responsibility for securing and isolating the target areas where action by the SAG is envisaged. However as stated earlier this tasking has been diluted and they are now primarily tasked with providing VIP protection to senior politicians, except for the Prime Minister and some former Prime Ministers or their families for whom security is provided by the Special Protection Group (SPG), under the SPG Act. In support of both these elements is the third element, which is manned by a mix of army and police personnel. This includes the NSG Training Centre, where all personnel undergo advanced training; the Force Headquarters, which is the controlling headquarters for the operational units and reports through an elaborate command and control set up to the Director General NSG, a three star police officer. Army personnel handle all operational and training aspects, while police personnel control logistics and budgeting.

There are a number of issues, which have increasingly resulted in a gradual erosion of the organisation's capabilities. To understand these aspects, one has to first look at and understand the divergent work environment, culture and ethos of the parent organisations that provide the personnel. The army has a strong apolitical working environment with a highly centralised command and control structure with extensive interaction among officers and men, with the officer's leading from the front. Personnel are used to clear cut and unambiguous directions, equitable division of responsibility and a relatively honest work culture with great emphasis on discipline and training.

As regards the Central Police Organisations, the Police Act of 1861 established the police system in India. The act, based on the draft prepared by the first Police Commission of 1860, had a limited aim – to perpetuate British rule in this country. The failure of the act to produce an efficient and a professional police force in the country was even recognised by the British. The second police commission set up under the chairmanship of Sir A.H.L. Fraser in 1902 concluded: "*The police force is far from efficient, it is defective in training and organisation, it is inadequately supervised, it is generally regarded as corrupt and oppressive, and it has utterly failed to secure the confidence and cordial cooperation of the people.*"[17] Unfortunately, "*the advent of Independence changed the political system, but the police system remained unaltered. The Police Act of 1861 continued to govern it, laws and courts continued to distrust it, its organisational structure stayed unmodified, the politicians and bureaucrats continued to exercise control and superintendence over it, the managerial philosophy, value system and ethos remained what it was, and its public unaccountability remained unchanged. It was a ruler appointed police and it continued to remain so. Only the rulers changed, the foreign ones being replaced by the Indians.*"[18]

As the Sri Krishna Commission Report to the Maharashtra Government states: "*The common man on the street has the image of an average policeman as a bloated, bumbling, comic figure holding a lathi in one hand with the other palm extended. Perhaps, the Hollywood by its "Keystone cops" and the Bollywood by its 'Pandu Hawaldar' helped perpetuate this image. But, truth is stranger than fiction! This image needs to be substituted with the image of a professional policeman who is sensitive to the problems of the law abiding public, but hardened enough to deal with crooks and criminals. The goal must be to project the image of the Bobby in London, Mounty in Canada or New York Police Department (NYPD) Officer in U.S.A., albeit translated into Indian idiom. The evidence on record clearly brings out that the authority of the keeper of law was flouted with impunity again and again. Curfew orders and ban orders were flouted with the knowledge that no serious consequences would entail. Preaching of communal hatred and incitement to violence continued unabated with the realisation that the law and order machinery was either unwilling or incapable of checking it. Exaggerated notions of the consequences of interdicting people, who were openly preaching violence, paralysed the administration. The will to prosecute failed against the contemplated consequences of what would happen if action was taken against leaders of certain party. There cannot be 'holy cows' in policing."*[19]

This is further substantiated by Mr. Dharma Vira, the Chairman of the National Police Commission, who states: "The basic recommendations of the Police Commission which were activated towards giving a different direction to the police and creating a force that was in tune with democracy and that was totally the servant of the law and not of any individual howsoever high he may be in stature in the country, was lost (sic). The rulers had got used to using the police force for their own purpose, according to their will. In fact, when I presented this report to the then Home Minister Sardar Zail Singh, he said, *"Dharamji, what sort of report have you produced? I can't even ask the sub-inspector what to do"*.[20]

Thus, one can conclude that with the background to the development as also the kind of baggage that they bear, the Police and the Army are two very different animals. Furthermore, with the SRGs now primarily being utilised for VIP protection, there has been a steady increase in factionalism within the organisation as personnel have developed individual loyalties and contacts with the VIPs they are protecting. This has also led to an incongruous situation in that the NSG leadership and the political and bureaucratic establishment place more emphasis and consideration on the SRG than on its elite assault units causing much resentment and heartburn.

The second aspect that needs consideration is the vastly different service profile of the personnel. All army personnel are specially selected, after meeting laid down criteria and are mainly from the combat arms with extensive combat experience. Due to differing service conditions the army officers tend to have more service as compared to their colleagues from the CPOs and other Para-Military organisations. Also due to the lopsided promotion profile of different services there are numerous instances of officers from the CPOs, despite being very much junior in service to their army colleagues, holding higher ranks. All this when considered with the fact that police personnel at all levels have very limited experience of terrorism or counter terrorism can lead to lack of cohesion within the organisation with the likelihood of disastrous results. So why has this not been visible or effected the organisation as yet?

The only reason for this may be the fact that the operational units, the SAGs are purely from the Army. There are problems, however, within the Headquarters and the training and logistic establishments, those establishments that have mixed Army-CPO manpower and there have been representations made against this aspect time and again. There is also a dichotomy in the fact that Army personnel have been placed under command of Police officers, an issue which needs legal examination since Army personnel can only be given a legal command by either a superior under the Army Act, or by a legally constituted superior under the constitution. Moreover, there is a prevalent and widespread belief within the Army that while the Army does the work, it is the police leadership that claims the credit.

A leadership lacking the professional expertise or experience to direct counter terror operations along with its lack of understanding of military ethos or experience in dealing with the military is a disaster waiting to happen. This has been further aggravated by the close interaction between police and army personnel which has led to some service personnel picking up some commonly prevalent malpractices that has regrettably afflicted our police forces, so much so that there is a distinct reluctance on the part of some units to contribute personnel, especially to the Force Headquarters and the Training Centre.

The connected problem that is faced is that due to qualitative requirements that are laid down, only limited personnel are available within units who are eligible for posting. As a result, it is common to find individuals who have done two to three tenures with the NSG. Also, since these units are located near Delhi and are seldom committed operationally, when compared to other infantry and Special Forces battalions of the Army, it is seen as a "cushy" posting by most personnel and these units have an overwhelming number of personnel from the vicinity, with its attendant problems.

In operational terms the SAG have proved themselves creditably on a number of occasions such as the intervention in Op Black Thunder, its actions at Bangalore to neutralise Prime Minister Rajiv Gandhi's killers, number of actions against militants in Punjab and Uttar Pradesh and its intervention in the clearance of the Akshardham Temple in the recent past. In Operation Black Thunder, for example, the hard-line terrorists who had again occupied the Golden Temple for the second time were neutralised and evicted not by a swift assault on the temple, as had been carried out in Operation Blue Star in 1984, but in a phased manner by "*neutralising the militant guns mounted on top of the 'Bungas' (guest houses on the periphery of the complex) from where they were dominating much of the complex... The strategy was to pin down the militants in their hiding places inside the complex by accurate long distance sniper fire and then step by step advance towards the Temple by first occupying the 'Sarai' and then other strategic places."*[21] Despite intense pressure from the local administration and police who were keen on an early resolution of the siege, being fearful of the impact on the local populace, the NSG was successfully able to bring the siege to a close with minimal casualties on both sides and the unconditional surrender by all militants being seen as a devastating blow to the militant cause.

While the NSG did receive some unwarranted criticism because of the casualties suffered by the organisation in its operations at the Akshardham Temple, it was the delay in its deployment during the hijack of the Indian Airlines flight to Afghanistan that caused much embarrassment. Though the facts on the issue have been kept under wraps, they appear to be as follows: -

- Indian Airlines Flight IC 814 entered Indian airspace at 1710 hours after departure from Kathmandu. It was at this stage that the hijackers acted and ordered the pilot to steer a course for Lahore.

- The Crisis Management Group directed the NSG to move to Amritsar at 1828 hours.

- The flight denied permission to land at Lahore lands at Amritsar at 1900 hours, low on fuel.

- The NSG reaction unit reports readiness to depart from Delhi at 1910 hours, within forty-two minutes of being ordered to do so. However unable to do so as hostage negotiators failed to link up.

Finally leave for Amritsar at 1955 hours, approximately three hours after the hijacking.

- Airport authorities at Amritsar fail to cordon off aircraft (cordon airport instead) and when ordered to delay (not prevent) flight from taking off, botch operation causing the hijackers to panic and force the aircraft to take off, without refueling for Lahore at 1944 hours.

The reasons for the Crisis Management Group to only inform the NSG to react ninety minutes after the incident defies logic as the NSG could have been simultaneously alerted and moved to the aircraft or even been airborne while options for dealing with the situation were being debated. The delay on the part of the NSG to co-opt its hostage negotiator with the SAG elements within the stipulated time as also the reasons for not moving the SAG element without the negotiators are difficult to fathom as they could have been moved separately if required. However, of concern is not the issue of tactical employment, but of doctrine as in such situations every operation is different based on the accuracy and quantity of intelligence available; and success cannot be guaranteed. Immediately after the hijack episode, there were suggestions made that increasing the number of SAG units and deploying them at different airports throughout the country could improve response times. While there is merit in the argument with regard to deployment of elements of the NSG outside Delhi, the need to raise additional units does not stand scrutiny. Fortunately this suggestion appears to have been rejected due to the inability of the Army to provide additional manpower. In fact, the most glaring weakness in the NSG is its inability to respond to a WMD terror attack and the lack of an institutional interface with the Army. There are a number of other fundamental issues with regard to doctrine, command and control and organisation that need to be examined.

Hard questions need to be asked as to whether the CPOs and Para-Military Forces are in a position to replace army personnel within the organisation as was envisaged at the time of its raising. The truth is that this does not seem a viable option at present as is obvious from the fact that even the SRGs are undermanned by a fairly large percentage due to lack of volunteers of suitable quality. Moreover, it is unlikely that senior police officers would willingly take on the huge responsibility of producing and maintaining a strike force; failure on whose part would have catastrophic results not only for the Nation, but also more importantly, on the individuals careers. This also needs to be viewed in the light of the fact as to whether such an assignment is worthwhile when compared to the other more lucrative appointments that are available to personnel of these organisations.

If this is not a suitable option, and many countries the world over utilise their army personnel for such tasks, then we need to consider if the Army elements can be organised to function separately. As stated earlier this is the *de facto* situation on ground as elements of the SRG are committed in VIP protection duties and are thus not available to the SAG for isolation of the target area. On the other hand is there a case for removing the existing SRGs along with the SRG training element from the NSG and placing them under a separate organisation, probably including the SPG as well, for utilising them only for the VIP protection duties.

Since terrorists can strike any corner of the country and the first requirement from the CT angle is the isolation of the target area, it may make more sense to have SRG type units at the state level that can then react quickly to isolate the area till the assault elements arrive. Such a force would have the added advantage of local knowledge and close interaction with the local police, aspects lacking in the present dispensation. There would be a problem of coordination with the SAGs as also of ensuring that these units are suitably trained and given the necessary importance and attention by local State Governments but these are not insurmountable. Such an option will also enable the NSG to convert to a purely military organisation.

Finally, the aspect as to whether there is a requirement for more than one SAG needs to be examined. The fact that the USA has only the Delta Force and that is the case with most nations except Russia, as also the fact that the SAGs have never committed more than two squadrons at a time for the type of operations it is required to carry out needs to be given due consideration. It may be more appropriate to have one Group with four squadrons than the existing organisation. Such a reduction will result in savings in trained manpower, an important consideration. It may also be worth considering if this force should be a homogenous unit, like other Special Forces units in the country, instead of the existing tenure system. Interestingly, as has been stated earlier, even the USA, which follows the tenure system within the services, has adopted the "Regimental System" for its SF.

*"The revolutionary war is a war of the masses; it can be waged*

*only by mobilizing the masses and relying on them."*

*-Chairman Mao Tse Tung*

## SPECIAL FRONTIER FORCE

The Special Frontier Force (SFF), established in 1962 in the aftermath of the war with China, is less well publicised by the Government. It has a number of parachute units, nominally subordinate to the Army and deployed along sensitive areas of the border with China. It also has a training centre, known as Establishment 22, along with its own Parachute Training School. It is primarily recruited from among border-area hill tribes and Tibetan refugees.[22] It is officered by personnel on deputation from the Army and has the role of carrying out guerrilla warfare in Tibet. It is believed that the officers on deputation are responsible for training of these units and are not expected to accompany units on their operational tasks.

By the late 1960s, the SFF was organised into six battalions with each battalion, consisting of six companies, which was the primary unit used in operations. Women also participated in the force and they were in the signal and medical companies. During this time, the SFF was never used against its intended enemy, China. However, the unit did conduct limited cross-border reconnaissance operations, as well as highly classified raids to place sensors in the Himalayas to detect Chinese nuclear and missile tests.[23] However, in 1975, a new rule prohibited the SFF from being deployed within 10 km of the Sino-Indian border purportedly due to several incidents involving unsanctioned trans-border operations by its men.[24]

1971 saw the SFF being used in major combat in the Indo-Pak War for the first time. Elements of the force were deployed next to the Chittagong Hill Tracts for carrying out cross-border attacks prior to the war. On commencement of the war the SFF was tasked to lay blocks in the Chittagong Hill Tracts along potential escape routes for Pakistani forces into Burma and fought some extremely successful actions including against elements of 2nd Commando Battalion of the SSG.

In addition to the guerrilla battalions, the organisation also has one unit, The Special Group, wholly manned by personnel on deputation from the Army. This commando type unit on the lines of the Parachute Commando battalions is organised and equipped for carrying out CT operations. The necessity for another specialised SOF unit for such tasks is difficult to understand in view of such units already being available in sufficient numbers within the army unless it has been organised for "black operations", that is operations of a covert nature which cannot be attributed to the Indian security establishment This unique option available to the Government, has never reportedly been utilised in such a manner, despite grave provocations that the Government has faced from Pakistan from time to time. Interestingly a core group provided by this unit first raised the NSG.[25]

The unit has also reportedly conducted counter terror operations against militants in Jammu and Kashmir in a similar manner to the commando units, with mixed results. There were also some reports in the media that the unit had at one stage carried out long-term pseudo militant actions with encouraging results. The reasons for ceasing these operations subsequently are unclear but may have been due to the difficulty in coordinating such operations with other security forces operating in the area.

While units continue to exhibit extremely high standards of professionalism, the force has over the years suffered seriously from a lack of relevance. Raising of an indigenous force that could be covertly committed against the Chinese in Tibet, in a guerrilla campaign that would result in the liberation of Tibet required use of personnel who were familiar with the terrain and had friends and family who would support them in their task. Passage of time and the consequent improvement in Sino-Indian ties has not only meant that the concept of a liberated Tibet is increasingly unlikely but has also implied a drastic reduction in the number of Tibetan expatriates with local knowledge of terrain, culture and language or even the required motivation. Added to this is the difficulty such a force would encounter in building up support because of the demographic changes and the systematic liquidation of opponents that the Chinese have been able to effectively implement. The issue has been further compounded over the years by the inability or unwillingness on the part of Government, for whatever reason, to employ them, despite clear provocation by the Chinese in the form of support to the insurgencies in the North East, especially in Nagaland and Manipur. This inaction on our part has been perceived as lack of political and national will and has led to distrust of and contempt for Indians and India.

Thus, over a period of time, the force has lost its motivated and dedicated fighters from among the Khampas who had in the past without outside support driven China to the wall. They have now been replaced by Tibetans who have been born and brought up in this country with no knowledge or interest in their former homeland. People, who would be unwilling to give up their comforts here to settle in the harsh environs of Tibet. For these people, the chief motivation for joining such a force has become a matter of earning a living. Moreover, as the number of Tibetan exiles willing to join has reduced, they have been gradually replaced by Gurkhas from Nepal. The viability of such a force to actually carry out its charter seems questionable. The Army on its part has further added to its woes by providing manpower, especially officers, who see themselves as being out of the mainstream and thus tend to be disgruntled and unmotivated. This problem has become even more acute in the past decade as the army has itself been facing increased deficiencies and has been hard pressed to meet its own requirements.

There is an even more serious issue, which stems from the inherent dichotomy in the way the force has been organised and is planned to be utilised, and needs to be examined. Since the force is to operate covertly behind the enemy lines it has been so organised that its Indian command and control element is not directly involved in actions within Tibet and controls these from own side of the border. This element is also responsible for training of all personnel of the unit prior to their being committed for operations. Theoretically, such a concept may seem sound but it is unlikely that any individual or sub unit will repose trust in any leader who is not leading from the front and is not to share the same dangers. This is further aggravated by the fact that all personnel of the force, apart from those on deputation from the Indian Army, are paratroopers.

The Special Group, on the other hand, has problems that impinge on its operational requirement and capabilities. It needs to be remembered that the Special Group was first raised in late seventies of about a company strength primarily as an anti-hijack and building intervention force on the lines of other such CT units. When the Government decided to set up the NSG, as would be expected, this unit was amalgamated into it and formed the core around which the SAGs were raised. Subsequently, however, the SFF decided to re-establish the Special Group with a more diverse mission profile, probably those of conducting covert strike operations. The problem that has hounded the group from the time of its establishment has been the lack of a cogent policy with regard to its employment. As we have seen time and again, the Government has established a number of organisations for covert employment across our borders, but has till date not employed these forces in this manner, despite the gravest of provocations, like the attack on Parliament.

This inability or unwillingness to carry out offensive actions, for whatever reasons, has placed the Special Group in a limbo and forced it to duplicate other existing establishments and take on other tasks such as its current employment in counter insurgency operations in Kashmir. Unfortunately, the fact that it is manned by personnel from within the Army on deputation for a three-year tenure, as is the case with the NSG, has led to some serious anomalies in its existing organisational structure that has not enabled it to perform at the same level as other existing SOF within the Army. Moreover, if this unit is for covert operations in third countries, manning by NCOs and other ranks from within the army needs to be re examined as these personnel are unlikely to have the cultural awareness, sophistication and the necessary education background to be able to operate in third countries under a plausible cover. Such operations are only feasible in our context if carried out by selected officers imparted with the requisite training. Also in the interest of secrecy such a unit cannot be organised on the lines of a commando battalion but be based on very limited numbers, primarily based on an officer-oriented organisation with limited number of other ranks for providing requisite logistic and administrative support.

It would also be appropriate to provide manpower for this unit from the Parachute Regiment, on a three to four year tenure basis, since it has an extremely large base of experienced special operations personnel at peak mental and physical standards. When required additional manpower could be provided to them to meet specific needs for a particular operation involving language or technical skills, detailed country knowledge or a specific ethnic requirement. There is also the option of a permanently seconding personnel from this unit to the Research and Analysis Wing (RAW) on completion of the tenure. This wll have the added advantage of providing RAW with desk/ controlling officers with field experience of the right type.

Any nation with great power aspirations, not only requires organisation and maintenànce of forces based on the ethnic nationalities from its area of interest and influence but also forces capable of covert strikes in third countries, as the Israelis have time and again shown. This will enable it to pursue its policies using unconventional military options if so required. Thus, the need for the Special Frontier Force with a regional orientation is inescapable but the quantum and type of force required, as also its concept of employment, need to be re-examined in the light of the strategic environment that it will be required to operate in.

*"By way of deception, thou shalt do war."*

-Israel's Mossad

## AVIATION RESEARCH CENTRE

Though the Air Force does not have any assets, earmarked for Special Operations at this time, there is the Aviation Research Centre (ARC), which like the Special Frontier Force, is directly under the Cabinet Secretariat. Some Air Force personnel on deputation along with a cadre of retired service personnel man this organisation.[25]

Not much is known of this force in the open domain except for the fact that it has some fixed and rotary wing assets for provision of transportation to the National Security Guard, Special Frontier Force and other Intelligence Agencies as required. In addition, as per reports, it also has assets for acquisition of airborne signal intelligence and photo-reconnaissance. Capabilities in this regard are not known, but reports indicate that this state of the art equipment is in use.[27] The organisation did come in for some adverse criticism for its inability to provide warning of the Pakistani build up and occupation of positions on the Indian side of the LOC prior to the Kargil Conflict.[28]

There is no data available as to whether this establishment is tasked to provide air assets for covert insertion of personnel into third countries. It, however, stands to reason that since this organisation does provide assets for conduct of airborne training of personnel of the Special Frontier Force, it is, in all probability, tailored for such missions.

Secrecy ensures that its efficacy and operational preparedness are not common knowledge, but it would not be incorrect to presume that since it is manned by highly skilled and extremely experienced former IAF pilots, it would maintain the highest standards of operational capability.

## NOTES

1. Littlejohn, *Foreign Legions of the Third Reich*, Vol.4, pp 130-138.
2. Lundari, *I Paracadutisti Italiani 1937/45*, p. 90.
3. Caballero Jurado, *Foreign Volunteers of the Wehrmacht 1941-45*, p. 31
4. Davis, *Flags of the Third Reich 2: Waffen SS*, pp. 21-22.
5. Sawhney, Pravin; Wahab, Ghazala, *The Maroon Beret*, Force, Jan 2004, pp. 12-27.
6. Khan, Lt Gen Gul Hassan, *Memoirs of Lt Gen Gul Hassan Khan*, Oxford University Press, Karachi, Pakistan, 1993 pp 188-234.
7. Praval, KC, *India's Paratroopers*, Vanity Books, Delhi, 1974, pp 291-297.
8. Salik, Siddiq, *Witness to Surrender*, Oxford University Press, 1982.
9. Mehta, Maj Gen (Retd) Ashok, K, *War Dispatches: Operation Iraqi Freedom*, Har-Anand Publications, India, 2004, p. 168.
10. Karim, Maj Gen Afsir, *The Story of Indian Airborne Troops*, Lancer International, New Delhi, 1993, pp. 202-235.
11. Praval, KC, *op cit*, pp. 298-309.
12. From the Net, *Indian Army in Sri lanka*, Bharat Rakshak. Com.
13. *Ibid.*
14. Sabharwal, Maj Gen (Retd) OP, *The Killer Instinct*, Rupa and Co, 2000, pp 221-231.
15. *Awoko Newspaper* 2002.
16. Kibbe, Jennifer D, *The Rise of the Shadow Warriors*, Foreign Affairs March/April 2004, pp104-105.
17. *Report of the Indian Police Commission, 1902-03*, Government Central Printing Office, Simla, 1903, pg 150.
18. *National Police Commission: Its Relevance Today, Papers and Discussions at a Seminar Organised by the Nehru Centre and Hindustan Andolan*, a Nehru Centre Publication, Mumbai.
19. *Sri Krishna Commission Report to the Govt of Maharashtra*, Ch V para1.2
20. National Police Commission: its relevance today, *op. cit.*, pp. 8-9.

21. Marwah, Ved, *Uncivil Wars: Pathology of Terrorism in India*, Penguin India, 1997, p. 189.
22. Kohli, MS, Conboy, Kenneth, *Spies in the Himalayas: Secret Missions and Perilous Climbs*, Harper Collins Publishers, 2003, pp. 16-17.
23. *Ibid*, p. 193.
24. Conboy, Ken and Hannon, Paul, *Elite Forces of India and Pakistan*, Osprey Press, UK, 1992.
25. From the net, *Bharat Rakshak. Com.*
26. Kohli, MS, Conboy, Kenneth, *op cit*, p. 17.
27. Ball, Desmond, *Signals Intelligence (SIGINT) in South Asia*, CIA World Fact Book, Library of Congress (Area Handbook).
28. Raman, B, *Kargil: Was There an Intelligence Failure?* SAPRA India, 04 July 1999.

4

# RESHAPING SOF

*"However absorbed a commander may be*
*in the elaboration of his own thoughts,*
*It is sometimes necessary to take the*
*enemy into account."*
Attributed to Winston Churchill.

## FUTURE WARS

It was way back during his presidency in the 1960s that President John F Kennedy foresaw the changing nature of war and warned that *"the free World's security can be endangered not only by nuclear attack, but also by being slowly nibbled away at the periphery.... By forces of subversion, infiltration, intimidation, indirect or non-overt aggression, internal revolution, diplomatic blackmail, guerilla warfare, or a series of limited war."*[1] He saw a need for a *"whole new kind of strategy, a wholly different kind of force, and therefore a wholly different kind of training"*[2] and directed the military to increase the size of the US Special Forces to the level that they have reached today.

The Vietnam conflict clearly brought out that a smaller nation, faced with a huge asymmetry in forces, when fighting a much larger and more powerful enemy, in this case a superpower, could, and in this case did, bridge the enormous gap between them by resorting to a different kind of war, a "people's war". In effect, changing the goalposts to confuse, demoralise and defeat the enemy with guile and cunning. Capture of territory and destruction of the enemy's military forces have always been central to all strategic and tactical doctrine till recently. A very Clausewitzian belief that the very nature of war was *"an act of policy to use violence to impose one's will upon another"* [3] and aimed to *"render enemy powerless"*–with emphasis on *"the destruction of his armed forces."* It was however Mao Tse Tung, the first to write extensively about insurgency, who saw military strength as not the only means to render the enemy powerless but believed that: *"our job is not merely to recite our political program to the people ... (we must) transform the political mobilisation for the war into a regular movement. This is a matter of the first magnitude on which the victory primarily depends."* [4] An emphasis on the concept of defeating the enemy primarily through political action which was clearly outlined in his famous three phases for the successful conduct of insurgency: the strategic defence involving building of political base; the strategic stalemate involving consolidation and control of bases; and the strategic offensive involving engaging the government in a final offensive using regular forces.

Mao knew insurgents could not match the government's conventional military forces initially. Therefore, he conceived the careful buildup of political, social, and economic organisations, a united front of all parties and groups with people from all walks of life, a people's patriotic front with one aim. He believed it was not just sufficient to gather supporters within but also used propaganda to undermine the political will of that enemy's allies and sponsors into withdrawing support for the war, and finally, generate material and economic support for the movement from friendly and neutral countries. To go with this Mao also conceived a military strategy that reinforced his political efforts. Mao wrote that while the final campaign would be a conventional attack, earlier phases must include a mix of guerrilla and conventional military operations. The dual nature of insurgency would place the enemy on the horns of a dilemma. If the counterinsurgent concentrated his forces to deal with the conventional threat, the guerrillas would thrive. If he dispersed to deal with the guerrillas, his outposts were vulnerable to the insurgent's conventional operations and guerrilla operations in the same area. "*A sophisticated understanding of the powerful political, social, and economic elements that constitute the base of military power*"[5] as Lt Col Thomas X. Hammes puts it in his erudite exposition "The Evolution of War: The Fourth Generation."

In their seminal and path breaking work, "The Changing Face of War: Into the Fourth Generation", William S. Lind, Colonel Keith Nightengale (USA), Captain John F. Schmitt (USMC), Colonel Joseph W. Sutton (USA), and Lieutenant Colonel Gary I. Wilson (USMCR) in the Marine Corps Gazette of October 1989, the authors have theorised on the development of modern warfare in generational terms. They suggest " *while military development is generally a continuous evolutionary process, the modern era has witnessed three watersheds in which change has been dialectically qualitative...and comprises of three distinct generations.*" In their view the first generation warfare reflected " *tactics of the era of the smoothbore musket, the tactics of line and column ... the line maximised firepower, rigid drill was necessary to generate a high rate of fire.*"[6] Second generation warfare was seen as "*a response to the rifled musket, breechloaders, barbed wire, the machinegun, and indirect fire. Tactics were based on fire and movement....*"[7] Third generation warfare was seen as "*a response to the increase in battlefield firepower. However, the driving force was primarily ideas. Aware they could not prevail in a contest of material because of their weaker industrial base in World War I, the Germans developed radically new tactics. Based on maneuver rather than attrition, third generation tactics were the first truly nonlinear tactics. The attack relied on infiltration to bypass and collapse the enemy's combat forces rather than seeking to close with and destroy them. The defense was in depth and often invited penetration, which set the enemy up for a counterattack.*"[8] This was pushed to a new level with the development of tank warfare and the tactics of the blitzkrieg and use of air power for close air support including airborne assault, thus, enabling forces to concurrently tackle forward and depth areas.

In their view, the two major catalysts for generational changes were the influence of technology and ideas. They identified four central ideas or elements that carried over and developed from generation to generation and which they feel help explain how fourth generation warfare is likely to evolve. The first is that each generational change has been marked by greater dispersion on the battlefield. Thus, fourth generation battlefield, in their view, is likely to "*include the whole of the enemy's society*" and therefore require even the lowest level to operate flexibly on the basis of the commander's intent. The second element in their view will be "*decreasing dependence on centralised logistics. Dispersion, coupled with increased value placed on tempo, will require a high degree of ability to live off the land and the enemy.*" The third element is of emphasis shifting from mass of men or firepower to manoeuvre because "*mass may become a disadvantage as it will be easy to target. Small, highly maneuverable, agile forces will tend to dominate.*" The final element is the "*goal of collapsing the enemy internally rather than physically destroying him."* In broad terms, therefore, they saw fourth generation warfare as likely to be widely dispersed and undefined with the line between war and peace, civilian and military being blurred to vanishing point. It would be nonlinear having no definable battlefields or fronts and actions would occur concurrently throughout all participants' depth, including their society as a cultural, not just a physical, entity. Views remarkably similar to Mao Tse Tung's concept of "people's war", except for differences in emphasis on social and cultural issues.

Interestingly, fourth generation warfare, as they saw it, could develop along two broadly divergent avenues driven either by technology or by ideas. They foresaw that the Western world with its rapid advances in communications, robotics, artificial intelligence, nano technologies and directed energy weapons would be driven by technology that allowed nations to wage war using fewer, but better equipped, soldiers capable of bringing down immense fire power, especially air power, at the point of decision. We saw the beginnings of this in the Gulf War and its further development in Afghanistan and in the campaign against Iraq in 2003. There has also been much discussion and debate in this country, as well, on the benefits of this revolution in military affairs and there have been many proponents advocating rapid induction of high technology weapons to ensure qualitative superiority in the region. Development of our military along such lines would require a move towards radically different force structures with emphasis on information warfare and psychological operations assets, induction of technologically qualified personnel and a quantum jump in our indigenous research and development capabilities.

The other proposition, made by the authors, which does not seem to have been given much attention here, probably as it is a low technology-low investment option, goes on to state that since the West no longer dominates the world, fourth generation war may develop through ideas rather than technology, primarily from non-Western cultural traditions, such as Islamic or Asiatic traditions, areas that are not strong in technology. Terrorism, they predicted, especially when combined with high technology and when based on a non-national or transnational element, such as an ideology or religion, can *"constitute at least the beginnings of a fourth generation of warfare?"*[9] They see a similarity between terrorism and the central tenets that they propounded, in that; a good terrorist operates dispersed at the individual level, lives off the land requiring minimal logistic support, depends on manoevure to hit at that critical point that will cause maximum damage and attacks from within as it takes advantage of the fundamentals of that society, such as freedom of movement, secular traditions and open communication, to attack it. Thus, fourth generation warfare developed along these lines, using technology and weapons of mass destruction, make conventional militaries irrelevant.

As recent events in the past few years in the Gulf, Afghanistan and our neighbourhood, and, in the United States, have shown the authors were prescient in visualising how future wars would develop, whether driven by technology or ideas. Thus a technology driven campaign will require forces equipped with extremely sophisticated state of the art weapon systems and equipment with real time Command, Control, Communication, Computers, Intelligence, Surveillance and Reconnaissance systems (C4ISR), capable of early detection and identification of suitable targets and their precise engagement with minimum collateral damage. These forces would require to be highly mobile, primarily mechanised, with vertical envelopment capability. However, just as warfare today is a juxtaposition of elements from all the three generations of warfare such as our attempts to bring linearity to the battlefield and the reliance on fire power, fourth generation war will include elements of earlier generations of war and, therefore, implies that our forces must be prepared to deal with the fact that not all future conflicts will be fought primarily using fourth generation tactics. If we accept that future war is likely to develop along the lines asserted to by William Lind et al, and developments in the interim tends to support their thesis, it would then be appropriate for us to examine how fourth generation warfare is likely to develop and be fought in our context. Towards this end it is necessary to examine the geo-strategic framework within which our armed forces would be required to operate, in the next decade or so, prior to visualising the nitty gritty of how we would have to do battle.

In the context of future developments in the South Asian region, the shape of Sino-Indian relations will be the most significant issue at hand. "*With sustained and even increased economic growth, India will attempt to play a bigger role not only in the region but also in world affairs. This may lead to friction with China over such issues as border demarcation, attempts to gain influence in Nepal and Myanmar, recognition of Sikkim, support for the Tibetan leadership in exile, support for Pakistan's nuclear programme and support for rebels in the North East.*"[10]

However, in the next decade or so as far as basic security is concerned, India is relatively well-off as the harsh terrain inhibits large scale offensives and our conventional capability is much superior to the Chinese in terms of fire power, training, defences and logistics. This is unlikely to change in the next decade or so given the overwhelming emphasis that China places on economic development. The declaration of our nuclear intent in 1988 and the continued development of our missile programme appear to be aimed at neutralising the huge imbalance vis–a-vis China with regard to nuclear capabilities. A minimum deterrent, capable of threatening Peking would nullify the existing Chinese capacity of nuclear blackmail. However, in the long term, once China is able to fully develop its logistic capabilities in Tibet, it would be in a position to enhance troop levels it can sustain thereby nullify the existing conventional advantage that we have.

The terrain along the Sino-Indian border is mountainous, open at high altitudes and greatly hampers and restricts movement. The depth areas both in Tibet and Ladakh, which hold all logistics and administrative elements, the key to sustained operations in the region, are located in high altitude desert plains devoid of cover and vulnerable to interdiction, especially from the air. Moreover, communications and supply lines connecting the hinterland to these forward logistics bases and ahead on to the forward troops are very limited, extended in nature, tenuous and extremely vulnerable to interdiction.

The first and second generation scenarios within which we are presently organised for hostilities along this border has not only vastly restricted our options to engage the enemy in depth, but also, because of restricted availability of surveillance assets, forced us to deploy a large quantum of troops. Despite the rapid technological developments that have taken place in the last three decades since our border war with China, we continue to prepare for and win the last war. Our reaction to the Kargil conflict, for example, has not brought about any drastic enhancement of our rotary wing assets in the region but instead has placed emphasis on increasing our animal transport assets. We continue to believe, wrongly as the recent operations in Afghanistan show, that technology has very limited applicability in high altitude terrain and have, therefore, given this sector the lowest priority for modernisation.

Available technology demands a radical shift in our operational concepts of war fighting in high altitude terrain and requires us to reorient and reorganise our forces with emphasis on the following aspects:

- Enhance our real time surveillance capabilities both at the strategic and tactical level with satellites, electronic assets manned aircraft and UAVs.
- Extend range of our operations in depth. The Tibetan plateau should be within our area of influence.
- Enhance manoeuvrability with increased emphasis on rotary wing assets with suitable avionics that will permit them to fly at night and in bad weather.
- Enhance firepower with new generation weapons, long-range artillery and increasing reliance on smart ammunition. Procurement or development of C130 "Spectre" class of gunships need to be examined. Increased emphasis needs to be placed on enhancing Air Force capabilities for interdiction and support operations, including airborne and heli-borne operations, in mountains and high altitude terrain.
- Enhance night fighting capabilities with new generation of night vision equipment being made available to each rifleman.

- Enhance survivability by equipping personnel with suitable lightweight cold climate clothing, high calorie rations, lightweight shelters and medical equipment. Personnel will need to be provided latest medicines that can prevent or reduce effects of high altitude sickness.

- Increasing reliance on specialised mountain warfare, such as cliff assault techniques, which will require units to be equipped with advanced mountaineering gear and suitably trained for such operations.

This ability to fight and win using fourth generation warfare in high altitude terrain emphasises the pre-eminence of technology, specialisation and training over mere numbers and demands a paradigm shift in our outlook. The need for specialised mountain infantry, armour and artillery trained and equipped to operate in high altitude terrain is unavoidable. In addition, SOF will provide additional options for enhancing our unconventional warfare, surveillance, interdiction and direct action capabilities that will become battle-winning factors.

The Kargil conflict was a watershed in defining how future conflict with Pakistan is likely to develop. Pakistan has been able to neutralise our clear superiority in conventional terms with its development of a viable nuclear deterrent. This emboldened it to launch operations in Kargil through which it sought to boost the ongoing insurgency in Kashmir which had vastly reduced in scale, change the status quo in Kashmir and force a withdrawal of the Army from the Siachen Glacier. It would in addition have restored some of the lost pride of the Pakistan Army after its disastrous showing in the 1971 War. However, it once again showed the inability of the Pakistani leadership to assess Indian reaction and resulted in yet another defeat with important lessons for both sides and the major lesson that the Pakistani leadership is likely to have learnt was that "*Kargil-like operations have high political costs, especially for Pakistan's international reputation. That said, the Kargil fiasco does not appear to have extinguished Pakistan's belief that violence, especially as represented by Low Intensity Conflict (LIC), remains the best policy for pressuring India on Kashmir and other outstanding disputes.*" This however does not rule out a repetition of such a misadventure since there "*continue to be many stakeholders in Pakistan who view Kargil as some sort of a victory lost. If such beliefs of Kargil—despite being fundamentally false in their details—represent the considered assessments of Pakistan's security managers, future policies could emerge that call for Kargil-like operations.*" The most important lesson learnt by us "*was that it (India) must be prepared to counter a wide range of Pakistani threats that may be mounted by what is essentially a reckless but tenacious adversary. India must therefore develop the robust capabilities it needs to thwart surprise and to win even if surprised by Pakistan. Another lesson is that if India is obliged to respond forcefully in future episodes, covert rather than overt action may be preferable.*"[11]

Thus, even to this day we are not quite clear as to whether Kargil should be viewed as the likely contours of future limited war, or as an attempt to expand the envelope of low intensity conflict. Whatever be our view, in essence, however, limited wars though not fully ruled out in the future, are unlikely given both side's inability to obtain a clear-cut and decisive victory, as also, the uncertainty with regard to the ability of Pakistan to restrict the scope of the conflict to only the conventional when facing adverse results. Such a situation could lead to escalation resulting in a nuclear exchange. In these circumstances it is more than likely that future Pakistani attempts will be restricted to not only supporting terrorism in

Kashmir but enlarging its scope to envelop other regions of the country as well. In this, policies of extremist right wing organisations will only assist Pakistan in exploiting anti Hindu sentiments from within parts of the Muslim minority population in various regions of the country. Supports of such elements in organising the recent Mumbai blasts, as also the attack on the Akshardham temple in Gujarat, are clear pointers in this direction. This "ugly stability" with which we are confronted is unlikely to change as Pakistan is seen to play a 'key role' in assisting the USA in its war on terror in Afghanistan and, therefore, its existing regime will not be subjected to undue pressure to change its policies.

Furthermore, Pakistan's lack of central control over some of its regions as also the widespread assimilation of militant Islamic ideology within the population and in the Armed Forces may lead to situations where the Federal Government has no control over the activities of the Pan Islamic terrorist organisations like the 'Al Quaida' or the 'Jaish-E-Mohamed' etc. An added and more dangerous dimension to this threat could be the use of WMD, either chemical or biological agents, against either population centres or, against military or right wing targets. The recent scandal involving selling of nuclear technology for cash by the Pakistani nuclear establishment is a pointer in this direction. Consequences of such an attack, especially since responsibility for such an attack will be diffused, are unlikely to lead to any strong response on our part, as has been the case time and again, though in somewhat different circumstances. Thus, in dealing with Pakistan, prudence dictates that we be prepared to fight and win a limited war as also be organised to combat low intensity conflict, much expanded in scope, that will primarily be fought in our hinterland. Even if in the next decade or so there are dramatic improvements in relations with Pakistan and China, not beyond the realms of possibility, there will continue to be fundamentalist Islamic forces inimical to India within the region. While the threat levels may reduce, there will continue to be a requirement of maintaining credible forces for dealing with such threats.

There is, however, a widespread belief, both within the Army as also in the administration and the intelligentsia, that the Army is not the organisation that should be carrying out such 'police' operations as this prevents it from preparing for its primary mission; that of defence of our borders. In fact, the stated Government policy required the Central Police Organisations (CPO), primarily the Central Reserve Police, to have taken over conduct of all such operations in the Kashmir Valley by December 2002, a policy that it has not been able to implement till date. Such a premise in the context of fourth generation warfare, more so for sub-conventional conflict that we will continue to fight against Pakistan, does not stand to reason as we see that the very nature of how future wars will be conducted has completely changed and defence forces, organised, equipped, trained and tasked as they are today, are fairly close to redundancy. However the premise that the police can by itself combat Low Intensity Conflict in the manner that it is developing seems at odds with reality since the police neither have the training nor the organisational structures or weaponry to be effective. Thus, the stated Government policy in this regard needs re-examination.

It is but stating the obvious that force configuration for both forms of warfare differ to some extent since conventional high/mid intensity combat requires an all arms bias while low intensity requires an infantry bias. This implies a need for two different types of forces with necessary interoperability built in to cater for unforeseen situations, though manpower constraints may in effect not permit such duplication. In no way is it suggested that a policy of this nature requires enhancement in force levels. In fact, if organised as has been suggested with regard to meeting the Chinese threat, forces for conventional operations can be drastically reduced with enhanced technological capabilities that will greatly increase the combat potential of units.

As regards units for LIC, there will be a need to enhance the number of units as also the adoption of a regional profile to ensure that units are permanently located in one particular area that permits them to be fully integrated within the community. These aspects, however,. need detailed examination and are beyond the scope of this book except, as they pertain to the organisation and deployment of SOF. It also implies recognition of the fact that there is a need for further specialisation, especially within the infantry. These are not new suggestions, as in effect; we are already implementing them to some extent with the raising of our Rashtriya Rifles units. Furthermore, conduct of combat operations in the Line of Control (LOC) Sector in Kashmir, which in all probability will be the contested ground, poses peculiar problems because of mountainous and jungle terrain in the region. There is, therefore, a need to reassess and reconfigure our force requirements for both mid and low intensity conflict scenarios in the context of fourth generation warfare. Ideally, SOF required to support operations in both these scenarios would also need to be differently organised and equipped with some amount of interoperability as has been suggested for other conventional forces.

The Mid/ High Intensity Conflict scenario will involve utilisation of air assets on a massive scale, simultaneous engagement and destruction of the enemy in his depth, intermediate and forward areas, real time acquisition of intelligence and accurate targeting by small mobile hard hitting teams that are capable of directing fire from artillery and aircraft with pin-point accuracy. With regard to the Low Intensity Conflict scenario, the following aspects need consideration:-

- Increasing dependence on suicide attacks.
- No value for human life or property.
- Aim at attacking soft targets to cause widespread panic and destroy national economy and, thus, harm growth of world economy itself due to the increasingly interdependent nature of the global economy.
- Increasingly sophisticated multiple attacks by groups using available communications and infra-structure network to coordinate attacks, which would increasingly be organised in cities and metros.
- Increasing cooperation between radical terrorist networks and criminal gangs regardless of ideological differences, supported by regimes of dysfunctional states.
- Employment of sympathetic personnel who have been able to infiltrate into key positions of target organisations or states.
- Attempts to procure weapons of mass destruction for use in such operations.
- Need for logistics and administrative support in target country for terrorists is less than that required for conducting a guerrilla war; but without support such operations are not feasible.

In the context of Low Intensity Conflict, irregular forces and procedures play paramount rather than supporting role in this spectrum in contrast to the high intensity spectrum. Psychological operations and civil affairs along with intelligence assume much greater importance since both sides aim to win over or coerce the fence sitters in the population. SF employment, both in offensive and in the defensive CT role can pay dividends. CT operations from the tasking point of view may thus be classified into the following:-

- **Strike Operations.** These include all actions taken to neutralise terrorist organisations, support groups and terrorists in hostile or third countries.
- **Reactive Operations.**
  - **Security Operations.** Those actions taken within the country to neutralise terrorist organisations, their supporters and sympathisers and includes actions such as rival and pseudo group operations, covert surveillance, counter surveillance and direct action such as raids, ambushes, and snatch operations.
  - **Incident Response Operations.** These include all actions taken within or outside the country to neutralise any terrorist incident that have occurred and include operations such as hostage rescue, anti hijack or neutralising attacks involving conventional explosives or WMD.
- **Support Operations.** These include actions taken to assist government and non-government agencies in preparation and conduct of CT operations outside the country such as protection and security advice to embassy staff.

Finally, on a different level wars are no longer going to be fought for capture of territory but for economic considerations. The focus will be on creation of wealth and jobs with the enemy being our competitors, be they friends, allies or foes. Economic and industrial espionage by countries against other nations and by companies against their competitors is well known and a documented phenomenon.

However, economic warfare involving attacks against infrastructure, industries and strategic targets will gain in importance, as it will enable us to achieve national aims without going to war. The ability to clandestinely send in personnel to carry out disruption of economic activity in Pakistan, for example, will in conjunction with our other CT actions force that nation to review its policies of conducting low intensity conflict against us. Moreover, as India emerges as a formidable economic power with its economic interests spread on the world stage, there will be a necessity to build up suitable capabilities to influence and assert policy beyond our immediate borders. In this SOF will play an increasingly crucial role as is the case with the more developed nations today.

*"Let your plans be dark and as impenetratable as night, and when you move, fall like a thunderbolt."*

- Sun Tzu, The Art of War

## CONCEPT OF EMPLOYMENT

As we have seen fourth generation warfare requires Nations to forego the concept of attrition or mass destruction and the necessity to utilise ideas, manoeuvre and accurate targeting to conduct its affairs by the use of small specialised forces exploiting accurate and actionable intelligence, high tempo, simultaneity and strategic surprise. In this context SOF operations constitute a variety of activities that serve offensive, defensive and deterrent purposes in every environment both in war and peace. While some tasks have limited utility and short-term effect, others serve a useful purpose right across the entire spectrum of conflict in which they are employed. Specialisation is needed to execute most of these tasks. Some tasks even call for super specialisation.

There are normally three requirements that are felt by any country. Firstly, there is a need to provide to the Armed Forces a force multiplier in the conventional war scenario. Secondly, to provide to the government and the army a viable, controlled response in the low intensity war spectrum and, finally, to provide a suitable force to respond to sensitive politico–military situations including situations other than war wherein orthodox conventional forces would find it difficult to operate successfully, if at all.

In the conventional limited war scenario, the primary task for SOF will be to support the field force at the operational and strategic levels. In this it will be primarily employed in support of the Corps

Operational Plan to prepare the tactical battle area for operations. Tasks executed in this spectrum assist the regular forces by physical and psychological means. These operations are meant to delay, deceive, disorganise and otherwise disrupt enemy command and control elements and degrade his communication and logistic support. They can if feasible degrade the enemy's combat power by direct action against his combat assets such as the raid and destruction of Argentinean aircraft by the SAS at their base on the Falklands during the conflict. Irregulars can also, either independently or in conjunction with SF, act as important force multipliers. Such forces were widely used in the Second World War by both sides. All such operations are of a "commando/ranger type" in nature and involve hit and run actions. In the present context the US 75$^{th}$ Ranger Regiment, the SAS and the Russian Spetsnaz are truly representative of units that have such a mission profile. Presently all our Special Operations Forces units less the NSG are trained and equipped to carry out such missions, though as we have seen there appears to be a dichotomy in the mindset with regard to employment of PARA (SF) in this regard. They can also be involved in blocking enemy reserves from being effective at the point of decision. In the context of the nuclear backdrop within which our forces will operate and its consequent effect on the depth to which our forces are likely to advance, these operations are likely to be fairly restricted in depth depending on the importance of the area of operations. In the conduct of defensive operations these forces can be utilised to interdict, delay and cause attrition to the enemy's follow up forces, command, control, communication and logistic elements.

The other important tasking of Special Operations Forces in the context of conventional operations would be in a "stand alone" mode in which they would be utilised for carrying out tasks of a strategic nature either independently or with the support of in-country intelligence assets or offensive air assets. Such actions would be carried out prior to and also after the commencement of hostilities. These actions may involve covert/clandestine insertions of teams/ individuals to carry out assassinations or designate or destroy targets of strategic importance. There is a need here to understand the difference between covert missions and clandestine operations. While both terms may at first glance appear similar, there is a subtle difference to the degree to which the Government's role can be acknowledged publicly in the operations conducted. It stands to reason that in covert operations deniability is of paramount importance as the Government can under no circumstances have its role brought out in the open without grave ramifications at the National or International level. In the case of clandestine operations the importance of deniability is lesser and the Government would be able to control or minimise the effect of loss of such deniability. In simplistic terms, for example, the assassination of President Zia-ul- Haq of Pakistan by organisations or countries that we are still unaware about, could be considered to be a classic covert operation while actions of the use of SSG by Pakistan in J&K or the Northern Light Infantry in Kargil, or even the Mukti Bahini episode for that matter may be regarded as clandestine operations. While covert missions are generally the province of intelligence agencies, clandestine operations can also be organised by SOF teams.

More often than not such actions would be carried out to only limited depth inside enemy territory. The attacks by the SAS on V1 and V2 sites located in France and Belgium during the Second World War as also the attack by the Coalition Forces against Iraqi Scud sites during the Gulf War are examples of such tasking. Operating at this level, in some situations, may call for safe havens, hideouts, intelligence and if possible transportation in the host/target country unless these operations are being planned in the proximity of the country's borders (trans- border). Active agents or friendly rebel forces operating in these countries can only provide such logistic support and without access to such agents, such tasks are extremely difficult to execute. While the exact modalities of how the USA and UK overcome this problem is not known, the erstwhile USSR had permitted its Spetsnaz to run agents. Also all SOF, with the exception perhaps being ours, organise covert visits by their key SF personnel to target countries/ areas during peacetime. India's SOF does not operate agents, hence, have only limited ability to operate in this realm at present and is a capability that we seriously need to consider establishing.

There is also a need for augmenting human intelligence sources as also supplement available electronic and satellite sources. SOF can perform this task both during war and in peace. They can do this both in the strategic sphere and in the operational sphere mainly in conjunction with one of the tasks discussed earlier. Though the US and UK have inserted SOF teams for this purpose just prior to operations or during operations itself such as the SAS employment in the Falklands and the Gulf War, the use of these troops has been in difficult terrain with low population and troop density. A fluid front-line, in particular, provides ample scope for this type of application. However, keeping in view the population density in the Indo-Pak border regions, such employment will be restricted to difficult, less developed areas with consequently less population. Employment in Punjab (less riverine terrain) and in the more developed areas opposite Rajasthan will be very restricted in terms of distance, personnel that can be inserted as also the duration they can be inserted for. This in no way precludes their employment as these are the only assets available that can bypass the permanent 'Maginot Line' type of obstacle belt that extends along the border in that sector. This, however, will not be a problem either along the Sino –Indian border or along our borders with our other neighbours in the region wherein extensive trans border operations are feasible because of either the terrain being suitable or the low population density or both.

Prior to examining the options available to the Army and the Government with regard to use of Special Operations Forces in a Low Intensity Conflict scenario some of the important deductions that can be drawn from the characteristics of the future CT environment examined earlier and which would form the very basis for future CT operations are as follows:

- The terrorist always has the initiative and can plan and launch operations at his own time and place of choosing. Thus, the pre-eminent importance of offensive CT operations and the requirement to tailor security structures towards this end.

- The necessity to integrate/network all agencies required to provide elements involved in CT operations to provide a seamless operational environment for own forces.

- The need for a responsive organisational structure that will enable us to bring down maximum force at the point of decision in the minimum time to neutralise terrorist capabilities at the earliest.

In the context of combating Low Intensity Conflict, we see that Special Operations Forces have a distinctive and delineated role in both offensive and defensive operations. In the conduct of offensive operations there are basically two major tasks that can be given to the Special Forces, both being in the realm of covert employment. These are:

- **Organising of Armed Insurrection.** Organising of "Fifth Columnists"and training and directing rebel groups or indigenous guerrilla movements is a common task taken on by most Special Forces, the world over. The US, for example, calls this unconventional warfare that requires them to "*organise, train, equip, advise, and assist indigenous and surrogate forces in military and paramilitary operations normally of long duration.*"[12] This requires a suitable environment, in that, there must be opposition to the existing regime within the target country and the area should be easily accessible to own personnel. The availability of similar ethnic populations on both sides of the border will be an added advantage such as is the case along all our borders. The training and employment of the Mukti Bahini prior to the 1971 operations against Pakistan is an appropriate example. The requirement would be for detachments of Special Forces, ideally of the same ethnic stock, to join up with these rebel groups and assist them in training, planning, coordination and conduct of guerrilla operations. They could also act as liaison and assist rebels in obtaining the required weapons and equipment. In addition they could also train rebels in camps established on own side of the border much in the way that the Pakistan Government has done since Independence. This has the added advantage of being treated as a "deniable operation" by the Government. Personnel posted in Special Forces units from the same ethnic background will be an added advantage and would then require that these units be oriented and based regionally.

• **Clandestine/Covert Intervention.** In those circumstances wherein the environment does not either permit supporting or training of rebel groups, or, where national interest may require the need to enhance our level of intervention, we could insert clandestine/covert elements to carry out similar destabilising ops that would otherwise have been carried out by rebel forces. Small detachments of Special Operations Forces may be clandestinely inserted across the border to carry out tasks such as harassment of the population, disruption of communications and raids on terrorist bases located in the region. The aim being to alienate the local population from the terrorist organisations based in the area as also from their own political and administrative leadership, all of whom would be held responsible for the problems created, destroy key assets, such as weapons and training facilities, and, assassinate key leadership of the terrorist organisations to demoralise and neutralise terrorist organisations and curtail their operations from the region. This will in addition reflect poorly on the administration and reduce their ability to govern. Such operations would need to be launched in difficult mountainous and jungle terrain, close to the border. The US, for example, did this in Vietnam, Cambodia and Laos in the 1960s and early 1970s, such as Operation Tailwind,[13] in which Special Forces detachments operated across the border from South Vietnam in Laos to try and destroy North Vietnamese and Vietcong elements operating or transiting the region. Similar operations were carried out in Cambodia and were, by and large, restricted to approximately twenty kilometres in depth. However, in Cambodia some such missions were more in the nature of a "reconnaissance in force" as up to company strength, at a time, of Special

Forces were employed. Secrecy and deniability of such missions was maintained by using irregular forces composed of tribesmen from the region as also the difficult nature of terrain made it inaccessible to the media apart from some control over media access. Such missions would require assistance of holding troops along the border for ground insertion that could otherwise be carried out using helicopters or stand off Combat Free Fall techniques. They would either live off the land as militants in Jammu and Kashmir or could be provided assistance either by agents in place or by covert re-supply drops from helicopters or aircraft using Remote Controlled Aerial Delivery Systems which provide stand off ranges. A variation of such clandestine intervention tasks would be the conduct of covert operations for carrying out assassinations or kidnapping of terrorist leaders or their sympathisers in third countries, an environment that is likely to be vastly different from what has been discussed earlier. Since such missions are normally the province of intelligence agencies it should rightfully be the Research and Analysis Wing (RAW) that should be conducting such operations. However, though no literature is available in the public domain on the effectiveness of RAW in such matters, it is unlikely to be of a very high order, otherwise well known terrorist and criminal elements who allegedly organised the Mumbai bombings would not have continued to live openly or in comfort as they do in the Middle East and Europe. There are numerous such examples of terrorists living in third countries who have carried out attacks against our population or our interests. Inderjit Singh Reyat, the Canadian resident who is alleged to have masterminded the bombing of Air India Flight No 182 in 1985 resulting in the death of

329 passengers, along with his alleged co-conspirators, Vancouver businessman Ripudaman Singh Malik and mill worker Ajaib Singh Bagri are yet to face retribution[14]. In this case the Israeli example of bringing down retribution is apt since it imposes caution on the terror organisations interested in carrying out such acts as also on their sympathisers. Though these would require to be carried out as deniable operations, the possibility of escalation or some of the detachments involved being taken prisoner should not be ruled out and catered for in the overall strategic plan.

In addition to these roles we will need to include the employment of SOF for Combat Search and Rescue (CSAR) of pilots downed in hostile territory. This is an aspect that has not been given due consideration by our Air Force despite adverse publicity and effect on morale the downing and capture of Flight Lieutenant Nachiketa had during the opening stages of the Kargil Conflict. One of the primary tasks carried out by the SAS towards the closing stages of the Second World War was recovery of pilots shot down over Occupied France. The US went even further and streamlined its procedures during the Vietnam War even going to the extent of launching an abortive raid by its SOF deep into North Vietnam to recover captured prisoners. The importance of assets capable of this task cannot be over emphasised, especially with regard to the positive effect on the morale of pilots who carry out missions deep in enemy territory. This issue is touched on subsequently.

Employment in the defensive role would restrict the use of SOF to conducting pro-active operations within our borders and for responding to terrorist attacks against our citizens or assets. In the former role, SOF would continue to be employed, as at present, to conduct covert surveillance, area domination, pseudo and rival gang operations, snatch operations and raids based on specific intelligence. Operations of this nature, especially in inhospitable terrain, must be carried out based on small teams that are able to live 'in country' for extended periods of time with aerial re-supply as required. The SAS for example carried out covert area domination and reconnaissance operations in Malaysia and Borneo for three to four months at a time wherein they sent in "patrols" of not more than four personnel who linked up with locals and built up their own intelligence network and either laid ambushes, carried out area domination or passed back actionable information to strangle the communist terrorists and their supporting elements. This is very unlike our operations that last no longer than seven days at the maximum and have extremely limited aims with no emphasis being given by our SOF on winning hearts and minds of the indigenous population. In our context, squad level detachments should be able to carry out such operations in Kashmir in the higher reaches of the Pir Panjal Ranges and in the jungles of Kupwara for extended durations of time. This would force terrorists to avoid such areas and move to more easily accessible areas where they can then be neutralised by other conventional forces.

However, such tasks require troops highly trained for light infantry commando type operations equipped with small arms and sophisticated night vision and communication equipped. Tasks that can best be performed by units organised, trained and equipped on the lines of 31 Rashtriya Rifles (Commando), leaving units of the Parachute Regiment for offensive trans-border operations. Employment of SOF units for responding to terrorist incidents involving hijacking of an aircraft, ship or bus, holding of hostages or the use of unconventional weapons or weapons of mass destruction require extremely specialised units with the necessary expertise, equipment and training. The National Security Guard is mandated this responsibility which it has carried out with élan and professionalism. However, as we have already seen, it suffers from some serious drawbacks that need to be corrected.

Finally, the most important role in the immediate future that the SOF will be called upon to perform are those missions that have serious political and diplomatic ramifications and may not provide a conducive environment for a conventional military response. These "special missions" are of paramount importance and can neither fail nor leave the perception of failure. Such missions include internal defense and assistance to third nations, surgical strike and recovery missions to prevent terrorist use of WMD and humanitarian assistance. As our influence in the region and the world increases, our citizens traveling abroad, our embassies and our other governmental and non-governmental agencies located outside are likely to become increasingly vulnerable to terrorist attacks by those opposed to us; the reports of threats to our embassy and consulates in Afghanistan from elements in Pakistan is a case in point. This would require conduct of threat assessment, advice on security and defensive measures, protection of staff and information on aspects that would need to be well known by our SOF in case they are required to conduct Incident Response operations at any stage similar to the US attempt in Iran or the SAS action to clear the Iranian Embassy in the UK. It would be necessary for SOF elements to be deployed for such tasks on a regular basis as also for them to maintain an exhaustive data on the subject.

In addition, the SOF would be the ideal force to respond to regional and internal contingencies, such as providing assistance in natural disasters, internal disturbances, assisting in the evacuation of nationals in the event of regional hostilities, and operating as a vanguard for conventional military in 'Out of Area' (OOA) tasks. As discussed in an earlier chapter, these will be operations in which commanders at the highest levels will have the option to respond using non conventional approaches because of the SOF's unique capabilities to do high-risk, high-payoff tasks no other force can accomplish within an acceptable level of risk, because of their manning, training and equipment profile. In addition covert operations involving economic warfare, wherein personnel, infiltrated using cover of business or tourism, could then strike at industrial and infrastructure targets using arson and other techniques before exfiltrating. Maintaining the capability to perform these missions should become the SOF's highest priority. Building up of such a capability will require some restructuring of units and command and control structures but will, more importantly require a deliberate decision at the highest levels to utilise these forces for meeting emerging contingencies instead of being held back as reserves and being employed piecemeal in a reflex action, as is invariably the case at present. This implies that SOF units will be the 'first in' as a situation develops from where they will provide real time intelligence and feedback on the emerging situation, thereby giving adequate time to commanders to plan and stage manage the most appropriate response. Once the situation has stabilised these units should be pulled out for rest and refit and subsequent preparations for upcoming tasks. It is a matter of interest that the US 75$^{th}$ Ranger Regiment, which is the USA's premier rapid deployment force, is at all times over manned by 15 per cent and has no organic combat support or combat service support and deploys with only five days of supplies. These operations can provide a low-cost means of promoting the long-term strategic goals of the country, especially within the region.

Having examined missions that can be entrusted to such forces through the complete spectrum of conflict and in situations other than war, there is a necessity to understand a few of the important principles that govern their employment for successful conduct of operations:-

- **Mission Profile.** Having seen the mission profiles suitable for employment of such forces, it is important to ensure that these tasks are suitable in that they are specific, with the end state to be attained being clear, and within the capabilities of the force being employed. If infantry can do the task it would not be worthwhile to employ SOF for the task. We have seen such forces being incorrectly utilised time and again in operations as well as in peacetime. The ongoing employment of SOF to protect Army Headquarters, probably against an expected terrorist attack, is a case in point. Troops holding defences without the ability to dominate the area of influence will always be susceptible to attacks by aggressive and well-trained and motivated terrorists. By limiting the SOF to a ground holding role, as "sentries" to protect buildings, is to not utilise their considerable skills and abilities and a complete waste of the months of rigorous selection procedures and training that they have undergone, especially so as there is no shortage of regular troops for such tasks. In addition, it also lowers their self confidence and self esteem and adversely affects their morale and motivation, to be treated at par with other troops presently deployed for the same task, albeit, the Defence Security Corps and the Territorial Army detachments, good troops no doubt, but not in the same league as the SOF soldier. However, more damagingly, in the unlikely event of being unable to foil a attack we would have also given a psychological boost to the terrorist groups and their supporters and damaged the credibility and confidence in our SOF no end. There, is thus, a necessity to ensure that selection and allotment of tasks to SOF are given due consideration.

• **Unity of Command.** To be able to out-fight an enemy who outnumbers you, one needs a command and control system based on outstanding leadership and effective monitoring. It follows the principle of forward command and silence implies approval. Such a method allows subordinates initiative, ensures security of operations while still retaining the ability to intervene and exploit fleeting opportunities or change the operational plan if required. Command and control should be vested in Headquarters in whose support such operations have been launched. This lends itself to efficient decision-making, which is a prime consideration for SOF operational success. Principle of centralised control must be adhered to get optimum results. More importantly, SOF missions are joint operations that will always involve tri service or even operations in coordination with other Central Police or Para Military Organisations or Foreign Special Forces. The necessity for a single Joint Forces Headquarters can only be ignored at our own peril. The conduct of the ill-fated US operation to rescue hostages from its Embassy in Iran, Operation Eagle Claw, is worth examining. As is well known, the operation had to be aborted prior to Delta Force reaching its target area due to a disastrous collision between a helicopter that had just completed refueling and one of the C 130 aircraft at the Desert One RV in the Iranian desert. An extract of the operation is illuminating and self-explanatory:

*"If the Carter administration had created Delta Force as a kind of insurance policy against terrorism they had neglected to read the fine print. Carter himself never took much of a personal interest, going to visit it only after the failed raid in Iran. However well-honed Delta's specialised skills may have been, other factors essential to direct action counter terrorist missions had been ignored and the type of understanding required at high levels to address these insufficiencies was just not there.... Almost a year before the hostage crisis a seizure of the Embassy had taken place, in February 1979, when demonstrators scaled the wall and occupied the compound for several hours... Delta immediately asked for permission to travel to do a detailed survey of the US Embassy and its surroundings... Permission for Delta was denied with no reasons being given... Similarly, the helicopter team assigned to Delta was chosen as result of decisions taken in the Pentagon that had more to do with inter service rivalries than with the mission's main requirement: to get in and out of a landlocked enemy capital surrounded by other states hostile to the US...Since the helicopters had to take off from an aircraft carrier, the Navy insisted that they had to be Navy helicopters because the Army ones were not equipped with folding tails and rotors, which would have allowed them to be stored below deck. Beckwith requested pilots with special operations experience who could be found in the Air Force Special Operations Squadrons and some Army aviation units, but the Navy insisted that they had to be Navy pilots. The only previous experience of the flight crews initially assigned was in minesweeping operations and in their first joint rehearsal they*

*proved so entirely inadequate that Delta had to insist they be replaced. But instead of agreeing to give Beckwith the pilots he wanted, it now gave a chance for the Marines to get a slice of the action in a special operation, which would make history. A Marine helicopter team was picked off the shelf with no special operations training or experience of any kind by the Joint Chiefs of Staff."* [15]

- **Intelligence.** Successful SOF operations call for timely, reliable, detailed, actionable and accurate intelligence. Operations based on vague information, individual appreciations and lack of background material are doomed to failure. While all Special Forces operations are high-risk operations these must be based on calculated risk being taken and not on a gamble. Intelligence also governs the level at which such operations can be launched. Lack of strategic intelligence usually pushes the Special Forces operations into the operational and tactical levels, where intelligence is usually available. There is also a requirement to institutionalize the interface between the intelligence agencies and the Special Forces establishment to ensure a seamless exchange of intelligence inputs. The British model in this regard is worth emulating.

- **Surprise and Security.** This is the main weapon of the Special Forces. It enables them to operate in enemy held territory against numerically superior enemy. It is by using surprise that Special Forces produce and exploit shock effect and paralysis. Surprise is achieved by unconventional, bold and daring actions in order to keep the enemy guessing as to their intention, target, timing and whereabouts. Surprise can only be achieved by rigidly applying the principle of security. There is a need to hide intentions; hence security of plans is a must. While communications are reliable and secure, these should be used sparingly in view of the potent electronic warfare systems being used by most advanced and modern armies. Troops should be moved to mounting bases and cordoned once they have been briefed and rehearsals have commenced. Information should be shared on a need to know basis. Most leading countries do not even publish the citations in respect of their award winners for security reasons nor publish their photographs.

- **Tempo, Friction, Simplicity and Simultaneity.** Special Forces operations attempt to reduce friction and exploit tempo in order to maintain their superior cutting edge. Similarly Special Forces operations assist regular forces by helping them to maintain/increase their tempo and also by degrading the tempo of enemy forces by manipulating the element of friction in the operation environment. Simplicity in operational planning is of utmost importance as complicated plans invariably go sour due to the number of variable factors involved. Operation Eagle Claw, the abortive US raid to free the hostages in Iran involved *"twenty one different agencies or units... using fifty one different radio frequencies, with more than 150 code words and call signs and... seventeen different landing zones and airfields..."* Thus *"the four commanders on the ground – one each from Delta Force, Rangers, Marine Corps Helicopter Crew and Air Force C-130s – were all on different nets and the only way that Charlie Beckwith could communicate with any of the other commanders within a hundred yards of him was via headquarters a thousand miles away."*[16] Simultaneous operations tend to divert the attention of the enemy commanders and make it difficult for them to make well-thought and logical decisions thereby seriously affecting their ability to react.

- **Manpower, Training and Equipment.** Suitable manpower is the most important asset that Special Forces require. In this the requirement of ensuring a higher education level at entry along with emphasis on selection of personnel with high calibre of moral courage and self discipline requires to be given due emphasis. These aspects along with focused training and state of the art weapons and equipment are important factors in ensuring that such forces perform to their optimum. This requires that the selection and retention procedures be well formulated and standardised. That all advanced training be conducted at training establishments that not only have the required resources and infrastructure but are also in a position to evaluate existing doctrine, tactics and specialist weapons and equipment and suggest changes and modifications as required. In the interest of economy and to ensure standardisation of training, it would be best if these were joint services establishments. It makes little sense for each of the Services to run their own establishments as is the case at present with the Air Force and the Special Frontier Force each running separate Paratroopers Training Schools and the Army running the Airborne Training School for imparting aerial delivery techniques. One joint services establishment could meet all our needs and save money to boot.

*"If you're in a fair fight, you didn't plan it properly."*

— Nick Lappos, Chief R&D Pilot,

Sikorsky Aircraft.

## VERTICAL ENVELOPMENT OPERATIONS

The latter half of the 20th century has clearly showed the critical importance of vertical envelopment, whether heliborne or airborne, in conduct of modern manoeuvre warfare in the conventional context. The numerous airborne operations in Europe against the Germans in World War II, the massive use of heliborne troops in Vietnam and the heliborne and airborne operations during the advance on Dacca during the liberation campaign in Bangla Desh in 1971 and the more recent employment in both the wars in the Gulf, are but a few examples.

While nuclearisation of the Indian subcontinent does not preclude conventional operations on a limited scale, as some influential thinkers would have us believe, there is a limit to what conventional forces will aim to achieve without its resulting in escalation in the nuclear dimension. In this context it would be unlikely that deep operations into our adversary's hinterland would be feasible without the risk of serious escalation. This implies that our offensive formations would require to operate laterally instead of in depth, as the recently unveiled doctrine, probably hints at. This in turn would mean that enemy reserves would be forced to deploy further forward in penny packets to be able to react with speed to the ingress of our strike formations. With such a deployment their ability to react against vertical envelopment forces would be extremely limited though the speed of reaction may be faster than was likely earlier. This has serious implications for vertical envelopment operations with regard to the roles, missions, tasks and the manner in which they would perform them in the context of a limited conventional war and there is a need for changes for such forces to be effective in the future.

In the context of this research there is a need to define the term vertical envelopment forces because while there can be no doubting the fact that airborne operations require specialised units there is a widely held belief that any infantry unit is capable of being utilised for heliborne operations with limited training on helicopters that includes aspects such as embarking, disembarking and RV drills and some practice in slithering. It is this fallacy as we have seen in an earlier chapter that was to some extent responsible for the debacle in Operation Pawan wherein Parachute Special Forces (PARA SF) and infantry elements were employed together in conjunction in a heliborne operation that went wrong resulting in elements of the PARA (SF) extricating themselves while the infantry elements were captured and killed. The fact is that in such operations while insertion by helicopter is a very small but critical part of the task, the ability of troops to deal with psychological pressures of operating behind enemy lines, the need for high levels of physical fitness and mental toughness, motivation and self reliance, flexibility and initiative along with exceptional junior leadership and high levels of individual and collective training are of paramount importance. With regard to the aspect of insertion by helicopter, especially during night, it is a well-known fact that there is fair amount of disorientation among troops during this phase that can only be neutralised by sustained and rigorous training that must include night exercises on a regular basis.

From what has been stated above and our experiences in the conduct of such operations it may be fair to conclude that heliborne operations can only be effectively undertaken by either selected personnel from infantry battalions or by selected units that have been given suitable manpower and ample time and facilities for heliborne training. Unfortunately, in our context, the limited availability of helicopters and air effort has severely limited the scope of training imparted and restricted it to slithering from fixed platforms with limited live training, something that is completely inadequate to meet operational requirements. To this if we add the problems caused by turnover of personnel in units and the rotation of units it will probably be just a matter of chance that a sub unit or unit required to carry out such an operation actually has any personnel who have trained for such a task earlier or have undergone such training within the past year, not the very best situation for launching such complex operations. It may therefore be more appropriate, as long as we are unable to provide adequate training, to treat heliborne operations as specialised operations to be undertaken by units of the Parachute Regiment only. This will ensure that specialised troops are utilised to the maximum along with focused use of all available air effort, as was the case a few years earlier.

## Manoeuvre – Attrition Warfare Continuum

"*Addicts of attrition*"[17], as Brig Simpkin refers to them, believe that all war focuses on the central theme of defeating the enemy by engaging and destroying his combat elements in battle. In this context manoeuvre is seen only as movement of own forces to meeting the enemy force and other intangibles such as psychological shock and effect on morale are seen as just force multipliers. The emphasis here is on massed fire support that aims at the destruction of the enemy. The raising of the Artillery Divison and the belief in some quarters in the absolute primacy of air power to defeat the enemy on its own are but natural corollaries of such an outlook. While attrition warfare involves force on force, manoeuvre warfare proponents, on the other hand, look to defeating the enemy through means other than destruction of his mass, ideally in a manner that makes his physical strength and the need to engage in battle irrelevant, by using force against his vulnerabilities. As Sun Tzu said *"To win one hundred victories in one hundred battles is not the acme of skill... To subdue the enemy without fighting is the supreme excellence."* [18]

Manoeuvre warfare in its very essence looks at war as a battle of wills involving minds of the population of the adversarial nations and thus hinges on the psychological impact of actions on the battlefield. It differentiates between destruction and defeat and holds that the former is not necessary to achieve the latter. This became amply clear in the recent operations in Afghanistan and Iraq where the regimes opposing the American Coalition were defeated without their armies having suffered debilitating losses during the campaign. In simplistic terms, manoeuvre warfare requires the use of a force to provide penetration of enemy defences and to fix the enemy (that Sun Tzu called ordinary force) while a second force (referred to as extra-ordinary or divine force by the great master) is then utilised to strike a vulnerability that the enemy is unable to counter using his mass thereby leading to his defeat. In this context, the role of the "divine force" required to strike at the enemy's vulnerability must ideally include by vertical envelopment forces as only that can permit full advantage to be taken of the essential ingredients of such warfare – that of pre-emption, dislocation and disruption.

If this hypothesis is accepted it implies that airborne/heliborne (AB/HB) forces should be employed against the enemy's weakest and most vulnerable points before he is prepared for such a response and in a manner that he is unable to react against it with an appropriate force at his disposal within an acceptable timeframe thereby believing that he has no option but to accept defeat. To ensure successful stage management of AB/HB forces in such a scenario requires emphasis on the following aspects: -

- Selection of suitable vulnerabilities as objectives whether they be headquarters, communication nodes, logistics or physical features, such as defiles, that the enemy does not visualise being neutralised at that particular moment in time and the loss or neutralisation of these will exert immense psychological pressure on the leadership. In the present context because of the limited depth that our forces will entail to reach, ground elements will not require AB/HB elements to establish bridgeheads or capture depth positions. Such forces may be more appropriately used to neutralise command, control, communications, early warning and logistics elements and more importantly capture defiles through which enemy reserves are likely to pass while attempting to move into the tactical battle area.

- To be launched at a suitable time in conjunction with other operations that will create a decision dilemma for the enemy commanders thereby offsetting both his troops to task and time and space calculations.

- Select objectives that are lightly held or not held and ensuring that the enemy is subsequently forced to fight in terrain of our own choosing.

Correct selection of objectives and timing of operations will ensure the following:-

- Requirement for limited forces for assault as this will have surprise and shock in its favour and thus a small number of troops will be successfully able to engage and neutralise larger forces. The conventional force ratio of 3:1 will not hold good. Numerous battlefield examples abound. Crete, for example, was captured by an airborne/ air transported force of twenty one thousand Germans pitted against an Allied force of twenty eight thousand. Even operations in Arnhem during Operation Market Garden resulted in two British parachute brigades encountering one infantry and one Panzer division located in the vicinity and despite losses sustained not only were terminal objectives captured but also held for more than forty eight hours longer than planned for. This reorientation in troops to task ratios will reduce requirement of air effort considerably thereby enhancing security of the task force and simplifying planning, coordination and conduct of the operation. Furthermore, the resulting reduction in the decision time required in conducting such operations will greatly increase momentum of the operation thereby further reducing the requirement of troops. In our context it will ensure that a viable option is available to the Air Force to carry out its task in the existing air defence environment without expending scarce resources.

- A company group task force of approximately 120 all ranks will require at best three AN32 aircraft for personnel and an additional AN32/ IL76 for heavy weapons or equipment, if at all. Such an aircraft requirement is easily available and can be easily inserted into enemy territory clandestinely without excessive need for protection and therefore does not pose too many problems with regard to air space management. In conduct of heliborne operations the issues involved would be similar with corresponding reduction in the number of helicopters required with advantages as mentioned earlier.

- Requirement of troops to hold the captured objectives will be lesser as the psychological aspects of pre-emption and dislocation along with actions to disrupt enemy's reactions would ensure he is unable to bring effective force to bear at the point of decision within the acceptable time frame. His reactions would be further degraded if we ensure that the enemy's reaction force is required to operate in unsuitable terrain. Thus, if the likelihood of the enemy reaction force being armour heavy is high, as is likely, it would be to our advantage to occupy built up terrain or hold defensive positions behind a natural or man made anti-tank obstacle.

- Tactics for various operations of war require complete re-evaluation, as conventional templates do not suit our purpose. For example, in the attack where the aim is to bring maximum force to bear at the point of decision and the aim is to preferably capture unheld territory, it makes little sense for a company attack to be launched conventionally with two platoons up each with two sections up, thereby using less than 50 per cent of our force on a narrow 200 metre front, which may turn out to be held. It would be preferable to attack with all sections up that would ensure that the frontage covered is approximately three times the conventional with 100 per cent force being employed at the point of decision. Thus, instead of keeping reserves to be used against opposition that stops or delays any of our assaulting elements we ensure that the complete force is capable of breaking contact and linking up and reinforcing any element that has been able to occupy unheld ground. Such a scenario has applicability even at a higher level up to that of the battalion. Similarly, in the context of defensive operations, the conventional mindset requires to be replaced by an innovative approach. For example, in the existing context a company group establishing a bridgehead on an obstacle would hold it with two platoons on the obstacle line occupying 600-800 metre with the third platoon deployed 300-500 metre ahead with some tank hunting teams being deployed even further ahead. While in the context of conventional forces such a task will invariably be given to a battalion or brigade thereby greatly enhancing the size of the bridgehead, in the case of an Airborne/Heliborne force such a task may be given to a company group as well. In this case if the Airborne/Heliborne force holds ground in a conventional manner, enemy deployed on the periphery of the company will still be able to engage and prevent use of the lodgment without its further expansion by additional forces. However, if this force deployed in a manner that it only had a section with the company headquarters element at the lodgment to prevent it being captured by a sneak attack, with the three platoons deployed 500-1000 metre ahead on the periphery in section strength with tank hunting teams even further ahead; such a deployment would not only ensure that the enemy is unable to bring down effective fire on the bridgehead from the periphery but more importantly because of the unconventional deployment pattern, which ensures a large area being held, he will be forced to take that much more time to gauge own strength and locations.

Similarly any attack by him along one approach gives the AB/HB force the ability to shift troops to meet the brunt of the attack as required. In simplistic terms, this implies that we either employ a AB/HB battalion group deployed conventionally to ensure a viable bridgehead or we use just a company/company plus deployed unconventionally to achieve similar results. The attendant difficulties in stage-managing a battalion group drop vis-à-vis that of a company group needs no elucidation. In this context, the innovative and unconventional employment of weapon systems also needs detailed examination. In our concept of conventional defence weapons are employed in a sequential manner so that weapon systems with long ranges such as artillery engage the enemy using indirect fire on which we build up fires by other direct and indirect firing systems as the enemy appears in their maximum effective ranges. Such a concept requires that the enemy be hidebound and completely lacking in imagination so as to ensure that he provides a suitable target for us for the maximum period possible. While actions by the enemy in this manner may have occurred in the past, especially in mountainous terrain with restricted approaches, it is unlikely to be the case in open terrain in our western sector. However, if we were to select a suitable killing area ahead of the location where the lodgment is required to be established and then locate our direct and indirect firing weapons in a manner that they are simultaneously able to engage the enemy once he enters the selected killing zone, much in the manner we plan sub-unit level ambushes, we would achieve far greater attrition on the enemy apart from causing disruption and dislocation of his command and control systems thereby neutralising his attack. Such unconventional employment of weapon systems reinforces the need to occupy defensive positions in small sub-units dispersed over a large area that have the ability to change locations based on the enemy's reactions.

- Such tactical techniques and innovations require not only advanced communications, preferably at the individual level, better night vision equipment and advanced weapons systems, but most importantly, highly skilled personnel and superb junior leadership. There can be no compromises in quality of manpower accepted in such units and each paratrooper would require to undergo extensive training in skills and character to ensure apart from physical fitness and individual field craft skills, all personnel are well versed in tactics and possess the required initiative and belief in their own abilities. Such troops using innovative tactical techniques with the element of surprise, shock and moral supremacy has a distinct advantage even if by some chance they are pitted against well trained and organised troops, which is unlikely, despite its size as was the case during the Beriwala Bridge action in the Fazilka Sector in 1971, where one Pakistani SSG platoon (later built up to a company) was able to withstand two to three battalion attacks using armour and artillery for over a fortnight till the end of hostilities.

### Role, Tasks and Organisations

We have over time adopted a mix of manoeuvre and attrition warfare concepts in the manner in which we intend to fight our likely enemies both in the plains and mountains. In this our vertical envelopment forces have the potential to play an increasingly pivotal role if employed imaginatively and unconventionally. While the nuclear dimension may hinder launching operations in sufficient depth that would ensure a decision dilemma in respect of the enemy's employment of his strategic reserves, the same can possibly be achieved by the lateral displacement of our forces in lesser depth. Thus a battalion group action behind enemy lines dispersed over 15-30 kilometres may have the ability to cause a similar decision dilemma as earlier once they are employed after tactical level reserves have been committed. While it would be true that our forces would be dispersed thereby lacking cohesion, the enemy too would have to not only make a decision as to whether his strategic reserves should be employed against where ground troops are achieving success or against the Airborne/Heliborne elements that have been interposed but also has the dilemma of deciding which element of the Airborne/Heliborne force to engage or whether he should split his reserves to attack all elements.

Since own troops will deploy in a manner that enables them to take advantage of the terrain and are also not required to hold till last man last round and have the ability to concentrate at their own point of choosing, they will have the ability to force the enemy to commit troops at least three to four times their size which tactically would imply that a battalion group should be able to keep up to approximately two brigades committed in neutralising its employment.

Thus, it appears that Airborne/Heliborne forces will continue to be able to perform all roles, missions and tasks that they are presently required to undertake though there will be a need for a shift in emphasis with regard to the manner in which they are employed, specifically with regard to troops to task ratios template they adopt, as well as a greater understanding of the fact that such forces are more effective when employed to cause psychological dislocation and disruption than to cause destruction of enemy forces as manoeuvre warfare doctrine demands. Such a capability requires limited reorganisation of existing parachute battalions and would result in savings in manpower which may then be better utilised elsewhere. Replacing of quantity by quality of manpower, training, weapons, equipment, leadership and appropriate tactics will ensure that these battalions will also add greater punch to our SOF capability and be comparable to our existing PARA (SF) battalions and enable us to utilise both type of units synergistically in conventional and Out of Area (OOA) operations. Thus, an urgent need for these units to be given similar status as our other PARA (SF) units.

*"We aren't going to try to train you,*
*we're going to try to kill you."*

- Soldier I, SAS

## MANPOWER AND TRAINING

Among the other important aspects that merit consideration, is the issue of manpower management and training. This issue has been receiving attention from the time that the units of Indian Parachute Regiment were disbanded in 1946 and replaced by battalions from a few selected Regiments. Volunteers from within their respective regiments met manpower requirements with personnel being absorbed by the units after they had successfully undergone a four-week probation. There was no change to this procedure, though a Depot Company was established along with The Guards Regimental Centre, on the raising of the Parachute Regiment in 1952 that processed documentation of personnel proceeding on discharge or retirement from the three Parachute battalions. These three Battalions of the Parachute Regiment, however, still continued their affiliation with their parent Regiments despite the acrimony the raising of the new Regiment had created.

However, this system was found to suffer from serious drawbacks with regard to quality and availability of volunteers from the feeding Regiments, which had no problems providing suitable manpower as long as these units had been a part of their own Regiment. This, along with the expansion of the Parachute Regiment undertaken following the 1962 Sino-Indian conflict, led to the raising of a Regimental Training Centre. Thus, ensuring that the Regiment was directly fed volunteer recruits by the recruiting organisation, who then underwent training at the Centre. This is a practice that continues, with a few changes, till date. This implied that these personnel no longer underwent selection in units, a serious flaw, since it enabled recruits unable to join Regiments of their choice (from their community) to still join the Army by volunteering for parachute duties. Moreover, since the Regiment had no laid down selection criteria, the standard of recruits fell drastically. The remarkable performance of these units, despite the average or lower than average quality of its soldiers can wholly be attributed to the very high quality of officers that units were able to select, since probation for officers had fortunately continued, and to their motivation and dedication to the cause.

Subsequently, in the late 80s a perception gained ground at the highest levels within the Army, that the performance of units, was hindered by the lack of quality of manpower. Unfortunately, this view, because of the conventional mindset that did not see parachute units as anything other than infantry. It was only restricted to an attempt at improving the manpower quality of the commando units by introducing a separate manpower policy applicable only these units which included the introduction of probation for recruits joining the commando battalions from the Parachute Regimental Centre. This resulted in the other parachute battalions perceiving themselves as second-class citizens in the SOF fraternity. A feeling that led to much turbulence within the establishment. This perception was generated to a large extent by the belief, especially held by some among the commando fraternity that quality manpower, among other things, was very limited within the army and would only suffice for the commando units and should, therefore, not be applicable to the Parachute Regiment as a whole.

The view that a million strong army can only produce a thousand or two thousand soldiers of the right quality is fallacious and does not stand scrutiny. The British Army, for example, despite its small size – it just has a total of fifty five infantry battalions including fifteen of the Territorial Army, has seven SAS and parachute battalions including from the Territorial Army and four Royal Marine Commando battalions on their Order of Battle. The fact of the matter is that the complete Parachute Regiment in its present form only requires approximately ten thousand personnel from a pool of approximately five hundred thousand in the infantry, a total of just two per cent and our inability to provide its requirements of the requisite quality has more to do with procedural issues and prevailing mindsets than with the availability of such manpower.

It has only been in the past couple of years that this anomaly has been corrected with the introduction of a new relatively standardised manpower policy that meets the requirement of the Parachute Regiment as a whole. This however underscores a dichotomy that needs to be rectified, in that, despite selecting and training its own recruits, the Regiment still has the powers to not accept them in its units, thereby not being accountable for its selection or training procedures. The logic behind this policy is based on the fact that an individual at the time of his recruitment is completely unaware of what is required of him when he joins such a unit. He has in fact volunteered because he is desperate for employment and though he may meet the qualitative standards laid down a percentage of those selected may have second thoughts once they start to understand the implications of what they have volunteered for. Thus, the needs to ensure that personnel undergo strict selection before being accepted by units. There have also been an increasing number of cases of recruits deliberately failing in the selection tests as it then enables them to join their own caste/class Regiments. There is a requirement to penalise such personnel so that this unhealthy trend is curtailed.

In order to ensure high quality of recruits, the Parachute Regiment Training Centre, unlike other such institutions, is required to carry out its own recruitment. For this it has not been given any additional staff and, therefore, does not have the ability to run regular recruitment camps all over the country from within its own resources. Thus, to meet its requirements it falls back on ad hoc measures such as requesting units and other regimental centres to run camps close to their locations. This hardly means an ensured quality recruitment on a regular basis. There is, therefore, a necessity to overhaul the recruitment system by laying down a suitable qualitative requirement for the SOF soldier including the laying down of minimum educational standards, which should be Grade XII pass, and utilising our recruitment organisation, already in place, to carry out the necessary recruitment.

This, however, brings us to a more pertinent question; is there a need to go back to the earlier system of induction to the Regiment? The truth is that other Arms and Services providing manpower to the Parachute Brigade have been able to retain their high standards because they only accept volunteers having three to five years of service in other units. In hindsight, the system of induction to the regiment that existed prior to 1963 probably produced higher quality manpower than procedures adopted later. The second aspect we need to consider is that with the increasing specialisation of our SOF soldier, would we be justified in keeping him away from his unit and utilising him for such mundane tasks as imparting training to recruits? It may also be worthwhile to look at other armies in this regard as most of them tend to man their SOF with experienced soldiers, rather than raw recruits. It may therefore be wise to reconsider conduct of recruit training at the Regimental Centre and instead have units manned by volunteers from within the Army. This will require education of the environment to ensure that not only availability of suitable volunteers, which aspects such as enhanced allowances and better terms and conditions will ensure, but also more importantly units do not hinder or prevent volunteers from applying for transfers. Units will need to look at move of such personnel as a long term investment, in that, a fair majority of them are likely to return to their parent units after a five to six year tenure as more experienced, combat hardened and better skilled soldiers in a position to make better contributions to the unit.

In addition there is a necessity for the Army Headquarters to put in place systems to ensure that volunteers are made available to the SOF by the environment. One such method could be that all briefings by formations, units and regimental centres to commanders at all levels must include a mandatory reference to details of personnel from their establishments who have volunteered and been selected by the SOF. This would in many ways reflect on the motivational and training levels within units and formations and provide commanders with an additional quantifiable input for assessing unit and leadership standards.

By and large, most agree, that selection is a necessity since requirements for the SOF soldier are different from that required in a conventional one. Moreover, there is also a requirement to ensure personnel who opt for such units because of their own compulsions. For example, an individual with serious disciplinary problems may volunteer to get away from his unit, and do not meet the criteria can still be sent back. However, the question whether such selection should be carried out centrally or left to units requires deliberation. The majority view, within the SOF, tends to be that since the individual must fit into the team there is a necessity for selection tests to be carried out in the unit he joins and will continue to serve with during his stay. This, however, implies that such selections are personality based and there tend to be wide variations within units. The selection schedule also tends to be affected by unit commitments.

The biggest drawback of a centralised selection system and an issue of which most units are very wary, is that conduct of such selection is wholly dependent on the motivation level and interest of the personnel conducting it and these personnel are in no way accountable for the quality of personnel they select. If both these crucial issues can be taken care of, conduct of centralised selection will pay dividends. The other aspect of selection that requires deliberation is that it is far too biased towards tests of physical fitness and endurance, no doubt an extremely important aspect, but more emphasis needs to be given to aspects of moral courage, self-discipline and ethical behaviour as small team operations depend wholly on an individual's ability to do the right thing without supervision, especially as immature and unethical behaviour can directly impact on the reputation of the nation as a whole.

It may, therefore, be appropriate to change existing manpower policies and man SOF with volunteers from the environment who have sufficient experience in regular conventional units and their activities. It may also be worthwhile to change focus of the Parachute Regimental Training Centre from training of recruits to conducting regular selection cadres for other ranks. For this it may be appropriate to have a board of officers from the units, with assistance being provided by the Centre, for conduct of the selection cadres. Units are then unlikely to object to the quality of personnel selected. In the case of officers it will be better to continue with the existing system since it has worked extremely well till now and units have only limited number of officers undergoing selection at any one time. It may also be appropriate to conduct formalised basic trade training at the Centre instead of at the unit where such training tends to be run based on unit commitments, availability of resources and time.

Ideally, this establishment along with the Special Forces School, where advanced skill training is imparted, and the Army Airborne Training School, where training on the use of heavy drop equipment is imparted, should be amalgamated to form the SOF Centre and School on the lines of the Armoured Corps Centre and School. In addition the Parachute Training School could also be incorporated as has been done by the US, Pakistan, Russia and China. There would be the problem of locating such diverse units together that has come up time and again. However, synergy requires that all these elements be brought together, sooner than later, as this is the next logical step for the development of such forces. An ideal situation would be to convert the NSG Training Centre into the SOF Centre and School with the Parachute Regiment Training Centre and the Special Forces School being moved to this location while the airborne training establishments continue to remain in Agra, though as a part of the same establishment, as suggested. The training of the Special Ranger Groups of the NSG, in whatever form, could continue to be imparted at this new establishment.

While in the final analysis the suggestion of establishing an SOF Centre and School is unavoidable, if synergy is to be obtained, it may be more appropriate to follow a step by step approach in that the Regimental Centre, without any major changes in its existing structure, could be reorganised in the following manner: -

- Have one company to provide basic recruit training for all directly recruited personnel, either recruited under the Unit Headquarters Quota or by the Branch Recruiting Offices. The personnel so recruited must not score below 90 per cent in the physical tests and 60 per cent in the written test. This will ensure that the Centre trains recruits of the highest quality.

- The second company should provide advanced training to all volunteer recruits opting from other regimental centres after they have successfully completed the basic phase of recruit training there.

- The third company should carry out selection cadres for all recruits who have successfully completed advanced recruit training and for those personnel opting from other Infantry Regiments and from Other Arms and Services.

The Special Forces School could then provide basic skills training for all selected personnel and advanced skills training as at present. Subsequently, once the SOF Centre and School has been formed with the amalgamation of all the SOF training establishments, the existing NSG training facilities could be utilised for providing advanced training in the required skills.

Finally, there is a need to look at the types of skills and trade specialisations that individuals need to undergo. In our case we have attempted to introduce skills and trade specialisations required by matching and mixing those followed by the SAS and the US Special Forces, not the ideal method, given the differences in our educational and cultural backgrounds as also our organisations, operational concepts and capabilities. The need for communication, medical and demolition as individual trades is unquestionable along with which it may be appropriate to have specialisations such as Pathfinders and Free Fall, Underwater Diving, Driving, Sniper, Support Weapons, Laser Designation, Languages, Intelligence and Interrogation and Heavy Drop Parachute Packers available within units on a laid down scale as required. Apart from this all ranks must undergo a survival, escape and evasion course prior to joining their units. In addition to regular specialised training the School should also be able to conduct adhoc training for specific requirements such as joint training with SOF of friendly foreign countries.

*"We ain't making no goddamn cornflakes here."*

-Col. Charlie Beckwith, founder Delta Force

## PROCUREMENT AND BUDGET

It is but a statement of fact that weapons and equipment that the SOF require should be the best available in the market. In our context, however, financial constraints require that the issue of equipping such forces be considered carefully keeping in view our needs and technological capabilities. There is also the tendency among such forces to select and procure weapons not so much for the reason that they require them, but, because other such forces have them. Invariably, as much of the military hierarchy tends to lack a clear understanding of SOF tasks and capabilities that we require to establish and maintain, which is only known to those at the very highest levels, most procurement choices tend to be left wholly to the SOF establishment. Selections, therefore, tend to be adhoc and based on personal preferences with no thought being given to formulation of any long-term equipment philosophy or policy. For example, while procuring the basic assault rifle of the 5.56 mm calibre for use at the squad level we were also planning to procure a 7.62 mm calibre squad automatic weapon, an extremely unwise decision of carrying separate calibre weapons within the squad. The fact that this has not yet happened is more due to chance than planning.

There is also an ill conceived notion prevalent among a fair part of the SOF community that standard weapons and equipment used by the rest of the Army are not suitable for SOF since they do not project a "different" image. Numerous examples are available though the issue of the "Light Strike Vehicle" (LSV) best illustrates the case. The US has equipped its SOF with the LSV, an extremely sophisticated and expensive all terrain vehicle with independent suspension that carries a crew of three to four and also provides a weapon platform. It can be carried and dropped from aircraft and helicopters in their inventory. We are now in the process of procurement of this class of vehicles for some of our SOF, though our requirement is for a larger vehicle since it would be required to carry the complete squad, with issues such as the inability of our helicopters to carry such LSVs inside and the questionable capability of such vehicles to operate cross country in obstacle ridden terrain opposite Punjab having been completely disregarded. That apart, cost and maintenance issues have also been ignored. The fact that the rest of the Infantry also requires this class of vehicles for use, as a weapon platform, is well known. It may thus have been far more cost effective to develop such a vehicle on an indigenous chassis, which may not quite have the capabilities of the LSV, but would be cheaper to produce and maintain.

The holding of the BMP 2 by the parachute battalions is another example of our inability to understand our needs. The erstwhile Soviet Union and the present Russian airborne forces utilise the BMD and not the BMP since the former is half the weight of the latter and double the number can be carried in an IL76 aircraft. However, because of our lack of knowledge about this infantry-fighting vehicle and also because of the lack of interaction within the establishment, we utilise the BMP-2, which is not the best for the task it is required to do. It may be worthwhile to note that the latest variant of the BMD, the BMD-3, has special crew seat capsules that allow the entire squad to be airdropped inside the vehicle, thus, avoiding loss of time due to crew and stick searching for their AFV on landing, a major innovation on the part of the Russian Airborne Forces. The BMD-3 features a better chassis, more room inside, more firepower and an amphibious capability so good up to sea state 5. The IL-76M can carry 3 x BMD-3s ready for airdrop. All BMDs have an adjustable suspension to raise or lower the vehicle's height and cushion it better for airdrop. A new PBS 950 parachute landing system has been developed for the BMD-3.[19] Interestingly, even China is reported to have procured the BMD3 for its Airborne Army.

It is also a well-known and accepted fact that most of our indigenous weapons and equipment lack quality control and tend to be bulky and heavy. Indigenous production, however, ensures availability of the item and its accessories as also serviceability of equipment at all times. There is no point in being equipped with state of the art imported equipment that cannot be fully fielded either because of non-availability of spares or some other connected problem, an issue which the Services have constantly faced. This problem is further aggravated, where weapons and ammunition are imported, as training invariably suffers due to limited or non-availability of spares and ammunition. The requirement for state of the art systems tempered by a realistic evaluation of their capabilities, limitations, cost effectiveness and availability vis-à-vis an indigenous system will enable us to select systems we need. There will be numerous cases where lower quality equipment may be preferable to the best available in the market based on either availability or cost effectiveness factors. This will in addition ensure that additional funds are available for procurement of weapons and equipment that are not manufactured indigenously. In the final analysis the numbers upfront are as important as the quality of the equipment fielded.

The lynchpin of our procurement policy for SOF weapons and equipment should, therefore, be to provide them with quality equipment from indigenous sources that is or will be in use with the rest of the

Army. Since research, development, manufacturing and issue of weapons and equipment to the environment follows a cycle that can take up to twelve to fifteen years and there are critical technologies that our research and development establishment has been unable to master, it may be appropriate to import such weapons and equipment, along with transfer of technology, for immediate use by SOF which can subsequently be utilised by the rest of the army once production lines have been established within the country. This will ensure that state of the art equipment is available to SOF at the earliest while also catering for its subsequent maintenance and replacement and enabling us to upgrade our technological threshold at the same time. This implies that General Staff Qualitative Requirements (GSQR) and the General Staff Policy Statements (GSPS) for both the SOF and the field army are in consonance to the extent feasible.

There is also a necessity to ensure that all SOF, regardless of service, have standardised weapons, to the extent feasible, keeping in mind their normal tasking. This is even more important with regard to compatibility of communication equipment. The belief that limited quantities can be procured quickly while larger quantities take more time holds good only when quantities involved are extremely large or very expensive. In fact, in our system, the procurement of ten thousand pieces of a weapon or equipment takes the same amount of time as would be required for procuring a hundred. There is every likelihood of a negative or poor response from a manufacturer if quantities involved are too small to be economically profitable for him.

Finally, there is a requirement to place emphasis on provision of extremely high quality of basic equipment, clothing and rations. It is these items of routine use that directly affect individual and sub-unit performance and efficiency. For example, despite an ongoing case from 1985, the army has yet to convince the financial experts in the Ministry of Defence for the urgent need to procure suitable boot for paratroopers, thereby incurring a loss in crores of rupees in medical treatment and non- availability of personnel due to ankle injuries sustained during parachute descents, a situation that can be easily rectified by an additional expenditure of not more than Rs. 300 per paratrooper. This unwillingness to provide quality footwear, clothing, headgear, load carrying systems, survival gear, shelters and packed rations points not only to the unhealthy connivance between contractors providing out dated equipment and procurement agencies but also to the warped bureaucratic system and the uncaring attitude of minions in the Defence Ministry and Army Headquarters who are unaffected by all this.

Thus, to a large extent our outmoded and cumbersome procurement system adds to our woes. In the existing system it requires a minimum of three years to procure any item through normal procedures. For one time procurement through the fast track route, the time required is between one to two years. As long as we continue with a system where authority rests with those without either accountability or responsibility no improvement is possible. If to this we add the functioning of the Defence Research and Development Organisation, the Director General of Quality Assurance and the procedures in vogue enforced by the Central Vigilance Commissioner, in the name of accountability, our cup of woe overflows.

One of the reasons behind our problems pertaining to procurement is the budget allotment. While revenue budgetary allotments deal with necessities such as routine procurements to maintain forces and equipment, rations, pensions, pay and allowances and training and other grants, the capital budget pays for new procurements. Thus, while all revenue allotments require hard cash, capital budgets are flexible and within the control of the politicians for dealing with unplanned expenditures. While it enables politicians to show their commitment and patriotism on the sleeve by allotting large amounts for modernisation of the Services, actual expenditures permitted, with connivance of Ministry of Defence (Finance), ensures minimal outgo that can then be squarely blamed on the Services' inability to utilise the allotted funds. Thus, year after year, the Services return unutilised funds while unable to push actual procurement because of procedural delays at the MOD level. An overhaul of our procurement and budgetary allotment systems will go a long way in enhancing the efficacy and capabilities of the Services, as also of the SOF.

In addition, budgets for other aspects of revenue expenditure such as training and other grants also require to be directly allotted to units by the highest headquarters instead of following existing procedures of following the chain of command. The connected issue of lack of delegation with regard to utilisation of the budget also needs to be corrected. An example of this is the present procedure involving allotment of funds for joint training with foreign armies. In the existing system various Directorates at the Army Headquarters push their cases for inclusion in the training budget, each asking for the moon, which is then reviewed and suitably amended by the nodal directorate for that particular event and finally approved at the highest level. Thus, planning is discordant with no agency to guide directorates in any specific laid down direction with budgets depending solely on the influence that the Director General's of each of the Directorates has with the decision making authorities and their advisors. Thus, individual Directorates do not have a fixed annual budget that would enable them to plan training on a long-term basis leaving no room for flexibility or motivation at the working level. In the event of a single agency organising all training with budgets and the broad aim of training being laid down there would be greater responsiveness, flexibility, creativity and innovativeness in the way this training is planned and carried out. Thus, for example, larger numbers could be sent abroad if existing rules with regard to free companion travel by Air India was taken advantage of.

Finally, it is a sad fact that all SOF personnel receive allowances that leave much to be desired. Grant of Rs 300 as Parachute Pay makes little sense. Moreover, the Navy and the Air Force have ensured that their personnel are better paid for such tasks, as are those with the NSG and the SFF. Thus, we have a dichotomy that the units that will, in the final analysis, pull out our fat from the fire are the least paid of all such organisations. There is, therefore, an urgent requirement to ensure that all personnel of the SOF from all Services have a unified pay and allowances structure that ensures existing anomalies are sorted out at the earliest and receive allowances commensurate with what we expect them to produce. The belief that an individual who joins such organisations is motivated by factors other than financial may have some truth in them but the requirement to be suitably compensated for the type of work that an individual is required to do is not only an unalienable right but an absolute motivational tool. The fundamental truth of this day and age that a person's worth is measured by what he is paid can only be ignored at a very high cost.

*"The summer soldier and the sunshine patriot will, in this crisis, shrink from the service of their country; but he that stands it now, deserves the love and thanks of man and woman. Tyranny, like hell, is not easily conquered ..."*

Thomas Paine

## LEGAL ASPECTS

As we have seen, SOF operations are not restricted to only times when war has been formally declared between nations, but also to periods other than war and in circumstances where it may be either difficult for these personnel to be covered by Article 4 of Geneva Conventions relative to the Treatment of Prisoners of War or they may be considered to be under the ambit of Article 5 of the Geneva Conventions relative to the Protection of Civilian Persons in Time of War. Furthermore, in certain circumstances these personnel are also required to undertake covert operations that target terrorist leaders or their supporters. Thus, there is every likelihood that such personnel, if captured in disputed or hostile territory, are unlikely to be treated as Prisoners of War or as protected persons under the Convention for Protection of Civilians. Therefore, there is an absolute necessity to ensure that such operations are conducted only when unavoidable and under the strictest of legislative scrutiny to ensure that personnel are not sacrificed to meet narrow political or personal goals.

In addition, and more importantly, there is a need to ensure that such personnel are not at any stage held for contravention of criminal laws pertaining to our country for operations in third countries that could lead to them facing criminal proceedings either within the country or being extradited to face charges in that country. The case of the two Libyan agents who have faced such action with regard to the bombing of Pan Am Flight 103 on 21 December 1988 over Lockerbie, Scotland, in which 270 people were killed, is too recent to be ignored. In this case, two Libyan agents, Abdel Baset Ali Mohamed Al Megrahi and Al Amin Khalifa Fhimah were charged with murder, conspiracy to murder and a breach of the 1982 Aviation Security Act, for having placed an explosive device on board the airliner. These two Libyan nationals were handed over by the Libyan Government to face the charges despite the fact that directions for such an act, was in all likelihood, to have been given by either Gaddafi himself or by a senior member of his Government since the Libyan Government has also agreed to pay compensation for the act.

This case brings to the fore two practical issues; the ordering of an indiscriminate attack and no responsibility being taken by the hierarchy for such a decision. Covert actions involving assassination of terrorist leaders must be executed in a manner to ensure that there is no collateral damage in terms of casualties to innocent people or their property and such a decision must have full government backing. This implies that such operations require written approval of the Cabinet Committee on Security or the Prime Minister before they are executed, as is the case in the United States and Israel. This would ensure actions are taken after thorough consideration and that specific directions are given on actions to be initiated. There must be mandated legislative scrutiny by a Parliamentary Sub–Committee for all such operations. In addition, all personnel participating in such operations must have legal immunity from being subjected to criminal prosecution.

The other important issue concerns maintenance of secrecy of such operations. Personnel in sensitive positions are required to sign the Official Secrets Act of 1923 which in all fairness may not stand scrutiny in a court of law in its present form as it applies to retired personnel and communication with the media. It may, therefore, be necessary to have personnel of SOF sign some additional clauses with regard to the sensitive nature of information that they may become privy to while operating in this environment. It is believed that the UK Government has such a clause that restricts their personnel from communicating information of a sensitive nature with the media.

Finally, since law and order is a state subject there may be a need for legislation that permits SOF to carry out searches, arrests and detention without a warrant even in areas not declared as disturbed areas. In the existing environment armed forces do not have such powers in an area that has not been declared as "disturbed". A comprehensive legislation that incorporates all aspects relating to the operations of SOF needs to be enacted to ensure such Forces are able to operate efficiently without fear of reprisal in an environment with the necessary checks and balances.

*" I took the one less traveled by,*
*And that made all the difference."*

- Robert Frost

## FORCE RESTRUCTURING

The doctrine of the western Special Operations Forces reflects their preference for deterrence and pro-active offensive action. They all have one common factor in that Special Forces activity spans the entire spectrum of roles that can be assigned to them normally and the entire spectrum is covered by a single agency. Responses have not been fragmented, though some functions may have been duplicated or even triplicated in some cases.

In our case, as we can see, this response has been compartmentalised and there is no holistic approach towards SOF. We have the SOF from the Army and the Navy that report to their own Headquarters with minimal interface being maintained between them only at the Service Headquarters level. The Air Force, which is required to support these forces, has no dedicated element either for covert insertion and extraction or for Airborne or Heliborne operations with the interface with the Army again restricted to the Services Headquarters level. Defensive counter terrorism is handled by the NSG and the Assam Rifles, which are under the Ministry of Home Affairs, and by the Army through its Rashtriya Rifles and deployment of regular units. Offensive counter terrorism capabilities are either non-existent or extremely limited and are handled by the Special Frontier Force, under the Cabinet Secretariat, and to a very limited extent, by the Army. To add to our woes cooption of the intelligence agencies in support of our Special Operations Forces is tenuous at best. Like most things in this country, how such organisations work together and achieve even a modicum of success can best be attributed to good karma.

To be able to carry out the complete spectrum of missions that we have discussed, there is a requirement for having the following types of forces:

- Intervention and rapid deployment forces capable of holding ground and countering conventional enemy forces for a limited duration as also providing forces for deployment and humanitarian assistance in third countries and for disaster and internal security stabilisation and management within the country.
- Forces for overt and clandestine direct action, reconnaissance, surveillance and target designation, offensive counter terrorism.
- Forces for covert actions abroad in support of national foreign policy objectives for tasks in which the role of the Indian Government is not apparent or acknowledged publicly, including economic warfare.
- Commando forces for Defensive Pro-Active Counter Terrorist Operations.
- Incident response forces capable of dealing with WMD attacks and hostage rescue situations. Special units for WMD response should, in conjunction with other SOF capable of direct action and intervention tasks, also be capable of conducting WMD recovery and strikes against such facilities.
- Forces for maritime intervention and protection of oil platforms and other maritime assets.
- Combat search and rescue (CSAR) and specialist air assets for covert/clandestine

insertion, intervention and rapid deployment tasks.

The existing Parachute Brigade, with slight modifications, will meet our requirements for intervention and rapid deployment forces as also provide required elements for WMD recovery or for strike on such facilities. In its present form it requires approximately thirty aircraft to drop each of its battalion level task forces, a requirement that the Air Force is hard put to meet, if at all. We need to accept that battalion group drops are passé except in certain scenarios because of a combination of factors. In conventional operations, the nuclear backdrop restricts the depth behind enemy lines at which these forces can be dropped and at closer depths, heliborne operations are likely to be more cost effective. The air defence environment along with the difficulties of air space management in the modern battlefield is likely to make insertion of a large airborne stream difficult. However, insertion by small air elements of four to six aircraft should not be ruled out. In mountains, where in all likelihood future conflict will take place, while the air defence environment may not pose a problem, the terrain, however, restricts formation flying and employment of a large number of aircraft in one wave. Thus, in the conventional context, employment of a battalion group simultaneously in an airborne and heliborne role in support of a corps offensive is feasible. In such a scenario, one to two companies could be utilised in the heliborne role and the other two companies in the airborne role. This would require approximately twelve helicopters and eight aircraft, well within our resources.

This, however, implies that there needs to be a reduction in the strength of our parachute battalions which can be easily achieved by doing away with the 81mm Mortar Platoon, the void being made up by introducing 60mm mortars at the company level and from fire support provided by long range artillery. Similarly, introduction of General Purpose Machine Guns at the section level can do away with the need for medium and light machine guns. The Mechanised Platoon should be taken away from the battalion and a Mechanised Company, holding eight BMPs (preferably BMDs), formed at the brigade level. There is also much scope for reduction of manpower from the Signal and Pioneer Platoon with the introduction of new generation of communication equipment as also in the administrative elements. On an average, unit strength can probably be reduced by approximately 25-30 per cent without any loss in its combat potential.

Two such battalions in the brigade will give it the capability to support the operations of two strike corps at any one time, a capability that should more than meet our requirement. More importantly, the requirement of aircraft and helicopters will be limited to just about a squadron each of IL-76 and AN-32 aircraft and a couple of squadrons of MI-17 helicopters. In addition, locating of a third such unit in high altitude for employment in that terrain will not only enhance our offensive capability and response times in mountains but also enable turn over of units in the brigade on a regular basis.

The requirement of artillery and other combat support and logistic elements presently authorised to the brigade would also need to be reviewed in light of the above facts and suitable reductions carried out keeping in view not only the employment of the brigade in conventional operations but more importantly its employment as a rapid deployment force for intervention in third countries and for carrying out humanitarian missions. In addition its use for direct action missions in a low intensity conflict situation similar to the raids carried out by the US Ranger Regiment in Panama and Afghanistan to capture leadership elements will be of importance. To ensure cost effectiveness, there is a need to ensure that support and logistics units must be organised and scaled with only essential elements that will enable this formation to operate in its required role, unlike as at present wherein these units are organised to assist the formation when it is planned to be utilised in the ground role as well.

Thus, raising of a combat support unit consisting of artillery, engineers, signals and air defence elements and a logistic support unit consisting of medical, supply, provost and ordnance elements to replace existing establishments needs to be considered. The aim must be to ensure that units of this formation are at all times utilised in their specialised role to the extent possible. However, if a situation does arise wherein they are utilised in a purely conventional role, additional elements required by them should be provided as additional resources from other conventional units. Finally, there is a need for a brigade pathfinder and reconnaissance unit, the role that the Presidents Body Guard (PBG) is supposedly earmarked to perform, but has not been tailored to carry out in the past. An element from this unit could be located along with the brigade for manning its mechanised elements since pathfinder duties should be the responsibility of the parachute battalions themselves.

As already mentioned, the Parachute (Special Forces) battalions are organised and structured for carrying out clandestine direct action, reconnaissance, surveillance and target designation (RSTAD) in the tactical battle area. There is a requirement for these units to be able to carry out some aspects of offensive counter terrorism and politico-military operations as well. These should be restricted to clandestine intervention, surgical strike and recovery of WMDs and assistance to third countries. It may be appropriate to have tailor made units so that some of them have a regional bias and are utilised for direct action and RSTAD in support of conventional forces as also for clandestine intervention in that area, while other units are capable of the usual tasks in support of conventional forces as also organised and equipped for surgical strikes and recovery of WMDs and for providing assistance to third countries.

The regional units should be organised in a manner that they have three assault teams for carrying out direct action and RSTAD missions and a fourth team for clandestine intervention. These units should have a regional bias with regard to their manning policies to the extent feasible with the clandestine intervention team being substantially manned by personnel from the ethnic communities along the border along which the unit is located. These units should also be responsible for participation in country to country defence cooperation activities, as and when that is feasible, with the countries bordering their area of responsibility. This will ensure that there is continuity in such activity over the long term as also those personnel are able to build up friendship and camaraderie amongst each other as also generate goodwill for the country, important facets in developing friendly and long lasting relationships among countries. The requirement of such units, not unlike the suggestion made by Pravin Sawhney and Ghazala Wahab in their article on the SOF[20], would be as follows:

- Two battalions for operations opposite Northern Command with a battalion each operating in areas opposite our 15 and 16 Corps Zones. The unit in the Kashmir Valley should provide elements for clandestine operations in the Ladakh Corps Zone with other special operations support being provided by the third Parachute battalion located in this region.

- Three battalions for operations opposite Western and Southern Commands.

- One battalion for operations opposite Eastern and the Andaman and Nicobar Commands.

In addition there is a need for one such unit to be kept as a part of Army Headquarters reserves to cater for unforeseen tasks. It should form the third battalion of the Parachute Brigade and would also be available for Out of Area Operations, WMD recovery (in conjunction with elements of the SAG) and for providing cooperation and assistance to third countries not a part of this region. It could also be given alternative tasks in the Eastern Theatre. In conventional operations this unit would provide additional assets for employment by the Strike Corps in conjunction with the Parachute Battalion's allotted to these Corps and the other Special Forces battalions in whose area of responsibility the Strike Corps may be employed. All our Parachute (Special Forces) battalions, already in the process of re-equipping and reorganising, will be able to meet the mission and deployment profile suggested with minimal changes in organisation, weapons and equipment, manpower or training. There will, however, be a need to raise one additional unit.

In addition to the Parachute (Special Forces) Battalions that will be carrying out only some facets of the offensive counter terrorism role, in addition to their tasks in a conventional war scenario, there is a need for other Special Operations Forces units that should be able to carry out other offensive CT tasks such as covert operations in third countries including economic and guerrilla warfare in the regional context. Deniable missions in third countries would primarily involve operations such as snatch actions, assassinations, sabotage and arson of infrastructural and industrial targets. Such operations would require use of very well trained operatives who have the ability to enter the target countries using genuine covers that they can sustain. In our context, by and large only officers have the requisite level of intelligence, basic training, initiative, sophistication and language and cultural awareness to be able to sustain a genuine cover and carry out such operations in a foreign country with limited training being imparted to them. Such missions demand, in the interests of uncompromising security, forming of mission oriented teams that can on completion of their task be disbanded with the personnel returning to their respective units.

This is the methodology that has been most commonly used by the Israelis using their assassination unit, known as the "Kidon" - Hebrew for bayonet. Kidon teams have been responsible for a number of high profile assassinations and snatch actions in the past such as the kidnapping and bringing to trial of SS-Obersturmbannfuehrer Karl Adolf Eichmann (1906-1962) who was head of the Department for Jewish Affairs in the Gestapo from 1941 to 1945 and was chief of operations in the deportation of three million Jews to extermination camps. At the end of the war, Eichmann was arrested and confined to an American internment camp, but he was able to escape unrecognised. He fled to Argentina and lived under the assumed name of Ricardo Klement for ten years until Israeli Mossad agents abducted him in 1960 to stand trial in Jerusalem that lasted from 2 April to 14 August 1961. Eichmann was sentenced to death and executed in Ramleh Prison on 31 May 1962. This was also the method used by them to assassinate Dr. Gerald Bull, designer of the Iraqi super-gun and Nasser Issa, also known as "The Engineer", a master bomb maker for the terrorist group HAMAS.

The Israeli response to the events leading to the massacre of eleven Israeli athletes during the Munich Olympics in September 1972 is instructive. Despite a massive retaliation by the Israeli Air Force and Army involving raids by approximately 75 aircraft against guerrilla targets in Lebanon and Syria, the largest such attack since the 1967 Arab-Israeli War, resulting in the killing of at least sixty-six and leaving hundreds injured. Despite this aggressive military response, a select group of high-ranking Israeli officials felt that more had to be done. They decided that a message had to be sent not only to those who participated in the Munich massacre, but also to those who might be considering terrorist attacks against their country in the future. Designated "Committee X" and chaired by Israeli Premier Golda Meir and Defense Minister Moshe Dayan, the group authorised the assassination of all individuals involved - directly or indirectly - in the Munich attack. There would be no captures, no arrests. The goal was to kill those they could find, and in so doing, terrorise those they could not. A list of thirty-five targets was drawn up including eleven terrorists directly or indirectly suspected to be involved in the Munich Massacre. Interestingly, only one of those targeted, Jemel Al-Gashey, the only gunman involved in the Munich operation who was still alive till as late as 1999, may have been able to get away by going underground.

Similarly, the former Soviet Union also used the Spetsnaz units of the GRU for similar assassination and snatch operations. For the conduct of economic warfare operations such teams can be inserted in a similar manner to carry out actions against the opposition involving destruction of water and power lines and other such acts that can damage their economy. Such acts in conjunction with other counter terror measures will force them to adopt a more cooperative attitude towards our country. Action by the Iraqi resistance towards US occupation involving repeated attacks against oil pipe lines is an appropriate example of what such actions can achieve. The Pakistani attempt at flooding this country with fake currency is another such example.

Such teams when temporarily raised would require certain essential back up establishment that would provide the necessary command, coordination, training and administrative facilities as also the necessary wherewithal to carry out the operation in terms of planning facilities, safe areas for training and rehearsals and the provision of the required weapons and equipment and the necessary cover and documentation. It is suggested that the Special Group that appears to have become irrelevant in its present form, as we have seen in an earlier chapter, should be completely restructured to provide the core establishment that would assist our special teams with their training operational preparedness, communications, control and logistics. It should, as a matter of policy, be ensured that personnel selected for such special missions belong to the Special Operations Forces community. However, depending on the sensitivity and complexity of the mission retired personnel and civilians should also be employed if they meet the requirement as is routinely done by the CIA. The most recent such example that has come into the public domain was the news of the death of a CIA operative, Johnny "Mike" Spann, during the rioting by Taliban prisoners at Kandahar in November 2000 during the recent Afghan campaign. It subsequently emerged that this CIA officer was a former US Special Forces soldier and that the CIA has many such personnel in its employ.

The capability to plan, organise and conduct guerrilla operations against countries inimical to our polices within the region is an option that needs to be retained for the next decade, even if the strategic environment appears to become conducive to a stabilisation of our relationships with our neighbours. Since such operations need to be organised with a great deal of finesse and complete deniability they are extremely difficult to set up requiring much time and effort. These operations differ from covert interventions in that they are conducted over a long period and are conducted by disaffected citizens of the target country. They must, however, have some control elements from our Special Forces to assist and advise them as also to ensure that these organisations do not divert their funding and assets to meet their own ambitions, as is commonly the case. This is exemplified in the manner Baba Yeshe, the CIA trained leader of the Tibetan guerrilla group, the Mustang Force located in Nepal, broke with the CIA and compromised most of their sources and groups located in Tibet. Moreover, such operations must only be contemplated if we are clear as to the end state to be achieved as otherwise such operations can go very wrong.

These forces would be deployed well before anticipated hostilities and may be the most suitable counter against hostile neighbours attempting to destabilise the country by providing training facilities, safe havens and weapons to disenchanted groups within. The requirement for irregular forces for such tasks should be restricted to just a few hundred as these personnel will form the core groups once inserted back in their country. This task should continue to be carried out by the SFF but with a vastly scaled down force of not more than a brigade. The force should, in addition to its present composition, include ethnic groups from all our neighbouring countries. Such an organisation will also enable insertion of personnel into their countries of origin on a regular basis, either covertly or under a suitable cover, to meet their supporters and others to gauge the social and political climate in the country as also the capabilities and future intentions of their governments. This will also provide the Research and Analysis Wing, our agency for acquiring foreign intelligence, with independent inputs in addition to their own sources on which to base their assessments.

For conduct of pro-active defensive operations in the Low Intensity Conflict scenario, as discussed earlier, commando type units would meet our needs in the most cost effective and appropriate manner. Rashtriya Rifles units, organised and equipped on the lines of 31 Rashtriya Rifles (Commando), would be the most suitable. These units need not be airborne qualified, since insertion by helicopters would best meet the tactical requirements, which will result in savings on manpower and training costs as also on air effort. These units should be raised at a scale of one per Force Headquarters for employment in Northern Command. There would also be a requirement for similar units in the Eastern theatre that could be raised under the aegis of the Assam Rifles, though personnel from the Army should wholly man them. The total requirement thus would be of four units in the Northern theatre and two to three, including one battalion for Assam, in the Eastern theatre. There is also likely to be a requirement of one to two units in addition for operations in areas affected by the Peoples War group (PWG), the Maoist Centre (MCC) and other such groups.

Since these units will be superimposed on the grid with no ground holding roles, there is the added advantage of flexibility, in that they can be shifted from one sector to another depending on the requirement or reconfigured and tasked to assist in a conventional war scenario in an early time frame, without degrading the efficacy of the existing grid. The removal of units from the grid in the Kashmir Valley and their commitment in the operations in the Kargil Sector led to avoidable voids in counter insurgency operations resulting in pressure on the terrorists being reduced with serious consequences later. Availability of nearly a division worth of highly trained and motivated troops will greatly add to the options available to the Army Headquarters in its planning and conduct of operations.

These units should continue to be manned by personnel on deputation or Extra Regimental Employment (ERE) with each of the battalions being provided manpower from a laid down group of regiments as at present. They may also be provided with some key personnel from the Parachute Regiment, if required. Such an arrangement will ensure that the Parachute units do not feel the pinch with regard to the type and quality of manpower they require. In addition these units should be validated by the Special Operations Command on an annual basis to ensure operational effectiveness.

In the context of conducting Incident Response Operations, the NSG that is presently mandated with this responsibility, will require to ask itself some hard questions with regard to whether the Central Police Organisations and Para- Military Forces are in a position to replace army personnel within the organisation as was envisaged at the time of its raising. The sad truth is that this does not seem a viable option, as these organisations have neither the motivation nor the discipline nor dedication that such a force requires. This can be seen from the fact that even the Special Ranger Groups are undermanned by a fairly large percentage due to lack of volunteers of suitable quality. Moreover, it is unlikely that senior police officers would willingly take on the huge responsibility of training and maintaining such a strike force; failure on whose part would have catastrophic results not only for the nation, but also more importantly, on the individual's career. This also needs to be viewed in the light of the fact as to whether such an assignment is worthwhile when compared to the other more "lucrative" appointments that are available to personnel of these organisations.

If this is not a suitable option, and many countries the world over utilise their army personnel for such tasks, then we must consider removing the Special Action Groups, along with its Force Headquarters, from the NSG and placing them under the Chief of Integrated Defense Staff or the Army. As stated earlier this is the *de facto* situation on ground as elements of the SRG are committed in VIP protection duties and are thus not available to the SAG for isolation of the target area. The other option could be to remove the existing SRGs along with the SRG training element from the NSG and place them, along with the Special Protection Group, under a separate organisation, for VIP protection duties. In this case, the Headquarters of the NSG can be provided replacements for the SRG units from within the police forces of each of the states located within the state. This would have the advantage that reaction to terrorist strikes anywhere in the country could be initiated at the earliest, as these units would be able to promptly isolate the target area and await arrival of the assault elements of the SAGs. Such a force would have the added advantage of local knowledge and close interaction with the local police, aspects lacking in the present dispensation. There may, however, be a problem of coordination between these units and the SAGs as also of their training being given the necessary importance and attention by local State Governments, but these are not insurmountable problems and can be managed.

Finally, there is a need to review if there is a requirement of more than one SAG on the establishment. The fact is that most countries of the world, barring Russia, have established very small assault units for this type of tasking, even the USA for example has only the 500 strong Delta Force, because such units are rarely used and when they are, they depend on very small detachments using speed and surprise to accomplish their task. Even in our context the SAGs have never committed more than two squadrons at a time for any of their operations. It may, therefore, be more appropriate to have only one Group with four squadrons rather than the existing organisation. Such a reduction will also result in savings in trained manpower. This Group would also require its communication and bomb disposal elements at an enhanced scale than at present. In addition it would need to be authorised specialist personnel and equipment for dealing with incidents involving attacks using nuclear, biological and chemical weapons. A more viable option may be to continue with the Force Headquarters in its present shape and authorise it one SAG with four squadrons and elements of communications and bomb disposal for intervention tasks and a second Group for dealing with WMD incidents on the lines of the NEST that the US has established. The latter unit can then provide elements that in conjunction with other SOF elements be capable of conducting offensive strikes against WMD facilities or for recovery of such weapons from terrorist groups and others as required.

Apart from a change in the organisational structure of this unit it may also be worth considering a change in manpower policies of this force to make it more in line with our other Special Operations

Forces. The tenure system that is presently in vogue does not give continuity or unit cohesion the importance they deserve; as a result unit performance tends to suffer when compared to similar units that are more homogenous, like our other Special Forces units. Interestingly, even the USA which otherwise follows the tenure system within its military establishment has adopted the "Regimental System" for its SF. It may thus be appropriate to make this unit a part of the Parachute Regiment as around fifty per cent of the existing strength of both the Groups is presently contributed by this Regiment. Volunteers from other infantry regiments, arms and services could however be permitted to volunteer for service with this unit on a tenure basis as at present. This will ensure that we are able to take advantage of unit cohesion and a wider manpower base as well.

The Special Operations Forces of the Navy and the Air Force are not being discussed at length. Suffice it to say that MARCOS in its existing organisation meets our requirements as long as it takes on tasks pertaining to maritime and amphibious operations with Army SOF providing support only if required. The non-availability of Air Force elements for specialised SOF missions, including Combat Search and Recovery, is a serious flaw that needs to be remedied at the earliest. The reality that our Special Forces elements conducting operations to rescue personnel belonging to our Army required to be transported by helicopters of the Royal Air Force during Operation KHUKRI in Sierra Leone, especially when own air assets were on station, does not reflect well on our Air Force, the favourable media spin within the country, notwithstanding.

As we have seen, the requirement of such fixed and rotary wing elements will be restricted to only four to five squadrons, which should be placed under a suitable Special Operations Wing. This will ensure that these units are fully integrated into special operations and understand the intricacies and problems associated with tasks involved. In the event of differing Air Force perceptions, the Army Aviation must raise such units, including fixed wing units as the Navy has done, to enable our SOF reasonable chance of success. This, however, should only be as a last recourse since logic suggests that the Air Force provide such units in the interest of economy.

This aspect can however be offset by a drastic reduction in the size of our transport fleet as most other tasks they presently perform can be contracted to commercial airlines and the Air Force should only retain the minimum cargo dropping and air transportation capability to meet operational needs that commercial airlines would not be able to provide. This would ensure a smaller cost effective force with no shortages of pilots. For its transport requirements the Air Force should then sustain aircraft to sorties ratio similar to that of commercial airlines; Indian Airlines with just sixty-two aircraft generates over three hundred sorties daily, as that would enable the IAF to reduce its transport squadrons. The savings incurred would enable the Army to raise specialised units as required to enhance its operational capabilities in this area.

The raising of the eleven hundred strong Garud Flight Commando Force by the Air Force in April 2003, reportedly as a "*composite commando force it seeks to earmark for its commando unit the role of a special force not only for anti- terrorist, SAR (Search and Rescue), para operation and special missions but also cross-border operations*",[21] on the lines of the UK RAF Regiment, which incidentally provides airfield defence and air defence cover, requires to be re-examined at the earliest. At the present time it is required to act as a 'Quick Reaction Team' for protection of airfields, not a task that would normally be given to SOF.

To also raise a force that will ultimately duplicate tasks that the Army SOF and the NSG are presently trained to do with the wherewithal and requisite combat experience for taking on such tasks appears an unnecessary waste of manpower, resources and finance. More so, when linked to the fact that ground operations in enemy territory will have to be in consonance with other forces operating in the area, which will wholly be from the Army, such tasks are best left to the Army to ensure close coordination. Further, unlike in the UK, where the RAF Regiment does have a parachute trained squadron for CSAR— area of operations of their forces are limited in scope because of the overall size of the Force available— our area of operations is much larger and therefore require larger number of units for CSAR as these units would have to be located on a regional basis.

The ability of the Air Force to build up a cadre of suitable manpower with the requisite proficiency or the combat experience appears to be questionable, especially on a long term basis, and it may be more appropriate to raise such units for providing the QRT component for airfield defence, presently an area that has scope for additional emphasis. It is suggested that the Air Force should continue to focus on its core competency and provide the necessary air assets, suitably trained and equipped for insertion into and extraction from hostile airspace for covert and overt tasks, as suggested earlier. It may be appropriate to base the Air Force SOF on the Aviation Research Centre, which presently carries out some of these tasks.

Finally an extremely important aspect that has not been given the serious consideration it deserves is the issue of manning of the Parachute Training School. While historically this establishment has been manned wholly by personnel from the Air Force based on the precedence set by our pre independence masters, without in any way denigrating the capabilities of the excellent personnel and training provided there, there is a basic dichotomy in following a training philosophy that requires combat jump training to be provided by instructors who have neither combat experience nor have jumped in either combat or simulated combat conditions. There can be no questioning the fact that personnel adapt and respond best to training that is provided by their peers and trainers perform best when they have experience of the environment in which the trainees are required to operate. Operationally too, the issue of manpower that remains behind in an aircraft when it could have been gainfully employed on the ground is unacceptable.

In the existing situation, an operational airborne mission at battalion level, for which it is unlikely that more than twenty aircraft would be available for personnel dropping, places severe restrictions on the number of combat troops that the unit is able to carry and the Commanding Officer is invariably left making tough choices regarding the type of personnel that need to be left out. However, each aircraft is required to be manned by a set of three dispatchers and jump masters who would be responsible for ensuring proper dispatch of personnel and for dealing with any unforeseen emergency that may occur. This implies that sixty personnel, or nearly a company worth, in most circumstances the difference between defeat and victory, would accompany the aircraft stream but would not be available on ground unless we adopted the US technique in which most accompanying jump masters and dispatchers belong to the same force and thus jump last in the stick after having dispatched the rest. This is however not feasible as Parachute Jump Instructors of the PTS have neither the training nor the skills or experience in ground combat, let alone in SOF operations.

There is therefore a genuine case to reconsider the manning profile of the PTS and bring in Army Jump Instructors who would then be available for inclusion as a part of the airborne group. Since at least one dispatcher would be required to remain behind in each aircraft to recover the static lines and parachute covers, it may be appropriate, in the interests of both Services, to man the PTS with Jump Instructors from both Services in equal strength. This will meet not only our need for preserving our traditional ethos but also meet the operational and training necessity. Interestingly, most countries such as the US, Russia, China and Pakistan among others use personnel from their SOF units as Jump Instructors and dispatchers.

*If you're not gonna pull the trigger,*
*don't point the gun."*

- James Baker

## COMMAND AND CONTROL

As we have seen, Special Forces are important for the role they play in dealing with situations covering the entire spectrum of warfare from nuclear to low intensity and now to what is becoming increasingly more important, unconventional scenarios that fall between the military-political dimension requiring an interface of all operating components of the conservative civil and military establishments to ensure a measured response to sensitive politico-military situations. The central nervous system of all Special Forces operations in such a complex environment is the command and control system. The decentralised and sensitive nature of operations calls for synergised and real time availability of information on the developing situation, early selection and deployment of suitable forces to respond, measured and speedy decision making and dissemination of orders to concerned units and civilian agencies and finally an interactive system that enables close coordination and control. It is for this very reason that despite the divergence of views regarding roles, tasks and the size of special forces that each of the advanced military power should have, the commonality has been on a centralized model, operating under the highest controlling authority at which level all political and military aspects can be easily and quickly resolved.

In our context the PARA (SF) units operate under the command headquarters, whose operations they support. The Army Headquarters has very limited control over them, except for the unit that is the Army Headquarter reserve, since Command Headquarters tend to be fairly possessive of their assets. Thus, more often than not their employment is dependent on the personality of the Theatre Commander and his views on the usefulness or otherwise of such units as also on his equation with the Director General Military Operations and the Chief of Army Staff. The Parachute Brigade operates under the Army Headquarters through the Command Headquarters. The MARCOS operates under the Naval Headquarters. All air assets that may be required are controlled by the Air Headquarters. The interface required is only at the Service Headquarter level and no routine coordination is feasible at the unit level, which ultimately is the functional level. Added to this, Air Headquarters sees no reason to organise and equip specific fixed wing and helicopter elements that would provide the crucial air element that is required for insertion of airborne and heliborne forces and utilises air elements from the Command where the operations are planned. This implies that the Air Force Task Force and Type Force Commanders are from the requisite Command and in fact may have had no prior inter action with the Army element earlier. More often than not commanders nominated have limited experience in current tactical airborne or heliborne operational concepts or liaison with the army units that carry out these operations or their commanders and thus tend to look at issues from a narrow parochial point of view. Moreover, the degree of cooperation between the services is wholly dependent on the respective personalities of the commanders involved and directly reflects on what exactly they are willing to do. Surely, not the best way to plan what are inherently complex joint operations. This recurrent requirement to 'reinvent the wheel' each time an airborne or heliborne operation or exercise is planned leads to immense frustration at the operating level, especially within the SOF community.

As regards the other Special Forces, the NSG operates under the Ministry of Home Affairs, while the SFF and the ARC operate under the Cabinet

Secretariat. Similarly, the intelligence agencies also operate under the Integrated Defence Staff, the Ministry of Home or the Cabinet Secretariat. Apart from this if operations are to be launched within the country, the State Government concerned, the State Police and Intelligence establishments and the district administration and any number of other agencies also come into the picture. The complexity involved in coordinating and launching operations can be well understood.

Thus, even this cursory examination of the command and control set up for Special Forces establishes that the political leadership is not well versed with the implications of the complex politico-military dimensions of the security problems that we face today. The civil service bureaucracy is too concerned with holding on to its perks and controls, insecure about its professional abilities and wholly bogged down in paper to be able to bring about any reforms to the existing structures. Professional dissensions, empire building, personality cults and the "CYA" syndrome ensure that the intelligence, security and defence establishments consider even the slightest whiff of change as heresy and are ardent status quoists. There are numerous and depressing examples to support this viewpoint. The inability to appoint a Chief of Defence Staff (CDS) till date, repeated intelligence failures, stalled reorganisation of Service Headquarters, outdated budgetary and procurement procedures, the endless wait to procure the Advanced Jet Trainer, the inability to produce a joint doctrine for operations ... the list is never ending. We have many times in the past, as all are aware, surprised our colleagues from the other services more than we may have surprised the enemy.

This complex and diffused structure for controlling our Special Operations Forces with limited institutional interaction and coordination, that too restricted to the Service Headquarters level, along with limited integration with our intelligence agencies ensures we are always reacting to situations in a piecemeal and discordant manner rather than proactively and in an organised manner, as we should. If this had not been the case we would not have had the ignominy of witnessing the Foreign Minister being forced to confabulate with a terrorist regime and had the option of using a mix of SOF to assault and capture Kandahar airport while other elements neutralised the hostage situation. Such an action would have surely enhanced our reputation worldwide.

Tragically, we have had the wherewithal and capability for such actions for over the past decade but have avoided establishing the required framework that would have provided the political and military hierarchy with appropriate advice and options after a comprehensive examination of the issues involved from the special operations perspective. There is an urgent need, therefore, to establish the required structures that will ensure that our Special Operations Forces are able to transcend the constraints within which they are presently required to work. This will only be feasible if national interest is given priority over self-interest and turf battles avoided. An extremely difficult proposition if the US experience in this regard is something to go by. It shows that despite joint command being the norm for decades, it required the Goldwater–Nichols Act of 1986 to bring about a reorganisation of the Department of Defence and force the services to adopt "jointness" as the required ideology for command, control and conduct of operations. Subsequently, even this Act did not suffice and required the Cohen –Nunn Amendment a year later to "*take immediate steps to repair a flawed organisation structure that leaves SOF [Special Operations Forces] at the mercy of inter-service rivalries and a military bureaucracy in which support for special operations runs counter to mainstream thought and careers...*"[22] The need for suitable legislation by Parliament in this regard needs to be given due consideration as it is unlikely that existing leadership will voluntarily accept a reduction in their own area of influence.

It may be more appropriate, therefore, to approach the issue bottom upwards so that functional aspects are given due emphasis. In the context of Army SOF, the placing of the Parachute (Special Forces) battalions directly under the Theatre Commands, with the Commanding Officer expected to advise the Theatre Commander on all aspects of special operations, is only feasible if he is fully conversant with prevailing and impending operational situation at all times. This requires his presence at the operations room or with the theatre commander at all times while simultaneously being required to supervise planning, preparation and conduct of operations by his battalion. This is not practicable, more so, with the unit spread over the complete theatre of operations, as at present. Furthermore, the Brigadier General Staff or the Chief of Staff who are required to validate standard of unit training and administration on an annual basis, are by and large unable to devote time to this aspect, sometimes with unhappy consequences.

With the proposed restructuring suggesting the deployment of Parachute (Special Forces) battalions with specific areas of operations that would approximately cover each of our holding corps and of Rashtriya Rifles/ Assam Rifles Commando battalions at the scale of one per Force Headquarters, there is a requirement for a controlling Headquarters at the Command level. This can be established either as a part of the Command Headquarters or as a separate entity. Since employment of the Parachute (Special Forces) battalions is to be restricted to Offensive Counter Terrorism operations in the normal course, the Low Intensity Conflict scenario being the prevailing problem, it may be appropriate to raise a number of SOF Headquarters on a regional basis which should interact with and provide SOF support to our operational theatres, where required.

There should be tri- service organisations and should control all SOF units, including those from other services, deployed in that theatre. It will, however, be more appropriate for such a Headquarter to be controlled at the highest level possible in view of the sensitive operations it would undertake as also in view of the fact that it will be a Joint Services Headquarters and should, therefore, be controlled by the SOF Command. It should in addition provide advice to the Theatre Commanders on SOF operations as also control these in a conventional scenario. Thus at the present time there is a need for three regional headquarters that would support operations of the Army Commands, the Naval Fleets and of the Andaman and Nicobar Command. As and when functional tri-service theatres on the lines of Strategic Forces Command and the Andaman and Nicobar Command are established, these SOF Headquarters could then be placed under the Theatre Commander with only technical control being exercised at the highest level.

Under ideal circumstances, all Special Operations Forces within the country should come directly under a National SOF Command Headquarters reporting directly to the Chief of Defence Staff, when appointed. It should be headed by a Lt General or equivalent with the status of a theatre commander. In view of the nature of operations he would be required to oversee, the Commander-in-Chief of the SOF Command must also have direct access to the Defence Minister and the Prime Minister as a political inter-face for such forces is of utmost importance. This Command would have operational and administrative control over all SOF units, except the Rashtriya Rifles or Assam Rifles Commando units, on whom he would only exercise technical control. The SOF Command Headquarters could be based on the existing NSG Headquarters; with additional increments being provided from savings accrued by restructuring of the NSG and the SFF. This will ensure substantial savings in manpower and infrastructure costs. Such a Headquarters would also be responsible for all specialised training. Manpower requirement for these forces would however continue to be the responsibility of the respective Service Headquarters. It will also need to establish intimate institutional links with the Defence Intelligence Agency, the Intelligence Bureau, the Research and Analysis Wing and the State Intelligence Agencies to ensure an integrated response to counter terrorist actions can be initiated even before the terrorist organisations are able to act. The recommended organisational structure is given at Appendix.

However since we do not live in an ideal world and bureaucracies do not follow conventional wisdom, a more practical approach to resolving the command and control conundrum would be to first establish a SOF Headquarter headed by a Lieutant General or equivalent Director General (DG SOF) who should control all SOF units of the three services and report directly to the CDS. In the second phase the NSG and the SFF could be integrated to form the SOF Command as suggested. However if this does not find favour with the Government it would be appropriate for this Headquarter to also exercise control over the reorganised Special Action Groups (incident response units), the reorganised elements of the Special

Frontier Force and the Special Task Unit, the erstwhile Special Group. The existing NSG Headquarters can then be reorganised to provide VIP security through the Special Ranger Groups. In addition it can be made responsible for training and control of State Police Units that would replace the Special Ranger Groups and provide Quick Reaction Forces (QRF) for cordoning and isolating the target area in a hostage situation. In this case, such a scenario would require intimate coordination and liaison between the SOF Command and the NSG Headquarters at the controlling level and between the Special Action Group and the State Police QRFs at the ground level.

In both the options given, there would be a requirement to integrate our intelligence and administrative elements to ensure a smooth and seamless operational environment that is essential. This would involve elements of RAW, IB, DIA and the administrative machinery at the Centre and State level interacting through suitably high powered committees established for the purpose, both at the National level and at the regional level. Also, in addition, such committees would require reliable and exclusive communication network that would provide would real time interface between operational units, headquarters and the decision-making apparatus. There also appears to be the necessity of establishing a separate intelligence unit, on the lines of the British 14th Intelligence Group for this purpose.

## CONCLUSION

The professional climate towards special operations is changing rapidly in their favour due to the proliferation of the unconventional low intensity threats. In this context Special Operations Forces are not competitors of conventional forces, but have the capacity to augment and complement them by utilising their wide range of specialist and unique skills and capabilities to carry out target specific surgical strikes with minimum collateral damage. This provides the Government with unique options for countering threats on the horizon in a pro-active manner, preferably without having to resort to the use of large-scale conventional operations.

As India emerges on the world stage as a power to be reckoned with it will not only have to look beyond its immediate borders but also develop the capacity to influence matters to its own advantage in those regions. With increasing dependence for raw materials and oil on the Central Asian Republics, Middle East and South East Asia for sustaining our rapid economic progress, there is a growing need for a capability not only influence but also protect our vital interests in these regions. Thus our sphere of influence has gradually spread from our immediate neighbourhood to include states in South East Asia, the Indian Ocean littorals, the states of the Middle East and the Central Asian Republics. It is in this context that Special Operations Forces will play an increasingly important and dynamic role. It is these forces that will assist in meeting our foreign policy objectives by providing security assistance and advice to our neighbours and also protect our vital strategic and economic interests as required.

These are roles that demand unobtrusive and low-key presence keeping host country sensibilities in mind. They also require the development of regional expertise on terrain, language and cultural aspects as also contacts within regional militaries to understand their operating procedures, capabilities and limitations. There is also a need to develop contacts with their leadership hierarchies to understand their perceptions on issues of mutual interest as also to be able to establish liaison to be able to function jointly if required. It is in this context that the dynamic cooperation between the SOF of India and the US that is presently being undertaken needs to be understood. Its importance has greatly enhanced with the on going operations in Afghanistan, an area of vital concern to India. It is possible to visualise an increasingly active role for Indian forces as the US and its NATO allies find themselves under increasing pressure and need additional forces on the ground. In such a situation Indian SOF will be required to play a vital role and its functional efficiency will be greatly enhanced by the close cooperation that has come about between the SOF of both countries. In fact, there is a need for us to greatly widen the scope and focus of this training effort and also carry out joint training with SOF elements of US Central Command and also with units from NATO.

Our SOF can only be effective if our political and military hierarchy have the vision to clearly appreciate their strengths and limitations as also the principles that govern their employment. While our Special Operations Forces have the manpower, ethos, state of the art equipment and training of a very high order, there is an urgent requirement to reorganise and reorient their command and control structures to make them responsive to our future needs. This demands sacrifices and willingness to look beyond narrow parochial boundaries and self-interest and work towards the common good. There is a need to travel the less traveled road, as Robert Frost says, so that we can find new ways to galvanise our national resources to meet our future needs beyond the narrow limitations of our existing structures.

## END NOTES


1. Kelly, Ross, S. *Special Operations and National Purpose*, Lexington Books, Lexington U.S.A. 1989.
2. *Op. Cit.*
3. Clausewitz, Carl Von, *On War.*
4. Biao, Lin , *Quotations from Chairman Mao Zedong*, Second Edition, Foreign Languages Press, Beijing, China, 1966.
5. Marine Corps Gazette, September 1994, *The Evolution of War: The Fourth Generation*, Lt Col Thomas X. Hammes
6. Lind, William S, Nightengale, Colonel Keith (USA), Schmitt, Captain John F (USMC), Sutton, Colonel Joseph W (USA) and Wilson, Lieutenant Colonel Gary I. (USMCR) *The Changing Face of War: Into the Fourth Generation* by Marine Corps Gazette, October 1989, pp. 22-26
7. Lind, et al *op. cit.*
8. Lind, et al *op. cit.*
9. Lind, et al *op. cit.*
10. Tellis, Ashley J, *Appendix D: The Changing Asian Political-Military Environment*, Rand 2001, pp. 203-240.
11. Tellis, Ashley J, Fair, C. Christine, Medby, Jamison Jo, *Limited Conflict Under the Nuclear Umbrella: Indian and Pakistani Lessons from the Kargil Crisis*, Rand 2001 pp. 5-8.
12. US Dept of Defence, *SOF Posture Statement: 2000*, Pentagon Press 2000, pp. 43-44.
13. Plaster John, *SOG: The Secret Wars of America's Commandos in Vietnam*, Simon & Schuster. pp. 263-71.
14. BBC World Service Report, 20 December, 2001.
15. Arostegui, Martin C. *Twilight Warriors: Inside the World's Special Forces*, St Martin's Press, New York, USA, 1995, pp. 175-177.
16. Connor, Ken, Ghost Force: The Secret History of the SAS, Cassel Military Publishers, U.K. 2002, pp. 338-339.
17. Simpkin, Richard E, Race To The Swift, Brassey's Defence Publishers Ltd, UK, 1985, p. 135.
18. Tao Hanzhang, Sun Tzu's Art of War: The Modern Chinese Interpretation, Sterling Publishing Co , New York 1987, p. 23.
19. Jane's Armor and Artillery, 1993-94, pp. 249.
20. Sawhney, Pravin; Wahab, Ghazala, The Maroon Beret, Force, Jan 2004, pp. 12-27.
21. Chakraborty, Dipankar, Out of the Wings, Force, March 2004, pp. 56-57.

22. Defense Issues: Volume 12, Number 34— *Military Operations in the Post-Cold War Era: Prepared remarks by H. Allen Holmes, assistant secretary of defense for special operations and low-intensity conflict, at the Intelligence in Partnership Conference, Joint Military Intelligence College, Andrews Air Force Base, Md., June 26, 1997.*

# Appendices

## Appendix A

### OPERATION URGENT FURY—GRENADA

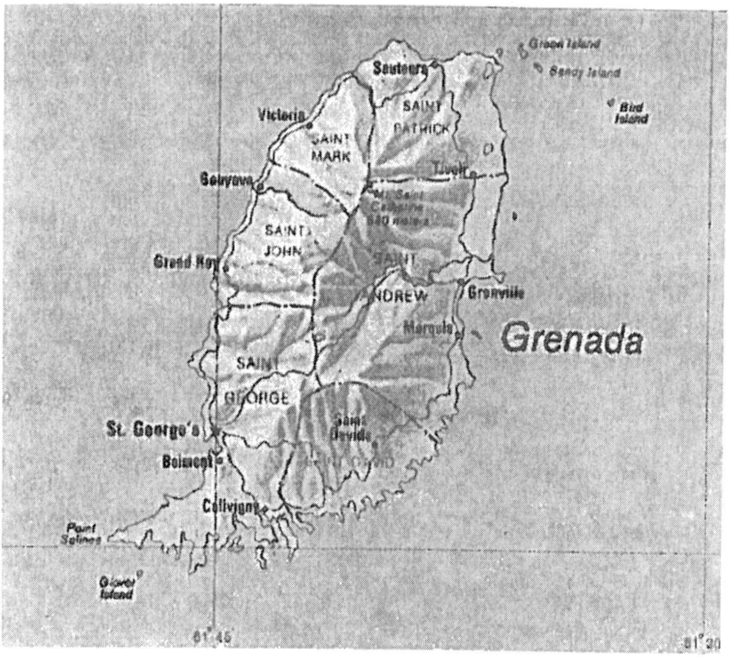

## Appendix B

## US SOF COMMAND AND CONTROL

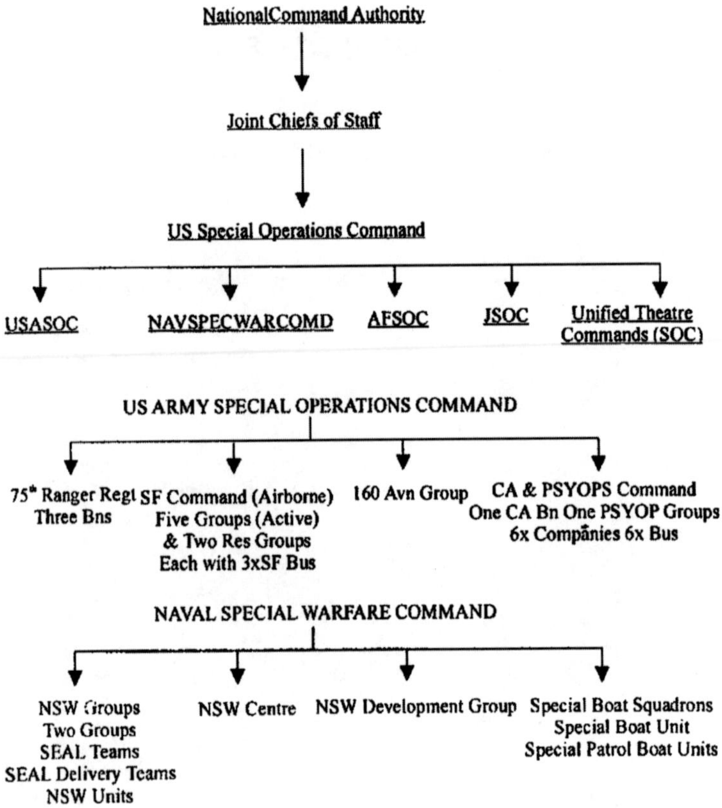

**US AIRFORCE SPECIAL OPERATIONS COMMAND**

- **Spl Ops Wing**
  - C 130 Tpt Sqns
  - C130 Spectre Gunship Sqns
  - C130 Tanker Sqns
  - Helicopter Sqns
  - Foreign Internal Defence Sqn
- **Spl Ops Groups (Two)**
  - C 130 Tpt Sqns
  - C130 SpeetGunship Sqns
  - C130 Tanker Sqns
  - Helicopter Sqns
  - Psychological Operations Sqn
- **Spl Tactics Group**
  - Spl Tactics Sqns (6)
  - Combat Weather Sqn

# Appendix C

## Organisation Setup: Pakistan Special Services Group

(Brig)

- HQ Coy
- PTS
- Musa Coy (Frogmen)
- Iqbal Coy (Signal)
- Zarar Coy (CT)
- Commando Bns (4)
  - HQ Coy
  - Assault Coys (4)
    - Combat Teams (3)
      - Combat Sections (3)
        - Detachments (2)
          5 Commandos Each

# Appendix D

## PROPOSED SOF COMMAND AND CONTROL FOR INDIA

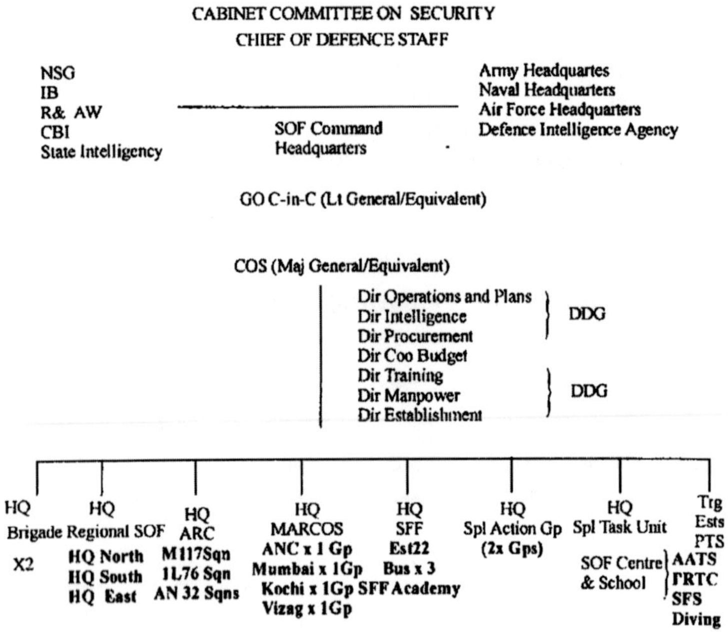


1. HQ Regional SOF will also deal with the Services Commands as follows:-

   (a) HQ North with Northern, Western & Central Army Commands.

   (b) HQ South with Southern Army Command and Western and Eastern Naval Fleet.

   (c) HQ East with Eastern Army Command and Andaman and Nicobar Command.

2. Elements of ARC, MARCOS, SFF and Special Action Groups will also be placed under command HQ Regional SOF as required.

# Bibliography


**Primary Sources**

'National Police Commission: Its Relevance Today', Papers and Discussions at a seminar organised by the Nehru Centre and Hindustan Andolan, a Nehru Centre Publication, Mumbai.

*Report of the Indian Police Commission: 1902-03*, Government Central Printing Office, Simla, 1903.

**Journals**

Chakraborty, Dipankar, "Out of the Wings", *Force* (March 2004), pp.56-57.

'Characteristics of the BMD3', *Jane's Armor and Artillery 1993-94*, p. 249.

Crawley, James W, "SEALs Give Glimpse Of Missions In Iraq", *San Diego Union-Tribune*, 27 June 2003.

Darragh Sham M, Lt ,"Rangers: The Long Road to Recognition", *Special Warfare* (April 1988), pp 19-27.

Ethan, Heral, "Yasotay and the Mangoday of Genghis Khan." *Armed Forces Journal International* (January 1985), pp. 38-69.

Hammes, Thomas X., Lt Col, "The Evolution of War: The Fourth Generation", *Marine Corps Gazette* (September 1994).

Holmes, Allen, "Military Operations in the Post-Cold War Era", *Defense Issues*, Vol. 12, No.34.

Kibbe, Jennifer D, "The Rise of the Shadow Warriors", *Foreign Affairs* (March-April 2004), pp102-115.

Lind, William S, Nightengale, Colonel Keith (USA), Schmitt, Captain John F (USMC), Sutton, Colonel Joseph W (USA) and Wilson, Lieutenant Colonel Gary I (USMCR),

" The Changing Face of War: Into the Fourth Generation", *Marine Corps Gazette* (October 1989), pp.22-26.

Raman, B, "Kargil: Was There an Intelligence Failure?", *SAPRA India*, 04 July 1999.

Sawhney, Pravin, Wahab, Ghazala, "The Maroon Beret", *Force* (January 2004), pp12-27.

Steiner, Carl W, General, US Army, "The Strategic Employment of Special Operations Forces", *Military Review* (June 1991).

Tellis, Ashley J, Appendix D: 'The Changing Asian Political-Military Environment', *RAND 2001*, pp 203-240.

—— do ———, Fair, C. Christine, Medby, Jamison Jo, "Limited Conflict Under the Nuclear Umbrella: Indian and Pakistani Lessons from the Kargil Crisis", *RAND 2001*, pp 5-8.

"Whither Russia's Elite Airborne Forces?", *Monitor*, Volume 7, Issue 156, 28 August 2001.

**Books**

Adams, James, *Secret Armies: The Full Story of SAS, Delta Force & Spetsnaz* (UK: Century Hutchinson Ltd, 1987).

Amstutz, J Bruce, *Afghanistan: The First Five Years of Soviet Occupation* (Washington: National Defense University Press, 1986).

Arostegui, Martin C, *Twilight Warriors: Inside the World's Special Forces* (US: St Martin's Press, 1995).

Beaumont, Roger A, *Military Elites* (London: Robert Hale & Co, 1976).

Beckwith, Charles, Knox, Donald, *Delta Force* (UK: Arms and Armour Press, 1984).

Biao, Lin, *Quotations from Chairman Mao Zedong*, Second Edition (China: Foreign Languages Press, 1966).

Burgess, William H, *Inside Spetsnaz: Soviet Special Operations a Critical Analysis* (US: Presidio Press, 1990).

Collins, John M, *Green Berets, SEALs Spetsnaz* (UK: Brassey's, International Defence Publishers, 1989).

Collins, John M, Col, *Special Operations Forces: An Assessment* (Washington: National Defense University Press, 1999).

Conboy, Ken and Hannon, Paul, *Elite Forces of India and Pakistan* (UK: Osprey Press, 1992).

Connor, Ken, *Ghost Force: The Secret History of the SAS* (UK: Cassel & Co, 2002).

Crawford Steve, *SAS Gulf Warriors* (UK: Simon & Schuster Ltd, 1996).

Crossland, Peter, *Victory Two* (UK: Bloomsbury Press, 1998).

David, Alexander, *Special Operations* (US: Berkley Publishing Group, Penguin Putnam Inc, 2001).

Farran, Roy, *Winged Dagger* (UK: Arms and Armour Press, 1948).

Gavin, John R, General, *Air Assault: The Development of Airmobile Warfare* (US: Hawthorne Books, 1969).

Joint Chiefs of Staff, *Dictionary of US Military Terms for Joint Usage* (Washington, D.C : Pentagon Press, August 1968).

Karim, Afsir, Maj Gen, *The Story of Indian Airborne Troops* (New Delhi: Lancer International, 1993).

Kelly, Ross, S, *Special Operations and National Purpose* (US: Lexington Books, 1989).

Kermit, Roosevelt (ed), *War Report of the OSS*, 2 Vols (US: Walker & Co, 1976).

Kirkpatrick, EM, *Chambers Twentieth Century Dictionary* (WR Chambers Ltd, , 1983.

Khan, Gul Hassan, Lt Gen, *Memoirs of Lt Gen Gul Hassan Khan* (Pakistan: Oxford University Press, 1993).

Kohli, MS, Conboy, Kenneth, *Spies in the Himalayas: Secret Missions and Perilous Climbs* (UK: Harper Collins Publishers, 2003).

Lang, Walter N, *The Worlds Elite Forces* (UK: Salamander Books Ltd., 1987).

Margolis, Eric S, *War at the Top of the World* (US: Routledge Press, 2000).

Marwah, Ved, *Uncivil Wars: Pathology of Terrorism in India* (New Delhi: Penguin India, 1997).

McNab, Andy, *Bravo Two Zero* (UK: Bantam Press, 1998).

Mehta, Ashok, K, *War Dispatches: Operation Iraqi Freedom* (New Delhi: Har-Anand Publishers, 2004).

Mitha, AO, Major General, *Unlikely Beginnings: A Soldier's Life* (UK: Oxford University Press, 2003).

Musa, General Mohamed, *My Version* (Pakistan: Oxford University Press, 1993).

Paschall Rod, *LIC 2010 Special Operations and Unconventional Warfare in Next Century* (UK: Brassey's, Inc, 1990).

Plaster John, *SOG: The Secret Wars of America's Commandos in Vietnam* (US: Simon & Schuster, 1994).

Praval, KC, *India's Paratroopers* (Delhi : Vanity Books, 1974).

Ransom, Harry Rowe, *Central Intelligence and National Security* (US: Harvard University Press, 1958).

Sabharwal, OP, Maj Gen , *The Killer Instinct* (New Delhi: Rupa and Co, 2000).

Salik, Siddiq, *Witness to Surrender* (UK: Oxford University Press, 1982).

Simpkin, Richard E, *Race To The Swift* (UK: Brassey's Defence Publishers Ltd, 1985).

Singh, Jasjit, Air Commodre, (ed), *Air Power and Joint Operations* (new Delhi: Knowledge World, 2003).Barber, Noel, *War of the Running Dogs* (UK: Collins, 1971).

Stanton, Shelby I., *Vietnam, Order of Battle* (U.S: News Books, 1981).

Suvorov, Viktor, *Spetsnaz: The Story Behind the Soviet SAS* (London: Hamish Hamilton Ltd, 1987).

**From The Net**

Ball, Desmond, 'Signals Intelligence (SIGINT) in South Asia', CIA World Fact Book, Library of Congress (Area Handbook), CIA.Org.

'Battles: The Battle of the Somme, 1916', First World War. Com.

Caballero Jurado, 'Foreign Volunteers of the Wehrmacht 1941-45', Feldgrau.com.

Davis, 'Flags of the Third Reich 2: Waffen SS', Feldgrau.com.

'Indian Forces in Sierra Leone', Awoko Newspaper. Com.

Jogerst, Colonel John, USAF, "What's So Special about Special Operations? Lessons from the War in Afghanistan", Global SpecOps.com

Littlejohn, 'Foreign Legions of the Third Reich', Feldgrau.com

Lundari, I Paracadutisti Italiani 1937/45, Feldgrau.com.

Mehdi, Col (Retd) SG, MC, Operation Gibraltar: Role of SSG Para Commandos, defencenotes.com

'SFF History and Organisation', Bharat Rakshak. Com.

'US SOF Posture 2000', Global SpecOps. Com.

# Index